To Raiha & Willson.

Hope you enjoy
as much as I enjoyed
writing it —

love & best wishes

Candice + Brian Reading

17th November 1992

↑

P.S. Happy Birthdays to
Candice & Willson!!

$\mathcal{J}\ A\ P\ A\ N$

The Coming Collapse

ƷAPAN

The Coming Collapse

Brian Reading

HarperBusiness
A Division of HarperCollins*Publishers*

This book was first published in 1992 by George Weidenfeld and Nicolson, Ltd. It is here reprinted by arrangement with George Weidenfeld and Nicolson, Ltd.

HarperCollins books may be purchased for educational, business, or sales promotional use. For information please write: Special Markets Department, HarperCollins Publishers, Inc., 10 East 53rd Street, New York, NY 10022.

FIRST U.S. EDITION

Library of Congress Cataloging-in-Publication Data

Reading, Brian.
    Japan : the coming collapse / Brian Reading. — 1st U.S. ed.
        p.   cm.
    "First published in Great Britain in 1992 by George Weidenfeld and Nicolson Limited... London"—T. p. verso.
    Includes index.
    ISBN 0-88730-607-1
    1. Japan—Economic conditions—1989.   2. Economic forecasting—Japan.   I. Title.
HC462.95.R4   1992
330.952′049—dc20   92-54421

92   93   94   95   96   RRD   10   9   8   7   6   5   4   3   2   1

Contents

Preface

I first visited Japan in 1974, just after the sharp rise in oil prices. I was then on the staff of *The Economist* and went as a guest of Nomura Securities. My next visit was in the early 1980s. Japan-bashing is now fashionable, particularly in America. Much in the country is rotten and wrong. But this is the product of history and institutions. We are all prisoners of our national past. The Japanese way of doing many things merits criticism. The Japanese people, however, do not merit the odium so often heaped upon them. In my experience they are normally courteous and kind. They are no worse than others, and in many ways much nicer. This book attacks a system and not a people; systems can be changed.

I began researching the book in August 1987 and started writing it in August 1990. No book written in an author's spare time can compete with one produced by an academic. Meticulous source references and numerous footnotes were a time-consuming luxury I could not afford. I also feel that they interrupt the flow of a book, designed more to inform than to contribute to the sum total of human knowledge. I have tried not merely to describe what goes on in Japan, but also to explain how and why things happen. Descriptive detail, anecdotes and much factual information have been culled from newspapers, journals and books. Other writers may recognise where I have drawn on their work. I hope they are as pleased as I am, when I recognise the use of mine. Although there are no acknowledgements in the text, this book could never have been written but for the superb reporting of Japan in such papers as the *Financial Times*, the *Wall Street Journal*, *The Economist*, the *Far East Economic Review*, and the *Nikkei Weekly*. Here I would like to express my appreciation to some of their contributors, Gregory Clark, William Emmot, Anthony Rowley, Ian Rodger, Murray Sayle, Charles Smith and Stefan Wagstyl. I should like to thank David Roberts and his successor at Weidenfeld & Nicolson, Hilary Laurie, as well as Anthony Hilton, who introduced me to them. A warm thank you is also due to Duncan McAra, who copy edited and corrected the text. His many helpful suggestions were greatly appreciated. Finally, I could not have completed this book but for the tolerance shown by my wife, Candice.

B.R.
6 February 1992
London

List of Charts

Introduction

'Just as the United States was once a colony of Great Britain, but is now the stronger of the two, if Japan becomes a colony of the United States it will eventually become the stronger.'

(Shigeru Yoshida, Prime Minister, on the terms of the
US–Japan Mutual Security Treaty, 1951)

Prophetic words, uttered only six years after atomic bombs destroyed Hiroshima and Nagasaki. Japan became a surrogate colony of the United States, which gave it most of the advantages of colonial status, without the disadvantages. Japan was given American defence protection, technology and markets, for which it paid little or nothing. Industrially, it has become the stronger of the two countries. People now say that 'Japan lost the war, but won the peace'. In one generation they caught us up. In the next they passed us. In another they will own us. Such views can be heard in any American bar or British pub. They are shared by politicians and reflected in the media of both countries. They seem not without substance.

In 1986 Japan, on its way up, passed the US, on its way down, as the world's richest owner of other people's property. The US now owes the rest of the world $360 bn, debts of $1480 per head; Japan owns net foreign assets worth $200 bn, $1625 per head of its 124 m population. Most of Japan's foreign wealth is recently acquired. Following the Plaza accord in September 1985, when Finance Ministers and Central Bankers of major countries agreed that the US currency was overvalued and should be allowed gently to fall, the dollar crashed 30% in a year against the yen. Foreign assets became ludicrously cheap to Japanese buyers. They went on an overseas shopping spree. They traded their cheap products – cars, cameras, video-recorders and the like – for American and European cheap assets – companies, factories, offices, hotels, shops, golf courses and homes. Headline-catching mega-deals included Aoki's purchase in 1987 of Westin Hotels, Mitsubishi's of the Rockefeller Center in New York in 1989, and Sony's of Columbia Pictures in the same year (which must have been particularly galling to Americans who remembered that Sony built its fortune on the basis of US transistor technology bought for a mere $25,000). But these were only part of the story. When the US real estate market weakened, the *Wall Street Journal* reported that individual Americans fell over themselves to sell condominiums, homes and ranches, to individual Japanese. Starting in 1985 at $2 bn a year, Japanese real estate purchases in the US rose to a peak of $17 bn in 1986 before easing back to $10 bn in 1990. Over 1985–90 they totalled $65 bn.

The Japanese shopping list included assets of many other kinds. Net purchases of US securities totalled $170 bn in 1985–90. In the late 1980s, it was not uncommon for Japanese buyers to take up 30–40% of all the US Treasury bonds issued at quarterly auctions. At each new auction the market asked, 'Will Nippon Life be buying this time?' The Japanese now own 10% of all US medium- and long-term Treasury bills outstanding. They took the world's art markets by storm. In March 1987, for example, Yasuda Fire & Marine Insurance Company paid $54 m for van Gogh's *Sunflowers*, to be beaten in May 1990 by Ryoei Saito, chairman of Daishowa Paper Manufacturing Company, who paid $78 m for the same artist's *Portrait du Dr Gachet*. Not content with this, Saito also purchased Renoir's *Bal au Moulin de la Galette* for $79 m, only to cause uproar and outrage in 1991 by saying he would take both paintings with him in his coffin to his cremation; it is a Japanese custom to take valued possessions to the grave. Fortunately hubris leads to nemesis; Saito promptly ran short of cash and had to reconsider.

The Japanese not only bought, they built. Their invasion of the US automobile industry was spectacular. In 1990, for example, while auto sales in the US fell by 5% to 4.8 m, US manufacturers' sales dropped 16.8% to 3.2 m. Sales of Japanese cars, by contrast, rose 27% to 1.3 m. Half were made in the US and accounted for one-fifth of US car production. Plans are afoot to expand Japanese car production in the US to around 1 m. With imports this means that the Japanese could capture half the US car market by the mid–1990s. That's assuming the Americans let them!

In 1990 things changed a bit. The Tokyo stockmarket crashed and the Japanese, squeezed for cash, scrambled to bring money home from abroad. The flood of Japanese foreign purchases abruptly diminished. But according to some, it was but a temporary intermission. The simple fact is, as the *Japanese Economic Journal* explained in February 1990 with regard to Japanese pension funds, their assets 'are too big for Japan's borders.'

Needless to say, the Japanese onslaught on America is bitterly resented. For one thing, it can be destablising. Nicholas Brady, who is now Treasury Secretary, was asked by President Reagan to study what caused the October 1987 Wall Street crash. He said that Japanese Treasury bill sales sparked it off. Two years later, the Japanese withdrawal from the United Airlines bailout helped to precipitate the October 1989 mini-crash. More worryingly, Americans see parts of their national heritage passing into foreign hands. 'Tinsel Town', Hollywood, is now mostly foreign owned. Sony's purchase of Columbia was followed, in 1991, by the biggest-ever Japanese buyout, when Matsushita Electrical Industrial Company paid $6.6 bn for the entertainments conglomerate, MCA. This purchase was particularly galling, as it included commercial properties giving exclusive rights to do business in the Yosemite National Park. The US Interior Secretary, Manuel Lujan, responding to public outrage, suggested that Matsushita might donate its Yosemite interests, worth $300 m, to the government. Matsushita was less than willing to oblige; but subsequently was forced to back down and parted with them to a charity at a knock-down price.

This insensitivity and lack of generosity should have come as no surprise. Following the Iraqi invasion of Kuwait in August 1990, President Bush asked Japan to contribute men to 'Desert Shield'. The Japanese Constitution forbad it. The former Prime Minister, Toshiki Kaifu, tried to change the law so that Japanese soldiers could serve abroad as non-combatants, but the Diet, Japan's parliament, threw out his bill. If not men, then yen; Kaifu's initial offer was derisory, less than ¥1 bn. It was also widely unpopular in Japan. Worst still, it coincided with news that the Japanese had just paid $1 bn for America's foremost golf course, Pebble Beach in Monterey, California. Later, the Japanese offer was raised to $4 bn, equalling the costs borne by the US for just six days. When 'Desert Storm', the shooting war, began in January 1991, the Japanese aid offer was increased by $9 bn – but it was made grudgingly. Japan buys 70% of its oil from the Gulf, so its interests were being protected by British and American lives. But many in Japan would have preferred to stand aside from the conflict altogether, bearing the cost of the outcome in higher oil prices if that was necessary. Writing in the *Financial Times* in October 1987, David Hale of Kemper in Chicago reckoned that 'financial servitude to Japan' would be a hot issue in the 1988 Presidential Election. He was a bit premature. But it should feature prominently in the 1992 Presidential Election.

Japan's financial muscle is founded on its economic might. Its postwar achievements have been considerable. Less than fifty years ago the

3

country was defeated, occupied and in ruins. Its government was in foreign hands; its industries were reduced to rubble; its money was worthless. The people could barely feed, clothe or house themselves; they had nothing left but their brains and their brawn. Yet by 1952 output was back to its pre-war peak. By 1955 reconstruction was complete. Income per head of the population, which had increased from 70 m to 85 m, regained its 1937 level. (For Japan the Pacific war started in 1937 with its attack on China.) But meanwhile other countries also had been expanding. With twice the population, America's GNP was twenty-five times Japan's; with half the population, Germany's was twice as large. But Japan's economy was expanding at a breakneck speed. In the 1950s real GNP almost doubled, with average annual growth of 9%. In the 1960s it tripled with growth of 11% a year. Meanwhile US real GNP rose by barely half in each decade. By the mid–1960s, Japan's economy was bigger than Britain's. By the end of the decade it had overtaken France and Germany to become the world's third largest economy, after the USA and the former Soviet Union.

The world economy in the 1970s was battered by the breakdown of the Bretton Woods fixed exchange rate system and two oil shocks. Growth rates everywhere slowed down, and though Japan's was almost halved it still outperformed all other advanced economies. The 1980s saw a further slowdown in Japanese GNP growth. Domestic demand growth was even more sluggish and a massive Japanese trade surplus emerged. America and Japan resembled two drunks, leaning against each other in order to stand up. The Japanese saved and lent; the Americans borrowed and spent. The Japanese lent their surplus savings to the Americans, who used them to buy Japan's surplus products. Between 1980 and 1989 the US ran a cumulative current account deficit of over $1000 bn; while Japan ran a surplus of nearly $600 bn.

Forecasts based on simple extrapolation predict that Japan will continue to grow faster than other countries. If 1980s growth rates are repeated in the 1990s, Japan's economy will climb to two-thirds the size of the US economy by the end of the century. If nothing changes, Japan will also continue to run huge trade surpluses, buying up more of other people's assets in the process. This alarming prospect prompted a study, commissioned by the American Central Intelligence Agency, to warn that Japan was threatening 'our country and way of life'. The report, entitled *Japan 2000*, feared that 'Given the situation in the US today, our economy will certainly be overwhelmed by theirs.... This will spell disaster for the American standard of living for our children – indeed for ourselves – if the pace of Japanese ascendancy continues unabated.' The yellow peril is a favourite American bogeyman: it was all a sinister plot,

4

said the report. 'Their economic power is based on a shared national vision for world economic domination.'

Exrapolation, however, is a poor guide to the future. After the Second World War, pundits forecast that Japan would never regain its 1929 level of industrial production: it would have to remain a coal-mining and agricultural country. Today it produces no coal and agricultural output is less than a twenty-fifth of GNP. Explaining the past is a better guide to the future than extrapolating it. The aim of this book is to show that Japan's post-war economic success is fatally flawed, while its political stability is dangerously fragile. There is no great plot or grand design. Japan is characterised by paralytic government, venal self-seeking politicians, pervasive corruption, gross inefficiency and inequity, lawlessness, latent violence and a total lack of any social purpose. The Japanese are not planning to take over the world. All they are doing is defending and promoting their own sectional interest against those of other Japanese. That this system has produced miracle growth and then massive trade surpluses was by accident rather than design.

Communism with beauty spots

Japan's role model is the collapse of communism, which took the world by surprise in the late 1980s. Centrally planned command economies could not handle the complexities of the technological revolution. They failed to provide the living standards to which their citizens aspired and which they observed were enjoyed in free market economies. Dictatorship by self-serving apparatchiks became intolerable. The speed with which the communist system came crashing down, once it started to crumble, amazed everybody.

Japan's economic system is not capitalist with warts, but communist with beauty spots. It is a half-way house between capitalism and communism, democracy and dictatorship. It is corporatist, with big business run for the benefit of stakeholders, management, employees and customers, not shareholders. It is a controlled economy, by bureaucratic regulation, designed to eliminate competition for the benefit of powerful producer interests. It is virtually a one-party state, corrupt, paternalistic and nepotistic, a neo-feudal system operated for the benefit of powerful and wealthy political and industrial dynasties, in which fear and greed dictate how unequal votes are cast in unsecret ballots to select politicians without policies. All are not equal under the law; barons of politics, business and finance consider themselves to be above it.

The story of Japan's coming collapse combines economic and political themes. The former exposes the flaws of corporatism and the latter

5

those of neo-feudalism. Both are presented within the broad sweep of Japanese history, which has been dominated by long cycles of stability culminating in violent change. There have been four such cycles in recent times. The first straddled the Tokugawa era, in which the country was closed to foreigners. The second began with the restoration of the Emperor Meiji, in which the country was opened and modernised. The third was the period of aggressive imperialism, which ended with the atomic bombing of Hiroshima and Nagasaki and occupation by foreigners. Finally, there is the present cycle which began in 1945, when the Japanese set out to rebuild their shattered economy. In it they evolved a system which secured miracle growth. But while it raised material living standards to amongst the highest in the world, it did little to enhance the quality of life for the average urban worker and his family. In pursuit of growth, the system encouraged a high rate of savings to finance the necessary high rate of investment needed to build a modern industrial economy. Once Japan had caught up with other advanced industrial countries, growth slowed and investment needs declined. But savings remained high and became excessive. Excessive savings lead either to large structural balance of payments surpluses, which annoy the foreigners whose markets are invaded by Japanese exports, or to economic stagnation.

Ever since the late 1960s, the Japanese have been struggling to suppress the malign effects of excessive savings. By one expedient or another, they have dealt with the symptoms without tackling the root cause. The two oil price increases in the 1970s temporarily diverted excess savings to Arab oil sheikhs. Increased exports were needed to pay for higher priced oil. During the late 1970s, in the interval between the two oil price rises, and in the 1980s, surplus savings pushed Japan's current account into an unacceptably large surplus. Other countries, particularly the US, demanded that Japan open its doors to imports and reform its domestic economy to eliminate unfair competition. But the government cannot easily dictate change in Japan; it operates by consensus. Before laws are passed, all interested parties must be consulted and their agreement obtained. This can take decades. Other governments have understood this and have been patient. Japan has been allowed a decade in which to tackle its problems. In the first half of the 1980s, the US saved the country from economic stagnation. Following President Reagan's supply-side tax reforms, the US moved into substantial balance of payments deficit. The Japanese were able to lend their surplus savings to Americans, who used them to buy Japan's surplus products. In the second half of the 1980s the US dollar collapsed and Japan was forced to fend for itself. It tackled its problems by pursuing a policy of excessively cheap and easy credit. This produced a 'bubble' economy, in which unbridled speculation caused share and property prices to soar. In each year from 1985 to 1989, the market value of privately owned shares and property increased by more than the nation's income. Investment boomed, consumers went on a spree, growth accelerated, the trade surplus declined and the savings excess was substantially reduced. But in 1990 the speculative bubble burst, leaving in its wake losses equivalent to three years' national income.

Today, the Japanese banking system is in danger of collapse. The credit explosion of the late 1980s could become the credit implosion of the early 1990s, akin to that which in 1929–31 led the US into depression. In the short term the only way to avert this disaster is to reflate the bubble. This may postpone, but cannot prevent, the day of reckoning; the next bubble will also burst. The Japanese will continue to save too much until land and property become plentiful and cheap. Ordinary Japanese should be given the room in which to live decent lives. Wealth should be more fairly shared, which means taking from the one-third of Japanese who own everything, and giving to the two-thirds who have only what they earn. This cannot be done by consensus; the losers will never agree. Before Japan's economic problems can be solved, its political system will have to be changed. This is the purpose of electoral reform, designed to end dirty money politics. The reform, when it comes, will destroy Japan's ruling Liberal Democratic party. It will disintegrate and parties will emerge representing sectional interests, i.e. consensus will be replaced by confrontation. Reforms will be imposed by the majority on the minority – and they will be bitterly resented and resisted. Japan has entered the period of violence and civil turbulence which marks the end of one long cycle and the start of the next. The last cycle made Japan economically great. The next will make it socially just.

PART I

Seeds of Success

From Sakoku to Surrender

Seen in the broad sweep of Japanese history, events have always moved in long cycles. Each cycle has had three to four phases. In the first, the nation is united in an effort to achieve some clear national goal. In the second, it usually achieves its objective, although it failed disastrously in 1941–5. In the third phase, it overshoots. It is reluctant to abandon the systems which have brought it success, even when circumstances, often external, require that it changes. In the final phase, the cost of doing nothing becomes greater than the cost of doing something. This is typically a period of acute political turmoil, involving civil or foreign wars. Only then can the Japanese unite to attack new common goals.

The explanation for these long cycles lies in the collective Japanese psyche. On the one hand, they are intensely loyal to whatever group they belong to; on the other, they are intensely violent towards any rival group. This is a product of the nation's agricultural and feudal past. Less than 150 years ago, Japan was a nation of rice farmers. A highly efficient basic food crop, rice will support more people per acre than most other crops, though it needs low-lying wet lands. The limited area of habitable land in Japan is of this nature. Rice cultivation requires communal investment, in dams, irrigation systems and water-wheels. Water has to be husbanded and shared. Growing rice is an easy job most of the time, but it calls for intense communal effort to plant out seedlings and harvest the crop. The growing season in Japan is short and the weather unreliable. At just the right moment, everyone must pitch in and work together. Murray Sayle, a distinguished expert on Japan, put it to me like this: 'You just never see a lone rice-farmer riding off into the sunset. Individualists starve.'

Working together was a matter of survival for the Japanese. 'Groupism' is not enforced but ingrained. As Murray Sayle went on to say: 'For instance, in the primary schools – with two children in the local village school I consider myself well informed on this topic – there are no individual sporting events on sports days. The nippers run in teams named after colours – red, blue, green and so on – and are supposed to put in their best efforts to keep blue ahead of red. How little Aiko Watanabe (or Alexander Sayle) did as an individual seems not to matter.'

Feudalism persisted far longer in Japan than elsewhere. It did not formally go until the 1870s. There was no legal system in the Western sense. Lines of authority ran vertically, rather than horizontally. Loyalty, duty and obedience were owed to one's superior, whose commands had to be obeyed without question. Punishment was meted out by that superior, rather than in the name of society by law courts. In return, the superior owed responsibility for the well-being of those in his service. Feudalism has not completely disappeared.

A nation's social and political values can well be gauged by those events in the past which remain clearly part of the national consciousness. The English remember the Magna Carta, the Scots the Battle of Bannockburn, the Americans their Declaration of Independence and man-made Constitution, the French their Revolution. The Japanese remember the story of the Forty-Seven Ronin, which started in 1701 when the Lord Asano was provoked into attacking and wounding the Lord Kira, a government official. He was ordered to commit suicide by disembowelment, known as seppuku. His lands were confiscated and his loyal retainers became leaderless. They determined upon revenge. To lull suspicion, they waited until December 1702, when they broke into the official's residence and cut off his head. They then gave themselves up to the authorities, who, after much debate, allowed them to commit seppuku near the small temple of Sengakuji, near Tokyo port. Thereafter the Forty-Seven Ronin were seen as heroes for their loyalty to their dead leader. Assassination, for selfless motives, remained forgiveable into the present century. Tranquillity in Japan must either be imposed by absolute authority or produced by consensus. Confrontation spawns turmoil and strife. Change, as the enemy of consensus, inevitably produces winners and losers. Thus Japanese tranquillity demands that change be resisted at all costs. Hence the long cycles.

There have been four long cycles in modern times. This chapter tells the story of the first three. It covers the history of Japan from the policy of excluding all foreigners, called sakoku, to the 1945 surrender and occupation by foreigners. The first cycle ran from the establishment of the Tokugawa Shogunate in 1603 to its collapse and the Meiji restoration in 1868. This period is important on two counts: first, during the long period of sakoku, the Japanese political economy developed distinctive and unusual characteristics, many of which still affect how the country operates; secondly, the story of the collapse of the Shogunate has many parallels with current events in Japan.

The second long cycle, following the Meiji restoration, began with a period of radical reform and rapid industrialisation, which by the early 1900s made Japan the first industrialised Pacific economy. Dramatic and traumatic change was achieved, but by authoritarian not democratic government. Strains and stresses were manifold. Disaffection was contained, not without bloodshed, by inculcating blind worship and obedience to the God-Emperor. Xenophobia, patriotism, ultra-nationalism, aggressive expansionism, invincibility, the belief in Japan's divine mission to conquer, rule and civilise the world, were the antidotes to domestic discontent.

The second and third long cycles blend into one another. They are different in that during the former, modernisation enhanced the nation's ability to engage in foreign adventures; whereas during the latter, foreign wars inhibited the economy's development. Modernisation decelerated sharply in the decade following the First World War, when the international economic environment turned hostile. As it did so, a period of political turmoil followed during which politicians and militarists struggled for mastery. Japan's political leaders could no longer control the forces which they had unleashed in support of radical reform; on the contrary, they fell increasingly under their sway. The fatal transition between the second and third cycles lasted from 1920, when a Japanese expeditionary army in Siberia refused the government's order to withdraw, to 1937 when the Lwantung army, acting without orders from Tokyo, attacked the Chinese in Manchuria. The third cycle can be described as long only in that it overlapped the second. It was not until the government was forced, against its wishes, into war with China that the militarists took full control of the country.

The first long cycle

The Japanese are a singular people, differing from all others; this is the product of geography and of history. They were originally Chinese, who migrated from the mainland through Korea around 2000 years ago. As newcomers, they pushed the Ainu, an aboriginal race of Caucasians, to the north into Hokkaido, Sakhalin and the Kurile Islands. There are only 200 pure-blooded Ainu left, although there are several thousands with some Ainu blood in them.

Mythology maintains that God-Emperors have ruled the country in an unbroken line for the past 2600 years. They are said to be descended from the Sun Goddess, Amaterasu. The dynasty was first chronicled in the *Nihongi*, written in the seventh century AD. Writing came to Japan late in the day, imported from China. Until then there existed only oral records of the country's history. The *Nihongi* did not attempt to give an accurate account of the past; it was political propaganda, designed to legitimise the authority of the Emperor, who was controlled by the Fujiwara family. The Fujiwaras were anything but legitimate, having just bloodily usurped power from rival clansmen. The *Nihongi* was written to secure their hold on it. If everyone believed the Emperor was God, he would automatically be obeyed. Since the Fujiwaras controlled the Emperor, they would become all-powerful. Indeed they did – for several centuries.

The country was run by warlords, called daimios, who owed feudal allegiance to the Emperor, but nothing to each other. Throughout the Middle Ages, they were in almost constant battle with one another. As different families struggled for power and wealth, rival alliances were formed, collapsed and reformed according to the fortunes of war. Towards the end of the twelfth century, however, a great daimio called Minamoto Yoritomo succeeded in bringing all Japan under single rule. He rewarded himself by forcing the thirteen-year-old Emperor of the time to appoint him to the hereditary office of Sei-i Tai-Shogun, meaning 'barbarian-subduing great general'. He also removed himself from Kyoto, where the Emperor held court, and set up a military government at his campaign headquarters, in a field at Kamakura near present-day Tokyo. This separate seat of government, subsequently moved to Edo, present-day Tokyo, became known as the Bakufu, or camp office, and the Shogun's rule went by the same name.

Shoguns ruled

The Shogun built a great castle at Edo, from which he ruled. The Emperor remained in Kyoto, where he reigned. But there he was the Shogun's prisoner and forced to do as he was told. The Shogun appointed and paid all the court officials. Their pay was abysmal and their duties negligible. To keep them from idleness and stirring up trouble, their time was fully occupied with meaningless ceremonials, the details of which were exactly and minutely defined. Detailed regulation by bureaucrats of all aspects of Japanese life persists to this day. Like communist countries, Japan has a controlled economy, but unlike communist countries, there is no central planning.

The relationship between Emperor and Shogun epitomised a deeply ingrained characteristic in Japanese life, the contrast between outward appearances and underlying reality, called tatemae and honne. On the face of it, the God-Emperor was all-powerful. Everything was done in his name. But nobody could remain a God if he actually did anything. He would be bound to make mistakes and Gods don't make mistakes. So the country was ruled in his name by others, who could then be blamed when anything went wrong. The Emperor was thus a puppet, whose strings were pulled by the Shogun. In Japan today, the division between tatemae and honne is all pervasive. Prime Ministers, for example, are now only figureheads, chosen and controlled by faction leaders.

The Shogun's power over the Emperor depended crucially on his remaining a barbarian-subduing great general. His overriding responsibility was to defend the insular integrity of the Japanese archipelago. One of Yoritomo's descendants earned his keep by defeating an invading Mongol army led by Kublai Khan in 1274. Seven years later, when Kublai Khan attacked again, with 4400 seagoing ships carrying 150,000 warriors, a Kamikaze, or divine wind, intervened to destroy the greater part of his fleet. These signal victories led to an upsurge in national self-confidence and a belief in Japan's divine destiny.

Tokugawa brought peace

Yoritomo was an exceptional leader and the Kamakura Bakufu which he founded lasted 150 years. But his later successors failed to maintain their hold over Japan. Much of the subsequent three centuries saw Japan ravaged by civil wars. Finally, another strong leader emerged, Ieyasu Tokugawa, who defeated all his main rivals at the great battle of Sekigahara in 1600 and became Shogun of a united and pacified country. The Tokugawa Shogunate, which he founded, brought two-and-a-half centuries of peace to Japan, albeit under a rigid and brutal dictatorship. The Tokugawa Shogunate was the stable phase in the first long cycle. Its stability was due to the ruthless steps Ieyasu took to control all other daimios. After the battle of Sekigahara, he re-allocated the great domains, taking land from the losers where he could, and apportioning it amongst his family and supporters. In this way he took control of all the best or most strategic land. He made sure that his family held at least half the country, particularly the fertile Kanto plain around Edo and along the strategic Tokaido road to Kyoto.

His defeated opponents, called the Tozama daimios, remained independent. Their lands were to the south-west of the archipelago; Choshu on the tip of Honshu island commanded the Straits of Shimonoseki connecting the Sea of Japan with the Pacific; Tosa, on the island of Shikoku, was separated from Honshu by the inland sea; and Satsuma and Hizen were on Kyushu island, the other side of the Straits of Shimonoseki. The Tozama daimios were feudal lords in their own rights, answerable directly to the Emperor and powerful rivals to the Shogun. A combination of two or three of them would be strong enough – and ultimately were – to overthrow the Tokugawa rule. The Tozama, therefore, were permanently excluded from office in the Bakufu government on the grounds that they were potential subversives. They were kept under control by a simple expedient: each one was forced to live every other year in Edo. When they returned home, they had to leave their families behind as hostages. This system, unique to Japanese feudalism, was known as Sankin-Kotai. Moreover, staying in Edo was deliberately made expensive. This kept them poor, helping to thwart their ability to rebel. Any who did so were mercilessly stamped out: a traitor's punishment was seppuku.

Below the feudal lords, society was rigidly stratified. The samurai – the warrior class – alone were allowed and obliged to carry swords. They did not own any land but, instead, were paid rice stipends. They lived in the castle-cities from which the country was governed. During the long period of peace which followed the end of the sixteenth-century civil wars, the samurai had little fighting to do. They therefore became the bureaucracy which administered the country. There were strict rules to determine who could hold which official positions and arising from this there was a detailed, precise and largely unchanging hierarchical order imposed on society. Everyone's place in life was clearly defined and largely immutable. Even speech had to reflect fine differences in status of the speakers. The lower the status, the lower the bow – if only to avoid decapitation.

The daimios and samurai comprised 7% of the population. Below them were the farmers, who grew the rice and paid taxes and who accounted for 80% of the population. They remained extremely poor and servile, and were controlled by hereditary headmen. Within the village, families were obliged to co-operate in groups of five to till the land. Within families, each member had to show absolute obedience to its head, regardless of his orders and demands. Villages, not individuals, were taxed according to standard rice crop yields. The rice tax was harsh, unfair and inefficient, as taxes today are in Japan. The village headmen determined how the bill was shared between families. They paid the least tax themselves and accumulated the most wealth. The tax was unchanged even when the actual rice crop failed and so fell short of the standard set for it. Taxes are never popular, but in Japan they were particularly disliked. There is still little social stigma attached to tax dodging.

Most peasant farmers were reduced to the status of landless serfs. They were nonetheless superior to the next class, the artisans, who worked in the countryside cottage industries. One group, the burakumin, were given all the nasty and smelly jobs. They were the butchers, tanners, grave-diggers and so forth – outcasts, unclean. So complete was their exclusion from Japanese society that their villages did not even appear on any maps. There are about a million burakumin descendants today, living mainly in Kyoto, Osaka and Kobe. They are indistinguishable in appearance or by name from other Japanese, but they remain untouchables and, so far as the Japanese press is concerned, unmentionables. Companies investigate potential recruits to discover and exclude any with burakumin connections. Families try to ensure that their sons or daughters do not inadvertently marry a burakumin. Discrimination against them is illegal, but this is simply another instance where appearances and reality part company.

Finally there were merchants, an undefined class with no formal status. Regarded by the samurai as parasites, they proved essential for the smooth running of the economy. Merchants were the lowest of the low, but became the richest of the rich. They lived in cities and cultivated commerce not land. As taxes were tied to rice production, they paid none. Small shopkeepers and the self-employed continue this tradition. From time to time, merchants were obliged to make forced loans to their daimios. But for the most part their strength lay in the fact that, in a highly regulated society, there were no rules governing them because they were not recognised as existing; while in a highly conservative society, nobody dared change any rules to bring merchants within them.

Samurai pay was fixed in rice. Living in the towns cost cash and was expensive. The samurai became increasingly impoverished and fell deeply into debt to the merchant class. But debt collection had its tricky side. A samurai had the right to chop off the head of any inferior for no better reason than to test the sharpness of his sword. All that prevented the solution of samurai debt at a stroke was that, in decapitating a pressing creditor, one might deprive a more senior samurai of a loan. He might then want to test the sharpness of his sword.

All change forbidden

Ieyasu Tokugawa established a rigid and detailed command economy. The object was to halt the development of Japan at the stage it had reached by the early seventeenth century. Position and jobs were all hereditary, with hierarchical status set out to an unlimited degree. People could sometimes be demoted for making mistakes; they were rarely promoted. No farmer could move from his village – he was even denied a family name. The individual had no legal existence. Families and communities were collectively responsible for anything and everything which went wrong. They were usually punished collectively, not individually. This ensured that groups exercised self-discipline over their members. The paranoiac Japanese desire to conform to group norms stems partly from this system. The individualist may bring down punishment on all, and therefore becomes an outcast.

Movement was tightly controlled. Roads and bridges were guarded, and no new ones could be built without the Shogun's consent. No ocean-going vessels could be built, although most transport was by coastal shipping. All aspects of life, dress, conduct, food and housing were meticulously controlled through detailed and immutable rules. Everyone spied on everyone else to make sure nobody broke codes so precisely laid down and so painfully enforced.

Tummy talk

Under the Tokugawa Shogunate, people had to be careful what they said to one another. Another's superior status could literally confer upon him the power of life or death over you. There were no civil rights or legal code. There was merely a hierarchical relationship between superior and inferior. Speech therefore was dangerous, words being used as much to conceal as to convey information. The result was 'tummy talk', which means that the hearer must guess at hidden meanings, as nothing is clearly stated. This trait also remains to this day. Japanese, who have lived in the West or who are used to dealing with foreigners, have become more direct in their speech. But when talking to each other their meaning is still often obscure. A Japanese colleague emerged from an hour's meeting with his superior. They had discussed whether to take a new advisory service. 'What did you decide?', I asked. 'I don't know,' he replied, 'but I think that we probably agreed to take it.'

Such an ordered, unchanging society maintained the power of the Tokugawa Shogunate at its peak. It made Japan a nation of rule obeyers, not problem solvers. Knowing the rules, however ridiculous, and scrupulously observing them, ensured personal safety. Problem solvers take the initiative – they do things differently. Under the Shogunate, that meant writing one's own death sentence. The Japanese still slavishly obey rules, particularly the unwritten ones which form part of their social code. Problem solving is largely a team effort. Individualism is frowned upon.

The Tokugawa Shogunate's prohibition of change of all kinds could not make the world outside Japan stand still. Contact with foreigners posed a direct threat to the country's stability. The Tozama daimios might become rich and powerful by overseas trade through their ports, and they could buy guns. Foreigners within Japan could undermine loyalties by converting discontented samurai to barbarian religious beliefs. Such threats had to be dealt with.

Doors to the world slammed shut

Europeans discovered Japan in 1542. The Portuguese from Macao were first to arrive, followed in 1549 by St Francis Xavier's Jesuits. The Portuguese came to trade (and introduced firearms) and the Jesuits to convert. Both were welcomed initially. Christianity spread to several hundred thousand converts, although not without some set-backs. Hideyoshi, Ieyasu's predecessor, outlawed the religion in 1587 and ten years later suppressed a small Christian community in Kyoto and twenty-six Christians were crucified in Nagasaki. The arrival of the Protestant Dutch traders in 1609 and the English in 1613 quickly stirred up further trouble for the Portuguese and Spanish. They revealed to the Japanese the threat that the proselytising Catholics posed. The Catholics aimed, asserted the Protestants, first to convert, then to subvert and finally to control the country. One Englishman in particular, Will Adams, influenced Ieyasu. He was the pilot of a Dutch boat, shipwrecked on the Japanese coast in 1600. He became an official adviser to Ieyasu and helped him to understand what was happening between Catholics and Protestants in Europe. (Will Adams has become famous as Blackthorne in James Clavell's historical novel, *Shogun*.)

Opinion in Japan, always xenophobic, progressively turned against foreigners. Finally there were sound grounds for action against them. Japanese Christians were deeply involved in a revolt against two daimios in the regions of Shimabara in 1637. The rebellion failed, but the rebels turned their resistance into a religious crusade. Some 30,000 Christians locked themselves up in the old castle at Hara and fought to the finish. They were all slaughtered, every man, woman and child.

Following the Shimabara revolt, the closed-country system known as sakoku was introduced: all foreigners were thrown out; foreign books were banned; and Japanese were prohibited from leaving and foreigners from entering the country, on pain of death. There was one marginal exception: Dutch and Chinese traders were allowed limited trading rights out of Nagasaki, which thereby remained Japan's one open window to the world. Sakoku gave Japan two centuries of comparative peace and prosperity, if not of progress. But meanwhile the industrial revolution was sweeping through Europe and America. Industrialisation created the need for ever larger markets and led to Great Power trade and territorial rivalry. This spilt over into South America, Africa and Asia. A country, frozen in the age of bows and arrows, swords and armour, was obviously ripe for exploitation and conquest.

Until the 'black ships' came

The Americans made the first decisive move. Commodore Matthew Perry was dispatched to Japan with a modern squadron, including two steam warships, the famed 'black ships'. His instructions were to force Japan to open its ports to foreign trade. Perry arrived on 8 July 1853 with presents and a letter from President Fillmore stating US demands. The former, which included a quarter-scale steam engine, carriage and tracks, were received with interest; the latter with consternation. Perry then departed telling the Japanese that he would return the following year with many more black ships for their reply. The Japanese had no wish to abandon sakoku. But nor did they want a war against a superior enemy. Perry could not invade Japan. But he could inflict a humiliating defeat on the Bakufu, by bombarding the coast and cutting Edo off from its food supplies, much of which came by sea. Defeat and humiliation would undermine the authority of the 'barbarian-subduing great general' as surely, but more immediately, than abandoning sakoku. So when Perry returned in February 1854, the Japanese tried prevarication and procrastination. But Perry was intransigent: he forced the Shogun to open the ports of Shimoda and Hakodate to American ships.

Britain's Rear-Admiral Stirling put into Nagasaki in September 1854 to demand that the Japanese give no aid or shelter to the Russians during the Crimean War. Unfortunately Stirling, a stuffy old windbag who talked in the obscure and convoluted manner of Western diplomacy, was not accompanied by an interpreter. Faced with tummy talk, he failed to make himself understood or to understand what the Japanese were saying. He came away, without knowing it, with the same treaty Perry had obtained six months earlier. The Russians followed suit.

These treaties of 1854–5 were only a start. Mercantile interests in Europe and the US were unsatisfied. They wanted Japan fully and freely opened to their trade, so they pressed for more. The Shogun favoured bowing to the inevitable. But the Emperor and the Tozama daimios wanted to reject the foreigners' demands. The result would be defeat for the Shogun in Edo, not for the Emperor in Kyoto. Nonetheless, 'unfair treaties' were signed in 1858 with the Dutch, Americans, Russians and British to open several more ports.

Collapse from within

The Shogun had to force the Emperor to endorse these treaties and the Tozama daimios to obey them. Even in the Bakufu's heyday, this would have been difficult. The Japanese did not take kindly to being pushed around by barbarians. But by the time that the black ships arrived, the developing cash economy was already undermining Japanese feudalism from within. For half a century before Commodore Perry's vessels arrived, the Japanese political economy was in a state of suppressed crisis. The samurai were impoverished and rebellious. Taxing farmers had been taken to the limit and beyond. There were numerous agrarian riots. The central Bakufu government and many provincial governments were bankrupt. They survived thanks to growing debts to merchants, the one class which had no recognised place in society. With all these stresses and strains the Tokugawa's grip on power was weakening.

Foreign war or civil war?

Perry's arrival heralded the overthrow of the Shogunate. Thenceforth, the Bakufu was in a dilemma. It could not control the powerful Tozama daimios of Choshu, Satsuma, Hizen and Tosa. When it made agreements with the foreigners, these daimios broke them. If any toed the Tokugawa line, their own samurai deposed and killed them. Tozama daimios had either to rebel or risk assassination. From the signing of the 1858 unfair treaties onwards, anarchy ruled. Foreigners in Japan were always in danger, and there were several assassinations. The British and American legations were attacked. Satsuma samurai, on the Tokaido road from Edo to Kyoto in 1862, bumped into a party of Englishmen out for a ride. The English did not grovel, so the samurai attacked them, hacking a merchant, Charles Richardson, to death. Immediately, *The Times* thundered: reparations were demanded, together with the death penalty for Richardson's murderers. The Shogun paid the damages, but could not force Satsuma to punish the assassins. The Royal Navy therefore bombarded Kagoshima, the Satsuma capital. The Shogun's failure to impose his will on Satsuma encouraged others to take the law into their own hands. Choshu forts bombarded foreign ships in the straits of Shimonoseki; in retaliation, an allied fleet bombarded the forts into oblivion.

The alarmed Choshu daimio decided to knuckle under to the Shogun. His samurai promptly deposed and dispatched him. Rebels from other domains then flocked to Choshu. Leading samurai were now in control of the Tozama daimios, who, like the Emperor, became mere figureheads. With foreign help, the samurai formed, armed and trained a modern army. In 1866 the Shogun, to re-establish his authority, attacked Choshu. He was bloodily repulsed and shortly thereafter died. Satsuma and Hizen, following the Bakufu's defeat, joined forces with Choshu and took control of the Emperor in Kyoto. The Emperor promptly ordered the new Shogun to resign the Shogunate. Instead his army attacked Kyoto to recapture the Emperor, but was defeated. In 1867 the Tozama samurai announced the restoration of power to the young Emperor Meiji and in 1868 the remnants of the Tokugawa forces were finally defeated. The Imperial Court moved to Edo, renamed Tokyo, and occupied the Shogun's castle.

The civil war ended in victory for the Tozama. Control of the country passed from the central plains to the western provinces, into the hands of Satsuma and Choshu samurai. Although they had fought the Shogun to expel the foreigner, Japan's new leaders recognised the futility of opposing superior technology. The policy of isolation was dropped. The unfair treaties remained in force and the country remained open. The aim henceforth was to learn from and catch up with foreign technology. The Japanese were determined to become a Great Power in their own right.

The Meiji restoration

The Meiji restoration marked the start of the second long cycle. It was one of the most outstanding periods in the country's history. In a quarter of a century, a backward feudal country was transformed into a modern military power. Industrialisation took rather longer, another quarter-century to the end of the First World War. The Meiji period was distinctive in another way. In times of danger and crisis, great national leaders – such as Peter the Great, Napoleon or Churchill – often emerge, boldly to steer their nation's destiny. No single great leader emerged in Japan; instead, a group of samurai carried their country forward. The only precedent which comes to mind is the Founding Fathers after the American War of Independence. The analogy is close. Both groups had to create a national government from almost nothing and over the heads of existing state or domain governments. In each case the existing rulers had been swept away violently by rebellions. As usual, these were led by relatively young men, who then remained in power for many years. Masayoshi Matsukata of Satsuma, Taisuke Itagaki of Tosa, Shigenobu Okuma and Hirobumi Ito of Choshu were the most notable, the Japanese equivalents to Alexander Hamilton, Aaron Burr, John Adams and Thomas Jefferson.

Although called the Meiji restoration, the term is misleading. The Emperor still did not rule. A council of his closest advisers ruled in his name, and an oligarchy established which collectively acquired dictatorial powers. It was natural that no new Shogun emerged after the fall of the House of Tokugawa. The domains, which had combined to topple the Shogun, were too suspicious and jealous of one another to allow any one family to take over. In any case, the Emperor's name was essential to unite the nation. So an appearance of substance had to be given to the claim that power had been restored to the Emperor. Therefore, by Imperial decree, new court advisers to a senior council were appointed from the ranks of samurai from Satsuma, Choshu, Tosa and Hizen, the men who had been actively involved in the *coup d'état*. Then, to allay public suspicion, a statement was issued in the Emperor's name, the Charter Oath of April 1868, asserting that policy would be determined only after the widest possible consultation. It would not, this implied, simply be dictated from above.

The abolition of feudalism

But, of course, policy was imposed. The Council set to work immediately to obtain power. The confiscated Tokugawa domains, with their tax revenues, were not shared out between other domains as spoils, but reverted to the Emperor, giving him property for the first time. The next crucial step was to strip the daimios of their power. In March 1869, those of the four most important domains were persuaded 'voluntarily' to hand over all their lands to the Emperor. In return each received a fat pension and the empty title of Imperial Governor. In July 1869 the remaining daimios were brusquely ordered to follow suit. Any who thought that the change was without substance were quickly disabused. In August 1869, the Emperor took control of all domain tax revenues, and in August and September 1871 the old domains were abolished and replaced by prefectures controlled from Tokyo. The domain armies were simultaneously disbanded, to be replaced by an Imperial army based on universal conscription.

In the Emperor's name, the country's real rulers had gathered power into their own hands with notable rapidity. They had reason to do so: they were embarked upon nothing less than building a new Japan. While they did not all agree on the details, they were totally committed to rapid modernisation. Having obtained power, they moved swiftly to use it.

The feudal system was next on their hit list. The samurai system had to be tackled. First, they lost the right to use their swords on the lower classes; then they were no longer forced to wear swords; and, finally, they were forced not to wear swords. They were freed to go into farming, industry or commerce. Marriage with commoners was allowed. Finally, in early 1872, the whole feudal system was abolished. In its place a peerage was created, a gentry and commoners. But everyone was freed, not only to do what they liked, but also to move around as they pleased. Overnight this created a mobile and motivated labour force.

Next, the financial system had to be reformed. The ban on land sales was lifted in 1872 and ownership titles issued to farmers. In 1873 a cash land tax was introduced at 3% of market valuation in place of the old rice taxes. This was fairly steep and helped to shift land ownership from the feudal farmers to landlords. Samurai stipends were next to go. At first these could be voluntarily commuted into lump sums. But then, in 1876, samurai stipends were compulsorily commuted into government bonds. A Bank of Japan was established in 1882 with the sole right to issue paper currency. Joint stock companies were introduced and on 1 January 1873 Japan adopted the Gregorian calendar.

In other fields, a postal service was started in 1871. The first railway, from Tokyo to Yokohama, opened in 1872. Compulsory primary education was introduced that same year and a nation-wide system of schools and universities established. A criminal law code was promulgated in 1882. Even with these reforms it was unlikely that modern industry would develop rapidly. The government therefore took the lead by establishing state-owned industries: shipbuilding, iron and steel, armaments, textiles and the like.

Another civil war

This was not all accomplished without opposition, at times violent. The oligarchy itself split in 1873, when some of its members wanted war with Korea. Ironically, the Japanese complaint was that the Koreans had continued a closed-country policy and were refusing to open ports for trade with Japan. But the split and senior resignations came after Korea had been persuaded to open its ports. The war party had hoped the negotiations with Korea would fail. It wanted a pretext for war. Some Japanese were already looking abroad to territorial expansion as a way both of uniting the country and of providing employment for a large number of disgruntled samurai.

The men who resigned in 1873 went on to lead violent opposition to the government. When the samurai's stipends were commuted in 1876–7, rebellion flared. But it was only serious in Satsuma, where Takamori Saigo led a major uprising. Unfortunately for him, the government's military reforms were already showing results. It had already not only created a modern Imperial army, based on universal conscription, but also had a reserve of trained soldiers. It took the whole of this army and its reserves, 40,000 men, to put down the Satsuma rebellion, but thereafter there was never any danger of the Meiji restoration being challenged.

In the economically depressed 1880s, the Korean issue did not go away. It was an early indication that, once strong, Japan would use its armies to assert itself. It also fostered political opposition, which emerged when the country finally established a Constitution in 1889 and an elected lower house, the Diet, in 1890. In no way was the Diet given any real power over the government. This remained with a Cabinet, appointed by and answerable to the Emperor, and a Privy Council established as the highest source of advice to him. The Diet was simply there to be consulted. In the event, despite narrow male suffrage based upon stringent property qualifications, it turned out not to say the things which the authorities wanted. It became a source of criticism and abuse of the government, and was regularly and speedily dissolved.

Foreign adventures

With the domains dissolved, feudalism abolished, national education and conscription introduced, better communications and power centralised in Tokyo, people were educated to think of themselves primarily as Japanese. Their old loyalties to their daimios and domains were replaced by absolute loyalty and obedience to the Emperor. Such a sense of national identity was a necessary condition for the reform and modernisation of the domestic economy, but one which was bound to lead to external adventures. These began even before modernisation was complete.

Korea, the stepping stone to the mainland, was a Chinese vassal state. Following internal troubles in 1894, the Korean King called upon China for troops to help him restore order. Japan had its own plans to control Korea and told China to withdraw. The Chinese refused and war was declared. The modern Japanese army comprehensively thrashed the Chinese and dictated punitive peace terms in the Shimonoseki Treaty of April 1895. Japan obtained a large indemnity, Formosa (now Taiwan), the Liaotung Peninsula, which includes Port Arthur, and Korean 'independence'. The Japanese people were delighted. But other great nations were not. The French, Germans and Russians ganged up on Japan and demanded it give back Liaotung to China. The Russians threatened war and the Japanese government was forced to concede, which produced a public howl of rage. An armament drive followed: the army was doubled; and the navy was supplied with battleships, cruisers, destroyers and smaller craft to make it formidable in size and thoroughly modern at a time when, with the coming of the dreadnought, ship design was rapidly improving.

In less than a decade, Japan was ready to deal with Russia. Japan attacked without first declaring war. In January 1904 it bombarded Port Arthur without warning – a precedent for Pearl Harbor. Powerful Japanese armies moved over the border from Korea. They beat the Russians, but not without bitter fighting. The scale of this war was bigger than is generally recognised today. The Japanese had some 400,000 soldiers fighting in China. It also involved modern naval battles in which the results were decisive beyond measure. The Russians sent their Baltic fleet round the world to raise the Port Arthur blockade. It left Europe in November 1904 and reached the Tsushima Straits in the early summer of 1905. It got no further. On 27 May, it was blown out of the water by a fleet under the Japanese Admiral Togo. Defeat for Russia and financial exhaustion for Japan led both sides to call a halt.

The foundations of modern industrial Japan

The decade from 1885 to 1895 saw the real industrialisation of the Japanese economy. In the early days of the Meiji restoration, industrialisation was on a limited scale. It came from direct government investment in factories, rather than from private enterprise. Western fertilisers produced a marked increase in agricultural output. This enabled the country to feed the workers who moved into the towns. But industry was on a small and a light scale. Textiles, as almost everywhere, led the way. Government factories were generally mismanaged. They made losses and were a severe drain on the Imperial government's finances.

The late 1870s saw the Japanese government using a series of inflationary devices to cover its widening deficits. Matters were not taken in hand until Masayoshi Matsukata became Finance Minister in 1881. He introduced an austerity programme, which included the privatisation of loss-making state industries. Both Mitsui and Mitsubishi were set in motion with the purchase of government shipyards and other enterprises. Only when private enterprise took over and made large profits did industrialisation expand rapidly. The industrialists reaped the rewards from the decade of reforms which had followed the Meiji restoration. There was a surplus of cheap, educated, skilled and mobile labour. Communications had been greatly improved. The lump sums the samurai had been given in exchange for their pensions provided capital. Japanese landlords, if not their poor tenant farmers, were prospering

26

from increased output and higher income. The Japanese phenomenon of high savings can be traced back to this period of industrial development. Finally, the armament programme of 1895–1905 gave the whole process a further substantial boost.

The process of industrialisation and modernisation reached its zenith in the first five years of the twentieth century. By 1905 Japan had been transformed into a great modern industrial power with an overseas empire. The fifty years that elapsed between the arrival of Commodore Perry and war with Russia witnessed a notable revolution. The unfair treaties of 1858 marked the beginning of a decade of trauma and confusion as the House of Tokugawa collapsed. With the Meiji restoration in 1868, the nation settled upon its new objectives, to industrialise and modernise so that Japan could no longer be threatened by the advanced nations of Europe and America. Militarily, by 1905 these objectives had been fully and demonstrably achieved; the work of the Meiji restoration was complete. The Emperor Meiji himself lived a further seven years, dying in 1912 to be succeeded by his son, Taisho, who unfortunately was mentally defective.

A return to anarchy

For the following two decades, Japan politically was like a beheaded chicken running round a farmyard. The samurai, who had run the country since the Meiji restoration, were dying off or becoming infirm and senile, with the result that a power vacuum emerged. The Constitution adopted in 1889 was seriously flawed. It was modelled on the Prussian monarchical system, not the British. In theory the Emperor remained an absolute ruler. But by custom he neither intervened in politics, nor spoke while his councillors were meeting. Their job was to reach agreement amongst themselves and then present the result to the Emperor for ratification. But because the Constitution pretended otherwise, it did not establish how those who wielded the power behind the throne were to be appointed. Rivalry between the old samurai had ensured that nothing had been done to choose their successors.

Had Japan then evolved into a parliamentary democracy, the Diet would have become pre-eminent. But ministers, though Diet members, were constitutionally appointed by the Emperor. Since he made no decisions himself, there was nobody to tell him who to appoint. The Cabinet was made up of the Prime Minister and ministers for finance, home affairs, foreign affairs, justice, agriculture, commerce, the army and navy. Each was answerable individually to the Emperor for the conduct of his department. The Prime Minister could not tell them what to do. Instead, the Cabinet was a collegiate decision-making body, with measures having to be agreed between all its members. Similarly, military matters were not within the province of the Diet, but in the hands of the Emperor as Commander-in-Chief. The army and navy ministers had to be serving officers, not civilians. The upper and lower houses of the Diet had equal power, except with respect to the budget which was in the hands of the elected lower house alone. If the lower house could not agree and pass a budget, government expenditure was limited to the level set the previous year. The elected Diet was supposed to advise and consent, not legislate and rule. There was no arrangement for the government to have the support of the Diet and no thought that the Cabinet would be formed from men belonging to the same political party.

There were many contenders for power. Court officials and the House of Peers sought to exercise authority through the new but infantile Emperor. Political parties emerged and endeavoured to make the Cabinet answerable to the elected Diet, which meant to the privileged few who then had the franchise. Others wanted the franchise extended so that the Diet, in its turn, was democratically answerable to the people, or at least the adult male population. Big business (zaibatsu), as their paymasters, wanted politicians to be answerable to them. Between 1890 and 1920 the urban population had risen from 10% to 50%. The conservatives in the country-side, who wanted to preserve traditional values, were pitted against the new salaried classes in the towns who were becoming increasingly West-ernised. But above all, the military wanted to control the civilian govern-ments. Even within the military, there was severe rivalry between the army, with its roots still firmly embedded in Choshu; and the navy, which was as firmly linked to Satsuma. These rivalries frequently overlapped: the con-servative countryside, which supplied the officer classes in the army and navy, was generally anti-democratic and supported the military; the cities and zaibatsu were progressive and supported the politicians. The pattern of developments, however, was substantially influenced by the prosperity, or lack of it, in the economy. In good times the liberal forces could make steady, albeit modest progress, through compromise and co-operation with the peerage, court officials, bureaucrats and military. In bad times consensus was replaced by conflict, much of it bloody.

The period of 1912–32 was, overall, one in which the Japanese nation, no longer united in the pursuit of an agreed common goal, was instead split into many rival groups whose interests differed markedly from one another. The process of their resolution led to rising anarchy, lawlessness and violence, which the political system was unable to control. The first crisis arose immediately after the Emperor Meiji's death in 1912, involv-ing a struggle for power between the army and the civilian government.

The Diet was controlled by one of the two major parties which had emerged. This was the Seiyukai party, supported by Mitsui. It had been formed to campaign for a more liberal Constitution. The government, led by the Prime Minister, Kinmochi Saionji, wanted to cut the 1913 military budget. The army objected and brought down the government by the simple expedient of forbidding any serving officer to take ministerial office. Without navy and army ministers, Saionji could not form a full collegiate Cabinet and had to resign. Saionji's place was taken by a Choshu general, Taro Katsura, who was acceptable to the military and could form a Cabinet. But Katsura could not obtain a Diet majority for his budget. Expenditure in 1913 was thus limited to its 1912 level. The impasse was broken by the appointment of a new government under a Satsuma admiral, who bribed and cajoled the Seiyukai party into support. The episode showed that a government needed military support to be formed and Diet support to function. The crisis led in 1913 to the repeal of the law that the navy and army ministers be serving officers. They could be retired officers, but not civilians. (The old law was re-introduced in 1936.) The army's stranglehold on government was eased, not removed. General Katsura formed a new party to support the military, which evolved into the Minseito party, the main post-war rival to Seiyukai. Mitsubishi, Mitsui's great rival, became the Minseito party's paymaster.

Wartime prosperity

The First World War brought an interlude to Japan's power struggle. The Japanese declared war on the Allies' side, and promptly pinched all Germany's Pacific and Chinese possessions. This aside, the country took little active part in the war. Instead it exploited the political opportunity for territorial expansion by making outrageous demands on the Chinese. Although not allowed to get all that it wanted, it did occupy the Kwantung Peninsula in order to control the South Manchurian Railway Zone.

Economically Japan prospered greatly during the war. Its rapid industrialisation from 1880 onwards had been based upon combining advanced Western technology with cheap Eastern labour. The wealth so produced went largely to the dynastic families who owned the great zaibatsu. But as they were a frugal lot, they spent little and ploughed most of their profits back into further expansion. Labour remained plentiful and cheap, largely because of the rapid growth in the population as diet, medical care and health improved, and because serious over-population in the countryside led to substantial migration to the towns. At first,

Japan supplied cheap and often shoddy products to their home and Asian markets. But as the European belligerents converted all their industrial potential to military use, the war enabled Japan to capture higher grade markets worldwide. Japan also became a substantial manufacturer and exporter of military equipment and munitions.

Japanese economic prosperity peaked in 1918. By this time the population had doubled to 60 million, from 30 million in 1868. It had become a major manufacturing country, which devoured vast quantities of imported raw materials. From being isolated from the world economy and self-contained, it was now dependent for its prosperity upon international trade. The post-war decade was one of acute disappointment. Japan suffered its slowest growth of any decade between 1880 and 1940. Its foreign markets dried up and its raw material supplies were threatened. The great Kanto earthquake in 1923 levelled much of Tokyo and Yokohama. The mass of Japanese people suffered straitened times after the war, with harvest failures causing famine in the countryside. Under these circumstances the latent tensions in society were bound to surface and in a violent form.

Hopes for democracy

Nonetheless democracy made some further progress against the military, but largely at the expense of persuading the anti-democratic forces in society to resort to violent and criminal means to get their own way. In 1918 Japan sent an army to Vladivostok in Siberia as part of a joint Allied expedition to support anti-communist forces. The army was 72,000 strong, four times as big as the government had authorised. Moreover it refused to return when requested. The Prime Minister, Kei Hara, the head of the Seiyukai party, attempted to impose his authority over it and, in 1921, was assassinated for his efforts. Despite this, the politicians won and in 1922 the army was withdrawn.

This episode was a warning. Over the following decade, the civil government's control over the military was to be steadily eroded. Within the army, the general staff lost control over the junior officers. Real control moved perceptibly into the hands of the colonels, who commanded the troops on the ground. This was particularly so with units stationed in the South Manchurian Railway Zone. Japan's expansion into Manchuria and thence to South China, which culminated in confrontation with the US, was led from below by soldiers in the field, not ordered from above by generals in Tokyo. Army commanders who resisted military expansion risked assassination by their junior officers; so did civilian politicians who stood in the army's way.

Nonetheless, from 1922 to 1925 it seemed as if Japan had been finally set on the road to democracy and peaceful co-operation with other Great Powers. The Anglo–Japanese Alliance of 1902 was replaced by a five-Power pact between the war victors: Japan, the US, Britain, France and Italy. There was an arms limitation agreement and Japan withdrew from Siberia and northern Sakhalin. At home, universal male suffrage was introduced in 1925. The military budget was reduced. The government and the Diet seemed to have obtained the upper hand.

The military takeover

The politicians' success in the early 1920s in controlling the generals led to the generals' loss of control over the army. The Kokuryukai, known as the Black Dragon or River Amur Society, was a secret society set up in 1901 to stir up trouble in Manchuria. Many of its members were serving army officers. Thanks to their influence, the Kwantung army in South Manchuria became a law unto itself. In 1928 it arranged the murder of Marshal Chang Tso-lin, the local Chinese warlord. The new Emperor, Hirohito, broke with convention to demand that his government discipline the army, but the military refused to take orders from the civil government. Instead of the Marshal's assassins being brought to justice, the government was brought down by the incident, which it had neither plotted nor condoned. Moreover, the Emperor's failure to achieve results on the first occasion he intervened personally in politics undermined his ability to do so at a later date. A new moderate government under the Prime Minister, Osachi Hamaguchi, was appointed. He tried to regain control of the Kwantung army, but in 1930 he, too, was assassinated. The Kwantung army became bolder. It staged a counterfeit bomb attack on a train and blamed the local Chinese. Without authority, it attacked the city of Mukden and took control of the remainder of Manchuria.

The Manchurian incident, as the affair was called, was the work of army officers who supported the Control clique, which advocated expansion into southern China. It was opposed by the Imperial Way clique, which saw the dangers of a premature clash with the US. The Imperial Way clique wanted Japan to suspend further aggression in China and concentrate on building a powerful enough navy to be able to confront the US, Britain and the Netherlands in the south Pacific. It was supported by another secret terrorist organisation, the Ketsumeidan or Blood Brotherhood, which was essentially fascist. Its target was the so-called democratic system, which was riddled with corruption. Politicians were blamed for the economic suffering in the countryside, for leading Japan away from its traditional values and for lining their own pockets. Big business was also among the brotherhood's targets. It wanted to engineer a Showa restoration akin to the Meiji restoration. Each member of the brotherhood, mostly young army and naval officers from farming families, was pledged to kill at least one politician. There were frequent assassinations and attempted assassinations. Moreover, self-seeking politicians were so unpopular with ordinary people that murderous attacks upon them were generally condoned.

The brotherhood was responsible for two famous incidents, named after the days on which they occurred. On 15 May 1932, nine army and navy officers took taxis to the Prime Minister's residence, burst in and murdered him, then left in the waiting taxis. During their trial, the assassins claimed to have acted in the public good: the murder was a warning to venal politicians. The public was on the murderers' side. More than 100,000 petitions for clemency were presented, some written in blood. Nine men offered to take the place of the accused and, as an earnest of their intent, sent their little fingers, pickled in jars of vinegar. Amputating one's pinky remains to this day one of the rites of gangster (yakuza) membership. The accused got off lightly: none was sentenced to death; all were free again within a few years. The murdered Prime Minister, Tsuyoshi Inukai, was the last pre-war party leader to become Premier. Thereafter, the military dictated who should hold office. As a result of the incident of 15 May, the Diet lost control over the government, even if it took another five years before the militarists gained complete control.

The second incident occurred on 26 February 1936. The finance minister, two former prime ministers (one of whom was an admiral) and an army general were assassinated and the centre of Tokyo occupied for several days by troops commanded by rebel officers. Again the excuse was punishment for corrupt politicians. The Prime Minister's brother was murdered by mistake. Okada himself escaped by hiding in a broom cupboard and was smuggled out of his residence under the eyes of his would-be assassins. Army leaders in Tokyo dithered, but remained loyal to their Emperor. For the second time in his reign he intervened, this time successfully. The rebellion was put down, the assassins were arrested, tried in secret and quickly executed. The Emperor, anxious to restore order, wanted the generals to re-establish command over the army. Public opinion had also shifted. People had despaired of politicians changing their rotten ways. Now they wanted stability under firm government to end the growing anarchy and bring back prosperity. Unfortunately, the incident of 26 February led to a purge of all senior officers who belonged to the Imperial Way clique.

Thus the Control clique gained the ascendancy. The military took over the government.

Between the two incidents, the occupation of Manchuria had been 'legitimised' by the formation in 1934 of the puppet state of Manchukuo under a child, the 'last Emperor'. At home, elections were held in 1937 and the Seiyukai and Minseito parties buried their differences to oppose the military government. They won an overwhelming majority at the polls – but the outcome was too late. The Diet had lost all control over the government; the generals had lost all control over the army. In July 1937, without authority from Tokyo, the North China army launched its attack on China. The general staff did its utmost to forestall war, but once the fighting started, it had no idea how to stop it. The Pacific War had begun. Patriotism demanded that the nation unite in support of its armies; the police made sure that it did.

In territorial terms, the army was immensely successful. It drove back the troops of Jiang Jieshi (Chiang Kai-shek) from Beijing; it took Nanking, massacring as many as 300,000 Chinese civilians after the city's fall. City after city surrendered to the advancing Japanese. But they did not defeat the Chinese army, which simply retreated further into that vast country. The Japanese army was being swallowed by space, just as Napoleon's had been in Russia and, later, Hitler's would be. The army high command sought desperately for a way to back off from the war, without losing face.

War in Europe and Hitler's 1940 victories changed everything. Japan's great opportunity to free Asia from the foreigners' stranglehold had come. As foreseen by the Imperial Way clique, the army's aggression in China had brought Japan into direct confrontation with the Americans. President Roosevelt had imposed an embargo on oil supplies to Japan. Stocks were low, less than two years' ordinary usage. In 1941 Japan's leaders were in a quandary: there were only two ways to end the American embargo. One was to withdraw from China – but that was unthinkable. The people had been told only of Japan's great victories. They did not understand that strategically Japan was stalemated. The army would rebel with the likelihood that the generals and politicians would be assassinated. The other way was to go forward by attacking US, British and Dutch installations and shipping. By expansion into South East Asia, the Japanese could capture raw material and oil resources.

The Japanese in 1941 were in the same predicament as in 1853, when the 'black ships' came. To withdraw from China meant civil war and the overthrow of the government and military leaders. Not to withdraw meant a foreign war, which everyone knew could not be won. It would be impossible to defeat and occupy America. The US was too large, too mighty, too populous and too far away. The only hope was that the Americans, once kicked out of South East Asia, would balk at the cost and casualties involved in getting back. They would throw in the towel and become isolationist. It was a forlorn hope, born of desperation. But to Japanese leaders, it was better than facing up to the truth that Japan's position was hopeless. Attacking the Americans would gain time, and who knew how the world might develop? The decision to go forward was taken; the order was given to attack on 7 December 1941 the US naval base at Pearl Harbor.

2

Save and Stagnate

It has been shown how, during the first long cycle, the policy of sakoku sustained the power of the Shogun at the expense of progress. But this policy of no change at all cost led, through foreign intervention, to traumatic change at great cost. It has been shown also how modernisation succeeded brilliantly when it harnessed the forces of Emperor-worship and ultra-nationalism in pursuit of radical reform at home, but failed miserably when those forces took control and led the country into external aggression. The foundations of the fourth long cycle were laid by the Americans by the reforms they imposed. They united the nation in its drive to reconstruct the economy and catch up with other advanced countries. The successful phase lasted to the late 1960s. The overshoot phase has lasted the last two decades, and the phase of political turmoil has now begun. In economic terms, high savings have played a crucial role in this fourth cycle. A little theory is needed to explain how and why.

Save and prosper

Savings are vital to an economy: they provide the resources needed for investment in new homes, factories, plant and equipment, roads, schools and hospitals. A saver earns more making things or providing services, than he spends buying goods and services others make or provide. He adds more to supply than to demand. An investor pays people to make things or provide services, which he does immediately use or sell. A company building a new factory does not then sell it; when completed, it makes goods which it sells. Investors add to demand, without immediately increasing supply. The more people save, the more a country is able to invest, the faster it grows or improves its social capital.

Countries at different stages of development need to devote different proportions of their current income to investment. First, they must invest to make good wear and tear, called depreciation, on their existing stock of capital assets. When machines are used they wear out and must be replaced. Roads must be mended, bridges painted. The larger the capital stock, the more must be spent on its upkeep. Total investment, which includes the sums needed to offset depreciation, is called 'gross' investment. What is left after deducting depreciation, called 'net' investment, increases the capital stock.

Most countries need to increase their capital stock. When the labour force is growing, additional workers must be supplied with plant and equipment. Backward economies, with too small or too old a capital stock, can raise productivity and output by providing existing workers with more and better equipment. Few countries have as good an infrastructure or as modern social capital as they would like. They need more roads, better railways and telephones, better schools, hospitals and homes. A country with a growing population needs more of all these things. It would seem there is no limit to the proportion of a nation's income that it could usefully devote to investment; in which case, the higher the level of savings the better.

Limits to investment

But there *are* limits. Once a nation has a large and modern industrial capital stock, it becomes unprofitable to increase it at too fast a rate. Producers need markets for the additional output which higher investment makes possible. But the more people save, the less they consume and the smaller those markets. A balance has to be struck, if investment is to remain profitable. The limit to spending on the social infrastructure, which improves the quality of life rather than increasing the level of output, is different. Much of such spending is paid for out of taxation or government borrowing. People object to paying high taxes, particularly where a tax system is unfair or inefficient. Borrowing builds up public debts on which interest has to be paid. These debts grow exponentially, if interest charges get so high that a government has to borrow to pay them.

The limits to the investment a country can sustain vary from country to country and time to time. They depend on a number of factors: the size and growth in its population and labour force; the size and nature of its existing capital stock; the rate of return on new investment in industrial assets; and the efficiency and equity with which it raises taxes and the size of its public debts. An advanced mature economy, with slow population growth and a static labour force, needs to invest a lower proportion of its income than a backward economy with rapid population and labour force growth. But people in the former have higher incomes than those in the latter, and will tend to save more out of their income. There is no

36

mechanism which ensures that the amount people *want to save* exactly equals the amount their country *needs to invest*.

Excess savings

High savings are benign when they are needed to finance a high level of investment. They become excessive and potentially malign, when the amount people want to save exceeds the amount businesses want and governments are able to invest. But there are mechanisms which ensure that the amount people actually *save* equals the amount that is actually *invested*. Most savers are lenders; most investors are borrowers. Interest is the price the lender receives for consuming less today, in order to consume more tomorrow. If people want to save and lend more than others want to borrow and spend, the rate of interest falls. This deters some savers, while encouraging increased borrowing. The lower the rate of interest, the better the prospects of the investor making a profit.

In normal circumstances capital markets ensure that savings equal investment through movements in interest rates. But this system can break down. Interest rates never fall below zero. Nobody lends if they get back less than they lent. It is better to leave the money under the mattress. People sometimes pay to have their money kept safe for them. That is not negative interest, but payment for a service. Prices, however, sometimes fall; when they do, the real cost of borrowing money rises. The investor must sell more lower-priced goods to make a profit. Since prices fall mainly when too much is already being produced, there is little attraction in borrowing to produce more. So when interest rates can go no lower, however excessive the level of savings, and prices are falling, a different adjustment mechanism comes into action.

The Keynesian liquidity trap

Excess savings mean that producers are paying people more to make things, than people are willing to spend buying them. Stocks of unsold goods build up at factories and on shop shelves. Businessmen then cut production, close plants and sack workers. Output, employment and incomes all fall. Even if they continue to put the same proportion of their income into savings, people save less because of their lower income. This is how excess savings can be malign and cause recession. The interwar depression is an obvious example. John Maynard Keynes described the phenomenon as the 'liquidity' trap. He prescribed a solution. If people saved too much, governments could dissave by running budget deficits. They, instead of businessmen, could borrow and spend. His solution worked when governments did just this, to pay for rearmament and to fight the Second World War.

The liquidity trap was a problem of excess world savings in the 1930s, which led to falling world prices. World prices have not fallen in any year since the start of the Second World War. Prices have fallen in only a few countries in only a few years. Excess savings have thus been a national problem for a few countries, for which there has been an international solution. Open economies trade with other countries. In consequence, an excess of one country's savings over its domestic investment results initially in foreign lending, which leads that country to run a current account surplus. The goods producers cannot sell profitably at home are sold abroad as exports. There are different ways in which such a surplus is produced, depending upon whether exchange rates are fixed or floating and whether capital movements are free or restricted.

International adjustment

When exchange rates are fixed and capital movements restricted, as under the post-war Bretton Woods system, excess savings at first slows growth in the surplus savings country. It therefore imports less. Slow growth also reduces inflationary pressures. Its exports become relatively cheaper or more profitable and it sells more of them. Its economy is buoyed up by the improvement in its trade balance. But those of its trading partners are depressed. Under the Bretton Woods fixed exchange rate system, payments surpluses tended to be small and short-lived, thereby increasing the demand for the surplus countries' currency on foreign exchange markets. Action had to be taken to prevent the currency from rising.

Foreign exchange market intervention was the first line of defence. Either the surplus country's central bank bought foreign currency with its own to keep its exchange rate from rising; or the deficit countries' central banks sold foreign currencies and bought their own. The pressure was always on the countries whose currencies were being forced down to act. Moreover, there was a limit to the amount of foreign currencies that they held in their reserves or could borrow. As this limit was approached, further action was required.

The second line of defence was fiscal policy. Either the surplus country's government reflated by running budget deficits – the remedy Keynes prescribed for excess savings but which few were willing to adopt – or the deficit countries' governments were forced to raise taxes or cut spending to slow growth in their economies. The Bretton Woods system could cope with a short-run cyclical excess of savings in one or two countries. The problem was soon solved as the business cycle moved on. It could not cope with persistent structural payments surpluses and deficits. Deficit countries, such as Britain and the US, with overvalued currencies refused to depress their economies indefinitely. So the Bretton Woods system collapsed.

Under floating exchange rates, when capital flows are restricted, surpluses and deficits are also short-lived. The surplus country's currency simply rises to the point at which its dear exports are choked off, while cheap imports flood in. If savings continue to be excessive, the escape route from recession through a trade surplus is closed.

The only system which will tolerate large and persistent trade surpluses is one where capital is free to move from one country to another. Falling interest rates in the excess savings country leads to capital outflows, which lower the value of its currency. The fall in its exchange rate causes it to run a payments surplus, instead of the payments surplus causing its exchange rate to rise. The surplus savings country lends its excess savings to people in other countries, enabling them to buy its excess products.

But trading partners, who run persistent deficits, amass foreign debts. There is a limit to how long they are able and willing to do so. Under some circumstances, payments imbalances can continue for many years. In wealthy, mature and advanced economies savings are usually high, while the returns from further domestic investment are low. More money can be obtained by investing in developing economies, where investment opportunities are attractive. Although the absolute size of developing countries' external debts increase, their size relative to their rapidly growing GDPs need not do so. Nor need interest payments to foreigners become burdensome, provided foreign money is productively invested in industries to increase exports or replace imports. In the two decades before the First World War, British capital exports averaged about 5% of GDP per annum and by 1913 Britain's total foreign assets exceeded its annual GDP. Britain led the way into the industrial revolution and its external lending helped other countries to follow.

This solution works where sound investment opportunities are plentiful and global savings are scarce. It does not work when world savings are excessive. It is often argued these days that German unification, the collapse of communism in eastern Europe and the former Soviet Union, the need to rebuild Kuwait following the Gulf War and the return of some debtor countries to the world's capital markets as creditworthy borrowers, has created a shortage of global savings. The former communist countries desperately need higher investment. But

39

while they remain in political and economic chaos, they are not creditworthy borrowers. Increased demands of those countries that are creditworthy is likely to be offset by the fall in investment, which is taking place in the mature economies with falling labour force growth. The world would not now be in recession were there a shortage of global savings.

People in one country can only save excessively provided someone else, somewhere else, is willing to borrow and spend those excesses. There is a limit to the amount thriftless foreigners will borrow to run payments deficits. There is a limit to the amount profligate governments will run budget deficits. In the end, a limit is reached to both the international solution and the Keynesian solution to excess savings. When these limits are reached, the excess savings country necessarily becomes depressed.

Big savers

The Japanese are big savers; they have been for the last four decades. The table shows how much the Japanese saved in 1988 compared with other nations:

	BY PERSONS	BY COMPANIES	BY GOVERNMENTS	TOTAL
Japan	10.4 (15.3)	20.8	2.1	33.3
Germany	7.9 (12.6)	18.7	−2.1	24.5
Canada	6.7 (10.4)	17.0	−2.6	21.1
Italy	10.0 (14.1)	21.8	−10.9	20.9
France	8.3 (12.1)	14.0	−1.8	20.5
Britain	2.7 (4.1)	12.6	1.1	16.4
USA	3.0 (4.3)	14.1	−2.0	15.1

Table 1   Savings in 1988 as % of GDP

[Figures in parenthesis show personal savings as a percent of total personal after-tax (i.e. disposable) incomes]

The Japanese save more than any other major nation. They saved one-third of their national income in 1988. People in Italy saved almost as much and Italian companies saved more, but the Italian government runs a colossal budget deficit of over 10% of GDP, which reduced Italian national savings considerably. The thrifty Japanese habitually save up to twice as much as the.spendthrift Americans. (See Chart 1.) In 1988 only the British and Japanese governments ran surpluses and

Save and Stagnate

CHART 1: Japanese and US Savings 1953–90
Total Savings as percent of GNP

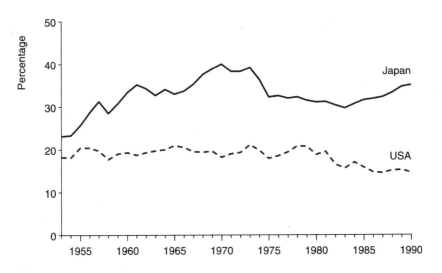

CHART 2: Japan's Excess Savings 1953–90
Percent of GNP

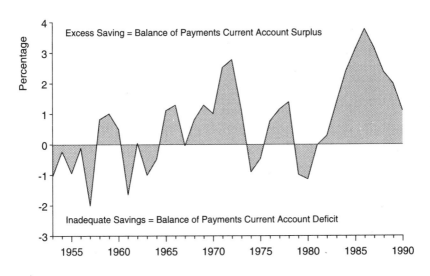

saved. The other five member governments of the Group of Seven (G7) nations, all dissaved, the Italians as already observed, to a massive extent. Since excess savings produce current account surpluses, it can be seen from Chart 2 that until the late 1960s Japanese savings were as often inadequate (i.e. produced payments deficits) as they were excessive. But when the Japanese economy caught up with other advanced economies, a high level of investment was no longer required. Growth slowed, particularly following the shock of the first sharp rise in oil prices. Japanese savings became excessive and a structural balance of payments surplus emerged. The next two decades were spent dealing with this problem.

The oil-price hikes both helped Japan. They turned the terms of trade against the country, meaning it had to export more to pay for the higher price of its imports. They effectively mopped up surplus savings, as can be seen by the Japanese payments deficits in 1974–5 and 1980–1. Between these years, the Japanese government acted to limit the country's excess savings by running big budget deficits. But the result was large government debts and this policy had to be abandoned in the early 1980s. After the second oil-price rise, the US bailed out Japan. The Americans borrowed and spent, running large budget and balance of payments deficits. The Japanese saved and lent. The Americans borrowed Japan's surplus savings to buy Japan's surplus products. The result was a record Japanese payments surplus of 4% of GDP in 1986, inflated by falling oil prices. This phase ended because the US took steps to reduce its twin deficits. The result was the period from 1985 to 1988 known as endaka, or strong yen, during which the yen doubled in value against the dollar. The Japanese economy stagnated.

Endaka was countered by a policy of cheap and easy money, particularly following the October 1987 stockmarket crash. The result was the 'bubble' economy, in which soaring asset prices in Japan encouraged people to save less and businesses to invest more. But the economy overheated, while asset price inflation destroyed the egality of income and wealth on which social harmony in Japan was based. So the Governor of the Bank of Japan burst the bubble by making money scarce and dear once again. In 1990 the Tokyo stockmarket crashed. In 1991 property prices fell for the first time in the living memory of most Japanese. Financial scandals followed. The economy slowed and the current account surplus began once more to soar.

Japan has now entered the phase in which high savings are malign. They threaten to cause deep recession. The Japanese have not faced serious economic hardship since the early post-war years. They are now about to do so.

3

Bamboo Shoot Years

The early post-war years were a period of great change and desperate hardship for the Japanese people. Their political economy was revolutionised at the dictate of a foreign power. For the most part it was a peaceful revolution. The Japanese establishment was not merely defeated, but also cowed and disgraced by the war; it was in no condition to resist change. Many ordinary Japanese welcomed it. But while American reforms laid sound foundations for future prosperity, American economic management caused unnecessarily severe and prolonged misery. The plight of the Japanese economy by 1950 was so serious that only the advent of the Korean War saved the country from renewed anarchy. But for the boost that US military spending in Japan gave to the economy, the occupation might have become an unmitigated disaster, instead of a brilliant success.

The costs of war

Excessive saving is now Japan's problem. But in the immediate post-war years the Japanese did not save – they were too poor to save for the future. Their problem then was to survive. Indeed the problem of survival remained so acute that as late as 1949 – regarded by many as Japan's darkest post-war year – there was real danger of a communist revolution. Violence, strikes, riots, assassinations characterised the domestic scene well beyond the end of the occupation and up to the mid–1950s.

At the end of the Second World War, the Japanese need and desire to save was pressing. The war left the civilian economy twice destroyed. The blockade on imports meant that every available resource was channelled into armament production and the war effort. By 1945, the production of peacetime goods had fallen 70–95% below pre-war levels. At the same time, stocks of raw materials, finished products, fuel and food were nearly exhausted. Clothing and household items were worn out.

Machinery, plant and equipment for peacetime production had been neglected for a decade, neither repaired nor replaced, only converted to the production of military supplies. The peacetime capital stock had been used up in the effort to sustain all-out war.

This economic destruction was followed by physical destruction. From 1944, air attacks on Japan had increased in intensity. The destruction was on a gigantic scale: 119 major cities were reduced to rubble. Only one, Kyoto, survived intact. In urban areas, 40% of all dwellings were flattened, 2 m homes were destroyed and 9 m people driven on to the streets. The countryside got off lightly, and in rural areas the majority of dwellings were undamaged. But communications were disrupted, and roads, bridges and port facilities were wiped out. Surprisingly, railways and electrical power supplies were little damaged.

A study by the Japanese Economic Stabilisation Board after the war put the loss of national assets at a quarter of their pre-war level. But this excluded the extent to which peacetime productive capacity was converted to wartime use. It also ignored the extent to which capacity had become obsolete because it remained based on early 1930s technology. Even so, the estimated loss included 82% of Japanese merchant shipping; while the ships that remained were so badly constructed during the war that they were unfit for long ocean voyages.

Heavy industry, on which the wartime machine was based, produced only half as much in 1945 as it did before the war. Peacetime production was one-tenth or less of pre-war levels. A striking illustration of the shortage of productive capacity is that, at the war's end, the rate of production of leather shoes was such that it would have taken thirty years to supply each person in Japan with one new pair.

There were also grievous human losses: 2 m servicemen and 700,000 civilians lost their lives during the war; thousands of children were orphaned. Trucks toured the streets of big cities collecting orphans, much as stray dogs are sometimes rounded up. But while the blockade and air raids left Japan in 1945 with no peacetime industrial capacity, the war also left in its wake millions of people jobless and homeless. When the military machine was dismantled nearly 8 m troops were disbanded and 4 m war workers lost their jobs. In addition 1.5 m civilian Japanese returned home from the former Japanese empire in Korea and China. Capital was non-existent, labour was abundant.

The need for savings was acute. Industry had to be converted back to peacetime use and re-equipped with modern technology. Roads, bridges and ports had to be rebuilt. The nation's housing stock required repair and reconstruction. Post-war inflation destroyed personal financial wealth. Real wealth, which had been concentrated in the hands of a few

44

powerful families, was confiscated by property taxes imposed at the command of the American occupation administration. Land reforms robbed landlords of their land, but redistributed it to former tenants at virtually no cost thanks to the rapid collapse in the value of money. Rural Japan again benefited in comparison with urban Japan. Corporate Japan was no better placed, and bankruptcies were rife. The big zaibatsu industrial conglomerates were broken up. Banks made horrendous losses on the loans they had been obliged to make to finance war production; their liabilities to their depositors were not reduced. In this situation, almost every Japanese family was poverty-stricken. Everybody needed to re-build personal wealth, to pay for education, sickness and old age and especially to guard against future misfortune. The state had no money for social security or welfare. The individual had to look to himself alone for his own survival.

The problem with saving is that income is necessary from which to save. During the war, Japanese living standards had been reduced to subsistence levels or lower. In 1945 the Japanese were unable to feed, clothe or house themselves. They had no surplus of income to be saved. Yet without such a surplus there was no way investment could be financed or industry recover. Savings could not rise until incomes rose; incomes could not rise until savings rose.

American occupation

It was no use looking to the victors for help. The American plans for post-war Japan were clear, simple and limited. They intended to dismantle the Japanese military machine and to destroy the industrial might on which it had rested. Economically, they aimed to return Japan to the state of industrialisation it had reached in 1926–30. Politically, they would impose democracy. Their overriding and almost only objective was to destroy the power, privileges and wealth of the Japanese ruling classes, who were blamed collectively and indiscriminately for Japanese militarism.

What remained of wartime capacity, mainly in the engineering and machine tool industries, could not be converted to peacetime use, but was earmarked to be dismantled and transferred to other countries in partial payment for reparations. The Pauley Reparations Commission of 1945 recommended that all aircraft, light metal and bearings factories be removed from Japan, together with half the equipment in shipyards, steam-powered electrical generating plant, steel, machine tool, aluminium sulphate and soda factories. With little peacetime capacity

45

remaining and most surviving wartime capacity scheduled for confiscation, there would have been no industrial basis upon which the Japanese could even hope to rebuild their economy to its pre-war level. It is not clear how democracy was supposed to take root under such circumstances. When a whole nation is reduced to penury, its people often turn to dictators for rescue from their plight. Democracy, and the feeble government which it usually spawns, is a luxury which the destitute can ill afford. Consequently, Japanese democracy had a weak and sickly childhood. The threat of revolution in 1949 was real enough, although it could hardly have succeeded while the Americans remained in occupation. It was fortunate that, when the Americans left in 1952, recovery was under way, the communists had been purged and the worst dangers were past.

The American attitude immediately after the war was that Japan was responsible for its own economic plight and would likewise have to bear responsibility for peacetime reconstruction. The US had no intention of lifting a finger to help. The only aid the Americans offered was emergency food, fuel and raw material imports, but on the minimum possible scale and only to avert the most desperate of crises. The US occupation authorities governed Japan indirectly through Japan's own government, bureaucracy, laws, police and judiciary. SCAP (strictly meaning the Supreme Commander for the Allied Powers, General MacArthur, but also loosely used to mean the occupation administration) issued directions to the government concerning legislation and reforms, yet also sanctioned or vetoed actions which the government proposed on its own initiative. In this way Japan's politicians shared the blame for the way things were managed.

Zapping the zaibatsu

SCAP, the administration, did nothing to encourage economic rehabilitation, limiting itself at first to its programme of demilitarisation and democratisation. It demanded the immediate and complete demobilisation of all the Japanese armed forces, together with the cancellation of all war supplies contracts, and then set about dismantling Japan's industrial machine.

From the Meiji restoration through to the end of the Second World War, Japanese production was concentrated in the hands of a few large zaibatsu: family-owned and controlled industrial and financial conglomerates. There were four major zaibatsu – Mitsui, Mitsubishi, Sumitomo and Yasuda – who between them accounted for a quarter of all paid-up capital in Japanese industry, and a further six – Nissan,

Asano, Furukawa, Okura, Nakajima and Nomura – which together accounted for a further tenth. These ten companies controlled 50% of Japanese banking and mining operations, 60% of its metal working and shipping, and 70% of all machinery production. The families owning them were amongst the richest and most powerful in the world. The zaibatsu customarily included banks, major trading houses, and a variety of large companies involved in steel, shipbuilding, heavy engineering, chemicals and other strategic industries. All were run by major holding companies owned by the immensely rich families. These dynasties actively managed their zaibatsu companies. Family members and their relatives monopolised all the top jobs. A good young manager from outside the family, could rise to a top job only if, on the way, the family elders decided to marry off one of their daughters to him.

The Americans intended to destroy the zaibatsu and to strip their owners of all personal wealth, power and influence. In November 1945 SCAP froze the assets of the fifteen largest zaibatsu, and then proceeded to split up the conglomerates into their component parts. Shares in the holding companies at the war's end accounted for 40% of all shares on the Tokyo stock exchange. By 1951 virtually all of these had been taken from their owners and sold. Holding companies were outlawed and tough anti-monopoly laws enacted. But the Americans did not stop there, they also broke up any large company which held a monopolistic position in its own market, e.g. Nippon Steel was split into Yawata Steel and Fuji Steel; Mitsui Mining into Mitsui Coal Mining and Mitsui Metal Mining; Dainippon Beer into Sapporo Beer and Asahi Beer.

Conglomerate-busting and anti-monopoly legislation were designed to change the corporate face of Japan. SCAP purged all senior public officials, politicians, zaibatsu families, industrial leaders and senior managers who had enjoyed positions of power, authority or wealth during the war. No attention was paid to what part any individual had actually played. Some had bravely opposed the military. No matter. All were regarded, prima facie, as having caused and conducted the war.

The owners and senior managers of the old zaibatsu were prohibited from any future activities in management and finance. Former politicans were forbidden from political activity and office. These steps were followed by a confiscatory property tax, levied in 1946, on all personal assets in excess of ¥100,000. Its graduated scale reached 90% of everything over ¥15 m. This harsh tax left formerly rich Japanese with very modest fortunes. These then evaporated with post-war inflation, which reached 400% in 1947. SCAP's measures destroyed the old nobility, the zaibatsu families and the landholding class, whose wealth and social position had enabled them to dominate Japanese society up to that time.

Creating the keiretsu

Measures to break up the corporate concentration of economic power were not entirely successful. It was too large and complex a task for the American administration to achieve on its own. The Japanese pretended to co-operate, the better able to mislead the Americans by hiding assets. The Americans also lost their enthusiasm for the task when, with cold war tension rising, policy towards Japan switched to reconstruction. The zaibatsu, in their old form, all ceased to exist; but somewhat similar keiretsu – also conglomerates of related companies – replaced them. But each member of a keiretsu family is owned by its own shareholders, and not by a family-owned holding company. Keiretsu family members are tied together by cross shareholdings and by board membership. They now centre mostly on major banks, which built up their original corporate shareholdings when bailing out cash-strapped or insolvent companies in the immediate post-war years. Keiretsu companies are managed by a professional management class instead of family dynasties.

Where companies themselves were divided, the result was intense competition as each part endeavoured to restore itself to the size and importance of the former whole. Dividing up Japanese industrial giants very soon resulted in there being twice as many such giants, whose competition for growth could not be satisfied by the domestic market and so spilt over into the export markets of the world.

Democracy designed by Americans

Democratisation involved establishing free trade unions, revising the Meiji constitution and land reform. Under the land reform measures, which the Japanese government was forced by SCAP to enact in October 1946, all land belonging to absentee landlords, and all but about two and a half acres belonging to landlords resident in rural villages, had to be sold to the government. It was then resold to sitting tenants. This measure changed Japanese agriculture from a feudal system, with a few large landowners and many small tenant farmers, to one of thousands of small peasant farmers each tilling a minute acreage of farmland. The proportion of land tilled by tenant farmers dropped from around 50% at the end of the war to 10% by 1950; the proportion of tenant farmers fell more dramatically. The money paid to former landlords either lost most of its value during the subsequent inflation or was confiscated by the 1947 property tax. The real cost to the tenant of purchasing their smallholdings was similarly reduced to a pittance by inflation. As in their

48

escape from the ravages of wartime destruction, so, as a result of American reforms, the rural population gained substantially relative to urban dwellers. This had major political and economic ramifications in the later post-war years. In particular, the land reforms produced a solid rural conservative vote which, together with over-representation of rural constituencies, did much to enable democracy – albeit defective democracy – to survive.

Trade union reform had more immediate and dangerous consequences. Unions were legalised, the right of assembly granted, together with freedom of speech and the right to strike. At the same time, SCAP ordered the release of all political prisoners, mostly communists who had been involved in the past in illegal trade union activities. The Communist Party was legalised. Communist exiles returned from abroad, mainly China. Not surprisingly, the communists took the lead in establishing the new unions and then applied their industrial muscle to political ends. They were particularly active in the large public-sector unions, the rail unions, Nippon Telegraph & Telephone, postal workers, teachers and so forth. They were less prominent in the private industrial scene, where the wartime, company-based Patriotic Industrial Associations re-emerged in new garb as company unions. Post-war labour relations in Japan were by no means harmonious and it was only after the reds were purged during the Dodge recession that the unions gradually became responsible and respectable.

The new Japanese Constitution, drafted by the Americans, was enacted in November 1946 and came into effect in May 1947. It contained three basic principles: the sovereignty of the people through their elected representatives; pacifism; and respect for individual liberty and human rights. The Emperor Hirohito was not dethroned or prosecuted as a war criminal. During the final days of the war, the Allies feared that if the Emperor were overthrown, Japan's resistance would have continued. Hirohito's co-operation was essential to the smooth operation of the Allied occupation. On 1 January 1946, Hirohito broadcast to the nation denying his divinity. Under the new Constitution, his role was changed to the titular but largely powerless head of state. The Diet, and more particularly its lower house, the House of Representatives, became sovereign in the people's name, and the Prime Minister and Cabinet were made answerable to it. Universal suffrage replaced male suffrage, giving Japanese women the right to vote for the first time.

Pacifism was written into the Constitution with the clause stating 'Aspiring sincerely to an international peace based on justice and order, the Japanese people forever renounce war as a sovereign right of the Nation and the threat and use of force as means of settling international disputes,' and 'In order to accomplish the aim of the preceding paragraph, land, sea and air forces, as well as other war potential will never be maintained.' While these clauses in the Constitution have not precluded Japan from building up 'self-defence' forces, popular support for pacifism has prevented defence expenditure from rising much above 1% of GDP and has kept Japan a nuclear-free nation. As such Japan has spent less money on defence in the post-war years than any other major nation, but has instead relied upon the US for protection under the Japan–US Security Treaty signed simultaneously with the San Francisco Peace Treaty in September 1951.

Post-war economic collapse

In the immediate aftermath of the war, the Japanese economy suffered a virtually total breakdown: industrial output dropped sharply to a low of 10% of its wartime peak; inflation accelerated; unemployment remained low, but only because the unemployed received no relief from their plight. Everyone eked out a living in whatever way they could, or lived off whatever real or financial assets they retained. The unemployed returned to the countryside, boosting the agricultural labour force from 14 m to 18 m by 1947. Others actively participated in the black market, trading in whatever they could.

With militarisation in the 1930s Japan had become a controlled economy. As the war progressed, disastrously, the regulatory system was tightened. By its end the Japanese government minutely controlled all economic activities through a comprehensive system of material and fuel allocation, product and food rationing, production quotas, war supplies contracts, financial directives, price controls, wage controls, labour conscription and direction.

Notionally this system of controls continued in force into the post-war period, together with the bureaucracy (other than its senior members and the military) which had operated it. In practice the system largely broke down. As in the former Soviet Union following the collapse of communism in the late 1980s, central directions from Tokyo were simply ignored. Officialdom was no longer obeyed. The authorities had no raw materials and fuels to allocate. They therefore had no levers to pull. Nor had they the ability to force farmers to supply food to the official distribution system. The newly created peasant farmers were not slow to exploit their independence.

While much of the framework of controls, other than conscription and the direction of labour, remained in operation, particularly so far as large companies and heavy industry were concerned, production, distribution, prices and activity generally operated through an unregulated free market. This was illegal and therefore designated the black market and its operators racketeers. Yet without a flourishing black market the Japanese economy could hardly have functioned at all during the early post-war years. The black market was capitalism in its natural state and it worked.

The official economy was in a parlous state. The industrial collapse resulted from severe shortages of fuel, raw materials and foreign currency with which to buy supplies from abroad. Japan was, in any case, initially prohibited from engaging in foreign trade. It had lost its major markets in Korea, China and the Pacific basin generally, while its major export industry, textiles, could not afford to buy the raw cotton needed for production. Coal output, the primary source of energy for Japan, ran at 3–4 m tons a month at the war's end. Immediately after the war, production dropped to barely 1 m tons a month. The reason was, as one Japanese author mildly puts it: 'With Japan's defeat, the Koreans and Chinese who had been subject to forced labour in the coal mines were refusing to continue, and coalmining was in a state of virtual collapse.'

It would seem that there were plenty of unemployed Japanese who could have replaced forced labour down the mines. But in no way could the Japanese have been made to work so hard in such arduous conditions. Restoring coal output to its end-of-war level required investment in new equipment, which, in turn, required steel. Unfortunately steel production also slumped. Without adequate coal supplies, the railways could not run and the steelworks could not operate. Without steel, coal output could not be expanded. When the prohibition on trade was lifted, Japan had nothing to export to earn foreign currency with which to buy additional energy supplies from abroad.

The agricultural situation was, if anything, more disastrous than the industrial one. Despite the sharp increase in the agricultural labour force, production fell. The 1945 harvest was barely two-thirds that of a normal year. Production recovered in 1946 and 1947, but only to three-quarters its normal level. At the same time, Japan was cut off from imports of rice and other food from China and Korea. The collapse in production resulted from exhaustion of the soil, starved of fertilisers owing to the rundown in the chemical industry and from the breakdown in the neglected water control systems which resulted in disastrous floods. Mass starvation seemed a real danger in 1945 and 1946, which miserably small emergency food relief imports from the US were hardly adequate to avert. It is in this context that Japan's present determination to shut out rice imports and remain self-sufficient must be seen.

Peeling bamboo shoots

Food shortages led to cuts in official rations, but the dangers of starvation were exaggerated. Peasant farmers in rural areas were able to supply their own needs and had surpluses to sell to town dwellers. Needless to say, these did not find their way through official channels at government regulated prices into the food-rationing system. Higher prices could be obtained on the black market and direct from city dwellers, who daily packed trains to the countryside on foraging expeditions. This produced what was labelled the 'bamboo shoot life'. Bamboo shoots have many skins and can be peeled like onions. In the same way city dwellers were peeled of successive layers of what savings and possessions of value they retained. Daily they would depart, some sitting on train bumpers for lack of room inside, clutching family heirlooms, returning in the evening having bartered them in the country for enough food for the family to survive a little longer. What wealth remained in Japan was increasingly concentrated in the hands of rural peasant farmers and black marketeers, while the city population was reduced to the absolute of material and financial poverty.

Printing money

Material and food shortages were accompanied by accelerating inflation, which ultimately became rampant. At the war's end, the economy was already over-supplied with money. To finance the latter stages of the war, the government had borrowed colossal sums from the Bank of Japan, which had raised the money by forcing Japanese banks to buy government bonds.

Government deficit spending continued apace after the war ended. Outstanding war supply contract payments continued to be settled. The future Prime Minister, Kakuei Tanaka, was paid for an armaments factory in Korea which his construction company never built. The government paid war damage compensation to the corporate sector. Disbanding the armed forces cost large sums in demobilisation compensation payments. The Japanese government was also obliged to contribute towards the cost of the occupation administration. Meanwhile tax revenues collapsed. The result was a continuation of deficit spending financed by further bond issues, flooding the economy with money which merely accelerated the rise in black-market prices. While the higher black-market prices rose relative to officially controlled prices, the greater the shift in activity from the regulated economy into the black market.

The corporate sector was reliant on war-damage compensation payments to repay bank loans and to finance the conversion of industry to peacetime production. The banks, in turn, were dependent upon repayment to meet withdrawals from their deposits. But in November 1945 SCAP stopped all further war contract or compensation payments. Notionally, the government was allowed to meet its payments obligations. But it was then forced to collect a 100% war profits tax upon them. The cessation of these payments caused a crisis for both companies and banks. The result was widespread insolvencies, which wiped out the value of shareholders' funds. Shareholders lost everything. But companies and banks were allowed to retain what remained of their real assets. They were simply re-launched as new enterprises, with new shareholders, relieved of the burden of dead-weight debt. This was how the keiretsu were born. But companies still had no money for reconstruction. The Japanese government, operating through the Industrial Bank of Japan, therefore established a Reconstruction Finance Compensation Fund through which it provided loans and subsidies. These were financed, like the war damage compensation payments, by sales of government bonds through the Bank of Japan. The Americans did not immediately object. They had stopped compensation payments as a way of confiscating wealth and breaking up the old zaibatsu. Government deficit spending went unchecked and inflation continued to accelerate. Black-market prices rose 30% between September and December 1945 and doubled by February 1946. In the six months to February money in circulation also doubled.

The first efforts to stabilise the situation were made in early 1946. The government froze bank deposits, allowing only limited further private withdrawals. It replaced old yen with new yen, only part of which was supplied in cash and the remainder had to be placed in frozen bank deposits. It redoubled its efforts to crack down on hoarding and black-market operations. It even raised official prices based upon key commodities such as rice and coal. The bank deposit freeze and currency conversion were successful in temporarily slowing the rise in black-market prices, but the crackdown failed. Deficit financing continued remorselessly and inflation soon accelerated once more.

Winter of discontent

The situation over the winter of 1946–7 was, if anything, worse than that in 1945–6. The powerful new Economic Stabilisation Board, established at the time of the 1946 banking freeze, reported on the condition of the economy in its first white paper, published in July 1947. It said that the limited stocks of raw materials and industrial assets, which had remained at the end of the war, had all been used up during the following two years. Nothing remained to support activity in the economy. Moreover, the 'bamboo shoot life' had continued so long that urban families were running out of personal belongings to barter for food. Far from recovering over 1945–7, the economy had drifted into a deepening crisis.

Labour unrest worsened. Workers, having been given freedom of speech, freedom of assembly and the right to strike, were not slow to exploit these. The left launched an extensive campaign aimed, amongst other things, at getting rid of the Emperor. He stood as the last representative of the old ruling classes and was blamed by many Japanese for having led the country into the war. While the communist unions, mostly representing public employees, organised widespread demonstrations and protests, company unions operated at a more mundane level. They fought redundancies following the crisis caused by the withdrawal of war-damage compensation.

In 1946 widespread strikes occurred against government plans to dismiss seamen, railwaymen, and other workers; 6 m working days were lost and the unions were largely the victors. The basis for the system of lifetime employment was laid in this period. There were communist-inspired street demonstrations in the spring of 1946. Half a million demonstrated in Tokyo on May Day demanding 'control of food for the people'. US troops had to use force to restore order. In general, however, the Americans stood back and allowed the workers to protest. New Dealers amongst SCAP officials argued that, having given workers freedom, it was unreasonable to prevent them from using it.

The run-up to the 1947 General Election was riotous: 70,000 workers demonstrated in Tokyo calling for the overthrow of the government. A general strike was called for 1 February. But by then American enthusiasm for free trade unions and the right to strike had waned. The cold war and developments in China meant that the US now regarded communism as a threat to democracy. At the last moment, on 31 January, the Americans forced the strike leaders to call it off.

The one bright spot in the deeply depressing 1947 scene was evidence that the government's 'Production Priority' policy was beginning to produce results. Under this system, all available coal supplies, not required for running the railways, were allocated to the steel industry, together with all emergency fuel imports. All additional steel output was allocated to the coal industry to enhance coal production. This process was continued until coal production was increased to the point at which a surplus became available to supply other sectors.

Inflation continued to accelerate during 1947 reaching 40% a quarter or almost 400% at an annual rate. A further effort was therefore made at stabilisation. In order to divert supplies back through official channels from the black market, official prices were increased to bring them closer to black-market levels. Unfortunately wages had also to be increased to compensate for these higher prices. The higher wages meant that producers made losses even when selling their output at the higher official prices. They were therefore paid subsidies to compensate them for the difference between their costs and official prices. This did nothing to reduce the government's budget deficit. It was, however, obliged by SCAP to suspend the sale of long-term bonds, those with a life to maturity of over one year. Since it still needed to borrow huge sums, it simply and sharply increased the issue of short bonds, rolling them over with new ones each time they matured. The measures, nonetheless, had some limited success. Helped by growing emergency imports, which flowed through official channels, rations and raw material allocations could be increased. But the subsidies required to keep official prices down proved prohibitively expensive.

By early 1948 American policy towards Japan had changed. The Democrat New Deal idealists, who had administered the programmes of demilitarisation and democratisation immediately after the war, were increasingly replaced by hard-nosed pragmatists. The cold war was intensifying and the communists in China were gaining the upper hand. Japan appeared to be America's only remaining potential ally in Asia. The Americans suddenly developed a marked interest in Japanese economic reconstruction.

Devastated by Dodge

American help, when it came, was of a kind that Japan could have well done without. It did not take the form of aid comparable with that given to reconstruct Europe under the Marshal Plan. Instead, it involved a US-inspired draconian stabilisation plan, which successfully pushed the feebly recovering economy into a deep recession. It made 1949 the blackest post-war year and took the country to the brink of revolution. The stabilisation programme was known as the Dodge Plan, after Joseph Dodge, a conservative Detroit bank president who designed it. Under the Dodge Plan, the Japanese government was prohibited from issuing any bonds at all. It was obliged to overbalance its budget, forbidden to incur any new debts and forced to repay all existing bonds as they matured. All reconstruction loans to industry were suspended and all indirect subsidies were ended. The multiple currency system which the Japanese government had been operating as another way of providing backdoor help to industry was abolished. In its place, a single ¥360 to the dollar exchange rate was set, and trading was freed. The ¥360 rate remained unchanged for twenty-two years.

The Japanese government was aghast. The Dodge Plan threatened to reverse all the limited economic recovery that had been achieved since the war. It caused a further wave of industrial retrenchment and bankruptcies, as well as the worst excesses of labour unrest since the troubles in 1947. When Japan National Railways was forced to sack 100,000 workers and the Post Office and Nippon Telephone & Telegraph a further 200,000, violence erupted. The body of Sadanori Shimouyama, President of JNR, was found on the railroad track; he had clearly been thrown under a train. Another train was deliberately allowed to run away, causing numerous casualties. Presidents of medium and small Japanese companies committed suicide in droves, some taking their entire families with them, in the tradition of Tokugawa Shogunate days. Assassinations became commonplace, as in the inter-war years, when the militarists seized power from the fragile Taisho democracy. But the opportunity provided by widespread redundancies was used to purge communist union activists from their jobs.

Fears of revolution

This red purge increased the danger of a revolution. It would have been futile while the Americans remained in power. But a failed revolution would have delayed the Americans' departure. As such it would have enhanced the growing hostility towards the occupation authorities and undermined the legitimacy of the elected Japanese government which was obliged to do their bidding. Had economic conditions in Japan not improved before the Americans did leave, doubtless there would have been a second and probably successful revolution. Not only might Japan not have remained a democracy, but it would hardly have remained an ally of the Americans.

The government did its utmost to moderate the severity of the 1949 Dodge recession. It recycled funds from the overbalanced budget back to stricken banks, and arranged for commercial banks to lend money they had not got to their corporate clients, allowing them to borrow heavily from the Bank of Japan to do so. Instead of the government running a budget deficit, private banks were encouraged to do so. Finally the bank-bailout of industry in 1949 accelerated the formation of keiretsu. They effectively operated as a unit, which was controlled by the bank at its centre. As that bank was itself controlled by the Bank of Japan, so were they. Bank loans exceeded their deposits and they borrowed the difference from the Bank of Japan. This over-loaned position became entrenched in banking operations. It subsequently enabled the Bank of Japan to control bank credit without raising interest rates. The Bank of Japan was able, through 'window guidance', to tell the banks how much they could lend and to whom. Since they were lending the Bank of Japan's money, they had no option but to obey.

The Dodge Plan succeeded in eradicating the inflationary excess in the immediate post-war Japanese economy. It did so not by increasing supply, but by ruthlessly cutting demand to the point that it fell below even the then limited capacity of the Japanese economy to produce. It created excess savings by destroying investment and eliminating, at a stroke, government deficit financing and dissaving. It left the Japanese economy, on the eve of the fifth anniversary of surrender and American occupation, in the midst of its greatest political and economic crisis since the war.

Rescued by another foreign war

The economic reconstruction of Japan would have been exceptionally protracted, and the chances of democracy taking root exceedingly slim, had not fate come to the rescue. On 25 June 1950, North Korean troops crossed the 38th parallel and invaded South Korea. The Korean War had begun, altering Japanese prospects out of all recognition. It saved the Americans from the consequences of their folly. It allowed the Japanese government to demonstrate its commitment to the Western alliance, accelerating the time-scale for the San Francisco peace treaty negotiations and the end of the occupation.

Ready for the great leap forward

These early post-war years had profound and long-lasting effects on the later development of the Japanese political economy. Had the Japanese been left in control of their own affairs in August 1945, there would not have been a new democratic Constitution. The Emperor's divinity could not have been challenged. Landlords could not have been forced to sell their land to their tenants. The great dynastic families, who owned and controlled the zaibatsu, could not have been dispossessed. The clash between those in favour of reform and democracy and those in favour of maintaining traditional Japanese ways, would have been bloody and violent. The Establishment would not have given up its power and its privileges without a fight. The country would have suffered instead a period of anarchy, as did Germany in the 1920s, before some great new military dictator took control once again.

In the event and despite the Dodge Plan folly, the US occupation was a brilliant success. It created the basis for Japan's subsequent economic miracle. The mass of Japanese responded favourably to SCAP's reforms and came to respect and like the Americans for the magnanimity they showed in victory. The Americans achieved a peaceful radical revolution in Japan, destroying Japanese militarism in the process, and succeeded in withdrawing gracefully. They left behind them a profoundly conservative, moderately democratic and surprisingly stable nation. The American occupation reforms, achieved in the space of six years, had as profound an effect as those in the twenty years following the Meiji restoration in 1868.

4

Miraculous Growth Machine

If the Japanese saved little during 1945–50, they saved considerably during 1950–70. For two decades the Japanese saved at twice the rate the Americans saved. In 1953–4, the first years for which there are meaningful figures, the Japanese saved 23% of their income, while the Americans saved 18%. But between the early 1950s and 1970 Japanese savings climbed to a peak of 40% of income, whereas US savings remained broadly unchanged at around 20%.

Japanese savings rose as soon as Japanese incomes started to rise. It was the Korean War in 1950 which 'jump-started' the economy. It eased the shortage of foreign exchange which, by denying Japan adequate supplies of fuel and raw materials, inhibited the recovery of industry during the 'bamboo shoot years'. American procurement expenditure almost doubled Japan's foreign earnings in the space of one year. Japan was the base from which the US fought the war. It was where their troops went for rest and recreation. Much of American local expenditure was on services, the supply of which could be rapidly increased given the abundance of under-employed labour. Some of Japan's increased foreign earnings came from sales of Japanese-made goods, although these remained in short supply; but whatever goods the Japanese could make, could be sold, even at ridiculously high prices by international standards. Japan's aged, inefficient and labour-intensive heavy industries were at last supplied with energy and raw materials and, despite high production costs, were able to sell goods at prices which produced profits. Given this chance to get going again, they rapidly expanded their production.

Incomes rose as soon as output began to grow; savings rose as soon as incomes started to rise. But consumer spending was slower off the mark. The Japanese people after the Second World War had three simple demands: enough to eat, clothes to wear and somewhere to live. Once these needs were met, at however basic a level, they worked and saved.

Every extra yen they earned went into savings. These savings were devoted entirely to financing corporate expansion, since under the Dodge Plan the government, far from being allowed to borrow, was forced to save because it had to run budget surpluses to repay maturing bonds. Japanese companies ploughed every spare yen back into modernisation and expansion.

So the miraculous growth machine roared into life and ran at high revs for the next two decades. During the 1950s, Japan's real GNP almost doubled and average annual growth approached 9% a year. During the 1960s real GNP almost trebled and average growth exceeded 10% a year. By 1970 the output of the Japanese economy was over six times what it had been in 1950. By contrast US GNP increased by only about a half in the 1950s and the 1960s, with average growth of between 3–4% a year. The size of the US economy doubled in twenty years, whereas the Japanese economy doubled every seven to eight years.

Following an initial burst of speed, Japan's real GNP regained its pre-war level in 1951. But since the Japanese population had meanwhile risen from 70 m to 85 m, it took until 1955 before Japan's living standards regained pre-war levels. The reconstruction period was then officially declared over. Nonetheless, with a population half that of the US, Japan's real GNP by 1955 was still less than 4% the size of America's. It was only half West Germany's GNP, while the West German population was barely half Japan's. Little more than a decade later, in 1968, Japan's GNP overtook Germany's. Exactly 100 years after the Meiji restoration released it from medieval feudalism, Japan became the free world's second largest economy, and this from the ashes of utter defeat barely a generation earlier.

The more one saves, the faster incomes can grow and the easier it becomes to save more. This was the virtuous cycle which the thrifty Japanese enjoyed during their miraculous growth years. They were able both to save more and to spend more. Although growth in consumption lagged behind the growth in incomes, it was nonetheless rapid. The Japanese developed a pattern of behaviour in which consumption went in waves. Confucian ethics encouraged frugality, but 'group conformity' demanded that when one family acquired something, all others wanted the same. As everybody started out equal, nobody wanted to be seen to have been left behind. New products were at first shunned as luxuries, until as incomes rose, they suddenly became necessities. In the late 1950s, Japanese families had 'three dreams': to own a black-and-white TV, an electric clothes-washer and a refrigerator; by the late 1960s the dreams had become the '3 Cs': a car, a colour TV and a cooler, i.e. air-conditioner.

Unstable growth

Although Japan enjoyed exceptionally rapid growth during the 1950s and 1960s, it was far from stable growth. The economy experienced marked business cycles. Periods of hectic growth were punctuated by sudden slowdowns. But even in the stop phase of this stop-go cycle, Japan's economy expanded faster than those of the US and UK in their boom years. Waves of consumer spending reinforced the cycle, but did not cause it. The instability came from reckless industrial expansion regardless of the costs in pollution, to the environment, the quality of life or inflation. The economy was encouraged to run flat out whenever there was a chance for it to do so.

Rapid growth was officially enshrined as top priority by the Prime Minister, Hayato Ikeda, in his 1960 'National Income Doubling Plan', the blueprint for the government's policies in the decade to 1970. Industry responded to every period of dynamic growth with wildly ambitious investment plans. Rival and intensely competitive companies strove constantly to outdo each other. If one planned a large modern steel works, all the others followed suit. Nobody worried that the result was excess capacity.

These were the years during which savings were a tonic, not toxic, to the economy, because they financed domestic investment-led growth. Indeed domestic investment growth was so rapid that there was never as much domestic saving as industry demanded. For the economy as a whole, there was a persistent tendency to invest too much rather than to save too much.

The miraculous growth machine had to be fed increasing volumes of fuel and raw materials imported from abroad. Together with food, these accounted for 80% of Japan's total imports, while much of the remaining 20% was imports of capital equipment. Japan spent next to nothing on imports of manufactured consumer goods. It could not afford that luxury, even though foreign goods were cheaper and better than home-made products. Its markets were therefore kept tightly closed, by fair means or foul, to cheaper and better foreign manufactures. Japan's infant industries were deliberately protected from foreign competition. It was right that they were. Had Japan imported consumer goods, the economy would not have recovered so rapidly. Nor could it have caught up with other countries. But the trade protection policies of these years left a legacy of resentment in other industrial countries, which freely allowed Japanese exports to penetrate their markets, although this meant slower growth for them.

To pay for imports, Japan had to export. But initially Japanese products, priced at ¥360 to the US dollar from 1949 onwards, were uncompetitive; industry was still inefficient and backward. At first, therefore, Japan was the marginal supplier. Its exports soared when world demand rose strongly, as during the Korean War boom. But whenever world growth slowed down, Japanese exports slumped. The varying rate of growth in world trade largely reflected the US business cycle. The growth path of Japanese exports was a magnified version of this cycle. But even though they had a bumpy ride, Japanese exports expanded mightily during the 1950s and 1960s. Japan's share of world trade rose rapidly. For the period as a whole, each 1% rise in world trade produced a 2% increase in Japanese exports.

Just as the domestic growth in investment was constrained by the availability of domestic savings, so the rate of growth of imports was constrained by the availability of export earnings. The Japanese business cycle followed a regular pattern. The upswing phase began with rapidly rising exports. Output expanded, stocks fell and capacity utilisation rates rose. A wave of new investment followed in plant modernisation and increased capacity. The investment boom further accelerated GNP growth, increasing employment and incomes. A consumer boom followed the rise in incomes. Imports rose rapidly, overtaking the increase in export earnings in a matter of months. As the Japanese current account balance slid into deficit, foreign currency reserves were rapidly run down trying to defend the yen's fixed exchange rate. Before long, the loss of reserves reached crisis proportions, obliging the Japanese authorities to apply the brakes to the headlong expansion in the economy.

The Japanese government was able to switch off growth almost overnight. It simply imposed a monetary squeeze through the Bank of Japan. The over-lent keiretsu banks were at the Bank of Japan's mercy. All the Bank of Japan had to do was to order them, through 'window guidance', to reduce their advances. They then reined back the over-ambitious expansion plans of their families of companies. The Ministry of International Trade & Industry (MITI) usually stepped in at this point to reorganise industries where excess spare capacity became a serious problem. When the large keiretsu companies turned off their investment programmes, they cut back or cancelled orders from their many subcontractors. Medium and small companies in turn reduced output and employment. Income slowed and imports declined once more, until they fell below exports. The Japanese balance of payments bounced back into surplus. Credit remained tight and reserves were rebuilt until the next surge in world trade sent exports soaring once more.

Small government, low taxes

This system of regulating the economy, and its keen responsiveness to government policy, meant that unstable growth did little to impede rapid growth. By rationing credit for investment, while keeping borrowing cheap, the 'stop' phase did not undermine the profitability of past expansion programmes or inhibit companies from future expansion. Fiscal policy meanwhile continued to operate under the balanced budget strictures of the Dodge Plan. The automatic stabilisers, which in other countries dampen the business cycle, were suspended. In the upswing, GDP growth regularly exceeded the cautious forecasts on which the government based its budget planning. During the financial year, tax revenues ran ahead of expectations and a budget surplus appeared. Balancing the budget required that this surplus be eliminated. So supplementary budgets were introduced, cutting taxes or increasing public works spending. This meant that, instead of an emerging budget surplus helping to moderate the speed of the economic upswing (i.e., the automatic stabiliser), tax cuts and increased public spending helped to maintain its momentum.

Japanese fiscal policy was biased towards low taxation rather than high public spending. When budget surpluses had to be eliminated, tax cuts were generally easier, quicker and more popular than spending increases. The Japanese government aimed to keep public spending at a low proportion of GNP. To achieve its target of about 29%, the Finance Ministry deliberately underestimated prospective GNP growth in each year's regular budget, thus keeping the lid firmly down on public spending increases. The balanced budget policy was thereby converted into a low tax and 'small-government' policy.

Response to a downturn in activity was not symmetrical. As the government persistently underestimated growth, its revenue forecasts were relatively accurate during a downswing. The budget did not move into deficit during the course of the year. There was no need to introduce a supplementary budget, cutting spending or raising taxes. This persistent caution lowered the underlying growth rate of public investment, which is not easily turned on and off, while ratcheting down tax rates as the tax base expanded.

Lifetime employment

The Dodge Plan's short-term effects were disastrous, but its longer-term effects were favourable. Inflation, the bane of slow growth economies, did not cause the Japanese authorities much concern until well into the 1960s. Indeed, at times they deliberately fostered faster wage growth. The miraculous growth machine always ran hot but rarely overheated. Throughout the 1950s and 1960s Japanese consumer price inflation exceeded the average of all the Organisation for Economic Cooperation & Development (OECD). But it was benign inflation, driven by the rapid rise in labour productivity in the advanced sectors of Japanese industry. Moreover it was the mechanism which pulled rural labour into the growth machine.

The Dodge Plan, red purge and the violence it spawned had a significant effect upon Japanese trade union development. The reds lost their jobs and consequently their role as union leaders. A wave of revulsion followed the assassinations and suicides of 1949. Labour unrest reemerged during the post Korean War recession of 1953–4 but on a reduced scale; instead, unions became increasingly responsible and respected.

The company union system fostered co-operation between management and employees in their joint interest in the success of their company. In the keiretsu and large companies generally, union resistance to redundancies during successive financial crises led to lifetime employment becoming entrenched in the system. Employees, recruited directly from school or university, expected to spend their whole working lives with the same company. Their pay on entry was set according to the level at which they entered, rising each year as they became more senior and experienced. Pay was not related to merit, but was the same for everyone in the same stream and with the same number of years of service. Graduate entrants in their stream always stayed ahead of high school entrants of the same year.

The seniority pay system was a reversion to the wartime system of wage control. But it too became entrenched in the post-war operations of large companies. Its graduated pay scale meant every permanent employee became better off each year, without the corporate wage bill necessarily increasing. This seeming impossibility illustrates the fallacy of composition: what is true of the individual is not necessarily true of the whole. We all get one year older every twelve months, but the average age of the population need not change; it falls when the birth rate increases and rises when the death rate declines. The same rules apply to the cost of the seniority pay system. In a rapidly expanding company, more young school and college leavers join the payroll each year than the number of older workers who retire. The average wage costs per worker falls, owing to the increased proportion of young workers on the payroll.

Lifetime employment and the seniority wage system contributed both to union moderation and labour flexibility. But it was coupled with a further feature which linked workers' interests with managements' in the success of their companies – the bonus system. Twice a year, permanent employees received a bonus, calculated at so many months' salary. Its size depended upon the profits the company had made. A year's bonuses could be as much as four months' regular salary and thus equal a quarter of total earnings. In some econometric analyses, these lump sum payments explain the Japanese worker's high propensity to save. He lived on his regular income, out of which his savings were as low as 5%; but he (or rather his wife) saved 80% or more of his lump sum bonuses.

Dual economy

By no means all Japanese workers were lifetime employees. Only the permanent staff of large companies, recruited directly from school or college, enjoyed such privileges. Large companies also employed temporary workers, who were, in effect, second-class citizens. They were hired or fired at will. Some were hired by the day, others remaining with their companies for protracted periods. But all received less pay than the permanent staff and no perks. In small- and medium-sized companies lifetime employment was rare, although such companies did still try to ensure the security of their workers' jobs. Only about one-third of Japanese workers enjoyed lifetime employment. The jobs and the pay of most other workers depended on the supply and demand for labour. The division of the Japanese labour market between lifetime employees of large companies and other workers was part of what was named the 'dual economy'.

Corporatist not capitalist

Japan operates a competitive market economy, but it is corporatist rather than capitalist. This is to say that the attitude towards shareholders, ownership and profits is different from that in Western capitalist economies. In a capitalist economy, companies operate for the benefit of their owners, the shareholders. The interests of managers, employees, suppliers and customers are secondary. They matter, but only to the extent that they affect profits. A Japanese company, on the other hand, operates primarily in the interest of its stakeholders, managers, employees, suppliers and customers. The senior management of major Japanese companies are self-perpetuating oligarchies. Cross-shareholding between companies limits the number of outside shareholders. It is virtually unknown for them to block the appointment of new directors or force the resignation of old. Senior Japanese company presidents and chairmen resign prematurely only when in disgrace. This is not so uncommon, because they take responsibility for any scandals affecting their companies, even when they are blameless. Since big business and scandals are inseparable in Japan, a healthy turnover at the top is assured. Nonetheless management, under little obligation to look over its shoulder at short-term share price movements, enjoys the luxury of putting longer-term profit and growth at the top of its agenda. In the end, the interests of stakeholders generally coincide with those of shareholders.

Japanese companies traditionally raise relatively little capital by new share issues. Their debt to equity ratios are much higher than is customary for American or British companies. Even the amount of equity outstanding is a misleading measure of the stake that the Japanese public has in Japanese companies. Companies and banks hold shares in each other. These cross-shareholdings exaggerate the amount of money borrowed from the public. Under the keiretsu system, company A issues, say, 100 new shares which it sells to company B for ¥1 m. In exchange company B issues 100 new shares which it sells to company A for ¥1 m. This operation costs A and B nothing, but it increases the equity base of both. Such cross-shareholdings bind members of the same keiretsu together and are a token of the goodwill each member shows for others in the same family. Keiretsu members co-operate in the interests of the family as a whole and in competition with those in other keiretsu families. Cross-shareholdings of this type account for as much as 40% of all shares issued by major Japanese companies.

Not only do Japanese companies have higher debt-to-equity ratios than British and American companies, they also pay out to their shareholders in dividends a lower proportion of the profit they earn. Their dividends to earnings ratio can be as low as 20% compared with 60–80% which can occur in Britain and the US. Under the capitalist system, profits are the buffer between costs and prices. When costs rise sharply and prices cannot be increased, profits suffer. Poor profits mean low dividends and depressed share prices, which expose American or British companies to take-overs. They therefore endeavour, as far as possible, to protect profit by passing on cost increases in higher prices, even when this means slower growth and a loss of market share. It is better to make high profits on low sales, than low profits on large sales.

American and British selling prices are a function of costs. Wherever markets allow, companies raise prices to earn maximum profits. Maximising shareholders' profit is the prime aim of every company in the capitalist system. In Japan it is the other way round. Companies' costs are a function of prices. Costs are stabilised by the bonus system, moderate unions, lifetime employment, cross-shareholdings, little danger of a hostile take-over, and the unimportance of shareholders. When sales rise, productivity and profits increase. The increased profits are either retained to finance investment or distributed to employees in annual wage increases and bonuses. When sales are squeezed and company earnings fall, workers' incomes are squeezed. This flexibility means that wages are directly related to productivity. Productivity, in turn, is a function of sales and output growth and hence of market share. Market share is won by keeping prices low. Japanese companies keep prices down to keep costs down. British and American companies, by contrast, keep prices up to keep profit up.

Rapid productivity growth amongst large companies in Japan's leading industries set the pace for wage growth. But the system for smaller and medium sized companies, particularly in distribution and service industries, operated in a different way. Wages were determined by the supply and demand for labour. At times they were markedly lower than those obtained by the permanent employees in the leading companies. Costs were controlled by hiring and firing workers. Wages were therefore sensitive to job security. They rose rapidly when small companies had to compete in hiring scarce labour, and slowed when demand was stagnant and workers were being laid off.

Benign inflation

Productivity growth was most rapid in large companies in Japan's leading industries. Smaller companies, particularly in services and distribution, were not able to match this productivity growth. But increasingly they had to pay wages which kept pace with those available in the large companies in order to compete for workers. Hence prices for such things as haircuts, train fares, entertainment, restaurant meals and the like rose faster than prices for manufactured goods. Rapid productivity growth increases service prices relative to product prices, causing consumer prices generally to rise. This relative price inflation is the means by which the benefits from rising productivity in manufacturing are shared by workers in other industries and services.

No government need worry about benign inflation of this kind. It produces greater equality in the distribution of incomes rather than growing inequality. It is just, not unjust. Moreover it helps rather than hurts a country's international competitiveness. Thus, whereas Japanese consumer prices rose faster than the OECD average throughout the 1950s and 1960s (see Chart 3), the price of Japanese traded goods, its export and import competing output, rose less rapidly. So while the

CHART 3: Japanese and OECD Consumer Price Inflation 1950–70
Annual percentage change

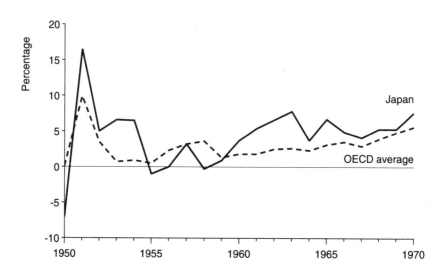

CHART 4: Japanese and US GNP Growth 1950–70
Annual percentage growth

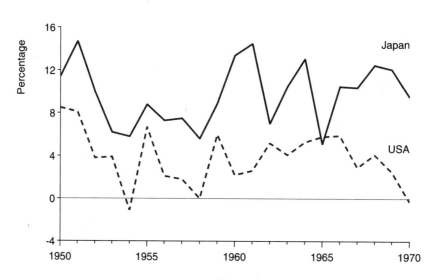

purchasing power of the Japanese yen to the consumer declined, the
¥360 fixed exchange rate became increasingly undervalued in terms of
the relative price of Japanese exports. Until the late 1960s, no Japanese
government was forced to slam on the brakes because of accelerating
inflation. The only constraint preventing the economy being run flat out
was the ability to export enough to pay for the imports needed for growth.

How the growth machine performed

The first post-war boom (see Chart 4) was triggered by the Korean War.
US military expenditure in Japan provided the foreign currency which
the economy needed to buy imports of energy and raw materials. But
Japanese heavy industry was uncompetitive even with ¥360 to the dollar.
Demand for its products would last only so long as the Korean military
build-up took place and wartime scarcity persisted. Realising this, the
Japanese immediately embarked on a massive programme of plant re-
newal and expansion, using the latest technology developed in the West.
This was just as well. In the spring of 1951, less than a year after the start
of the Korean War, the opposing forces had reached a stalemate on the
battlefield and truce negotiations began. The Allies' war aims changed
from beating the North Koreans to containing the Chinese and restoring
the division of Korea along the 38th parallel that existed before the war.
With this move to containment, the rearmament boom lost momentum
and American expenditure in Japan started to fade.

Dash for growth

The Japanese economy could well have relapsed back into stagnation,
yet it did not. The demand for capital to rebuild industry was intense,
and the government determined that it would continue regardless of the
cost. Steps were taken to plough funds into strategic sections of the
economy. The Japan Development Bank, established in March 1951,
raised money in its own right by bond issues, and was also given access to
funds accumulating in the government's hands. Vast sums from personal
deposits in postal savings and insurance funds flowed into the government's coffers. These funds were combined into one large investment
pool which industry could draw through the Japan Development Bank.
Special tax measures were introduced lowering or abolishing taxation on
a variety of corporate earnings or reserve funds. Companies were thus
encouraged to plough back the majority of their earnings into investment.

Shareholders did not mind that dividends remained meagre. The

CHART 5: Tokyo Share Price Index 1950–70
Nikkei Dow Index

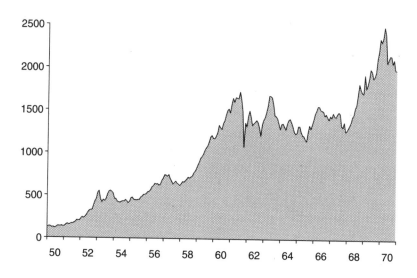

Tokyo stockmarket enjoyed its first post-war boom (see Chart 5). People made in capital gains far more than they could ever have expected to earn from dividend payments and, more to the point, capital gains were tax-free whereas dividends were taxed. Finally, the keiretsu banks were positively encouraged to continue lending more than they collected in deposits. They borrowed from the Bank of Japan to make up the difference, increasing their overloaned positions.

The plant and equipment boom of 1951–2 kept the Japanese economy expanding as Korean War demands faded. The boom was concentrated in basic heavy industries, with steel as the star, thanks largely to the government's role in promoting modernisation and exports. It set out to establish huge industrial parks. The first was on land reclaimed from Tokyo Bay. Kawasaki Steel, a new company, was given 3 m sq. m of land on which it built the most modern integrated steel facility in the world. Located close to a new, modern harbour, a continuous production line was established covering all stages of production from raw materials to finished products on the same site and using the most modern technology in the world. With labour still relatively cheap, Kawasaki steel became the cheapest in the world.

Here the results of dividing up the old zaibatsu came into play. Neither Yawata Steel nor Fuji Steel was prepared to allow a newcomer,

Kawasaki Steel, to steal a march on them. Both launched similar developments, creating a large and modern Japanese steel industry in the world-beating class. Nor was the steel industry alone in this process. Electric power generation, shipbuilding, chemicals and even the textile industry, to some extent, trod the same modernisation path. The automobile industry followed suit, but primarily to supply home demand. It began by building foreign-designed cars under technical co-operation agreements, such as with the British Austin and Hillman companies and the French Renault. Today the successors of those British companies build Japanese cars in Britain.

The 1951–2 investment boom launched Japan into its miraculous growth years. Hard on its heels came the 1952–3 consumer boom, which supported demand growth when the investment boom started to fade. This consumer boom was the first time ever that many Japanese families had a little income to spare after meeting basic living costs, and also some consumer goods to spend it on. It was nothing by comparison with later consumer booms. It simply meant that people could afford to buy a sewing machine or a fridge for the house, or take a weekend excursion into the countryside for pleasure. For Japan the 1952–3 consumer boom was important in another way. For the first time ever, incomes were equitably distributed. In periods of pre-war prosperity, the rich had merely become richer leaving the majority of workers in a continuing state of grinding poverty. As a result, large consumer markets never developed. This was one reason why the products of industrialisation were diverted to an alternative use, namely militarisation. Industrial prosperity provided the broadly based domestic consumer market necessary for infant Japanese industries, such as automobile production, to develop. In doing so, they were sheltered by the government from foreign competition. SCAP's reforms, by destroying the roots of Japanese militarism, created the basis for Japanese economic expansionism.

The first foreign exchange crisis

Japan's first post-war boom ran slap-bang into a foreign currency crisis. After the world rearmament boom, came the post-war recession. The US economy stagnated and world trade growth slowed decisively. Japanese exports faded (see Chart 6) while imports soared. In 1953, a large Japanese current account deficit emerged and the country's meagre foreign currency reserves rapidly dwindled. The result, in 1954, was 'Yoshida deflation', named after the Prime Minister at that time. The deflation was short and sharp. The Japanese economy had followed the US into the upswing of the cycle; it lagged into the downswing. So

CHART 6: Japanese Exports and US GNP 1950–70
Annual percentage growth

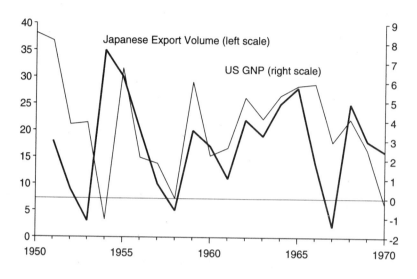

Japanese deflation in 1954 coincided with the beginnings of the US recovery. As massive new and modern capacity from the 1951–3 investment boom came on stream, domestic deflation forced the expansion in production into exports. The current account deficit was immediately reduced on both sides, by falling imports and rising exports. Japan's balance of payments bounced back into surplus.

People, who had been looking over their shoulders at the past, started to look instead to the future and to the world at large. They saw that while Japan had recovered, the world had moved on. Japan remained, apart from a few key sectors concentrated in heavy industry, a poor, backward and underdeveloped country. By 1955 reconstructed Japanese industry was still marked by the contrast between the advanced keiretsu sector and the rest. But the condition of the people had changed. They were now free, educated and politically aware. Wealth was evenly distributed. There was still a large farming population, primary industry employed 40% of the workforce. But tenant farmers had almost disappeared and peasant farmers were able to profit from the food they grew, instead of being left with barely enough to eat themselves.

The 'Jimmu' boom

From 1955 onwards the task was to catch up with prosperous Western economies, by creating for the first time in Japanese history a broadly based democratic industrial society, which would serve the needs of middle-class, mass consumers. The government gave absolute priority to rapid growth. The official catchwords were 'modernisation' and the 'technological revolution'. It aimed to narrow, if not eliminate, the income inequality which the re-emerged dual structure of the economy had produced, arguing that aggressive economic expansion was essential for this purpose. It was also essential if the bulge of school leavers in the late 1950s – some 800,000 a year – were to find jobs.

The timing could not have been better. The recession hit bottom in the final quarter of 1954. Thereafter recovery was led by exceptionally rapid export growth. By chance, 1955 was also a record year for agriculture. The rice harvest beat the pre-war best-ever level by 30%. This was followed in 1956–7 by a spectacular boom in private investment in plant and equipment. This new boom included a second wave of modernisation in the steel industry, but broadened to include petrochemicals, plastics and synthetic fibres, car production, electrical appliances and electronics. In 1956, for instance, Matsushita Electric (Panasonic) began producing electric rice cookers, vacuum-cleaners, electric juicers and electric blankets. In 1957, it introduced transistor radios and fluorescent lighting; adding the following year stereos, tape-recorders, air-conditioners, gas heaters, sewing-machines and mercury lamps to its product range; 1959 saw clothes-driers and garbage-disposal machines; and in 1960 came colour television.

This was called the 'Jimmu' boom, after the Emperor Jimmu whom legend said ascended the throne in 660 BC, ushering in a period of unsurpassed prosperity. From the trough of the Yoshida recession in the final quarter of 1954, the Jimmu boom rose to its peak in the third quarter of 1957. It spawned the first real consumer boom in Japan. Households began, for the first time, to acquire washing-machines, cleaners and, above all, black-and-white TV sets. The advent of TV in the Japanese home was itself revolutionary. Today, 95% of Japanese watch some TV every day and the average viewing time exceeds three hours.

The Jimmu boom launched Japan's drive to catch up with the West. Growth in the boom far exceeded planners' expectations. The government in 1955 looked for 5% a year economic growth to 1960, with a 7.4% a year increase in mining and manufacturing output. Instead real GNP grew by 9.1% and manufacturing output by 15.6%. The Jimmu boom produced relatively little inflation. Rapid wage growth was accompanied by sharply higher productivity. Costs of imported fuel and raw materials continued their secular decline from the Korean War peak. Fiscal policy continued to stoke the furnaces the hotter they became.

Another balance of payments crisis

A balance of payments crisis and shortages of foreign exchange forced emergency deflation in 1957. Again it was exceptionally rapid and successful. The Jimmu boom peaked in the second quarter of 1957 and the recession reached its nadir exactly one year later. Meanwhile imports fell 40% in value while exports recovered strongly. At all costs, private industry had to use its expanded capacity to the full, if only to employ its expanded permanent labour force. The 1957–8 recession was labelled the 'bottom of the pot' recession. This was a misnomer. The recession was expected to be U-shaped, deep and long like a saucepan. Instead it was V-shaped, short and sharp. The trough of the recession was in the middle of 1958 and the boom which followed peaked at the end of 1961. The speed of the recovery reflected, as usual, the rapidity with which deflation corrected the balance of payments deficit and so eliminated the foreign currency constraint on rapid growth. Japan was lucky to have growth limited by balance of payments rather than inflationary problems. Slower growth quickly eliminates a balance of payments deficit. By contrast, a recession takes years rather than months to cure inflation.

A bold 1957 budget contributed to the speed of the turnaround. The consumer boom quickly resumed its stride, adding to the upward pressure on demand from the rise in exports. The boom which followed was labelled the 'Iwato' boom again from Japanese mythology; music had lured the sun goddess Amaterasu from seclusion in a cave ('Iwato' in Japanese means cave).

Ikeda's National Income Doubling Plan

At this stage the government abandoned the practice of deliberately underestimating the country's growth. The Prime Minister, Hayato Ikeda, publicly recognised that Japan had entered an 'era of fast growth'. He capitalised on this in his 'National Income Doubling Plan' for the decade to 1970. (In fact, growth was again underestimated, as Japan's real GNP rose 2.7 times between 1960 and 1970). The main purpose of forecasting such rapid expansion was that it allowed a more rapid rise in public spending, without necessitating higher taxation or budget deficits. The way was thus cleared to remove the bottle-necks in the public infrastructure, which had restricted expansion in the latter stages of the Jimmu boom.

The government also planned a marked improvement in social welfare to bring Japanese standards up towards those in advanced economies. National Social Insurance & Pension programmes went into effect in 1961. A further element in the National Income Doubling Plan was trade liberalisation. Despite reconstruction and the rapid growth which followed it, Japan continued to operate a tough foreign currency allocation system. Barely a quarter of Japan's imports had been liberalised – imports having grown spectacularly – but they remained dominated by food, fuel and raw materials. While imports of foreign manufactures, other than capital equipment, remained negligible, Japanese exports had shown spectacular growth. This produced three-cornered trade: Japan bought from primary producers and oil countries and sold in the biggest markets of the world, those of the advanced Western industrial economies and particularly the US.

By the late 1950s, other countries had already started to put pressure on Japan to liberalise its trade. The post-war world dollar shortage was over and the US was beset by balance of payments deficits. At this stage the US had not lost its trading advantage. The weakness in its payments position was the result of heavy defence spending abroad, particularly in Europe, and a massive private capital outflow from the US, as American multinationals spread their tentacles. These put downward pressure on the dollar. But since it was the linchpin of the Bretton Woods fixed exchange rate system and the world's predominant reserve currency, it could not be devalued. The pressure had to be alleviated if the system was to survive. The US could have taken action to slow growth in its domestic economy. That would have reduced import demand and set resources free for increased exports. But it was unwilling to do so. Instead the US argued that other countries should open their doors wider to US imports.

Europe responded, and in December 1958 most countries dropped foreign exchange controls over current transactions and moved to full dollar convertibility for their currencies. This meant that anyone in Europe could import goods from the US without having to obtain permission to buy the dollars to pay for them. Meanwhile Japanese exports to the US reached record levels and the country moved into bilateral surplus with the US for the first time since the Second World War. Naturally Japan was singled out as a major offender because of its illiberal trade practices.

Ikeda conceded these demands; he had reason to do so. The Japanese foreign currency allocation system had skewed the development of industry towards the strong, established companies, whose import quotas reflected their past scale of operations. New and expanding companies had problems obtaining the currency they needed to support their development. Liberalisation would also keep prices down. Companies with large import quotas had been able to obtain monopoly profits at home from their privileged position. Finally, Japan's full admission to the advanced economies' club, the OECD, meant that it was obliged to eliminate government subsidies on exports and controls over imports.

A fourth element to the plan was to spread prosperity more evenly throughout the Japanese islands. The hectic post-war expansion had been concentrated on the Pacific coast, predominantly in Tokyo/Yokohama, Osaka/Kobe, Nagoya and northern Kyushu. The result was excessive concentration in these four regions with little development elsewhere. The National Income Doubling Plan set out to limit further development on the Pacific coast and to encourage expansion in other parts of the country. Other areas were designated key centres for large-scale industrial projects and the government undertook, in its expanded public investment programme, to supply the necessary infrastructure. At this time all regions clamoured to be designated special development areas, an attitude which later changed as pollution and the environment became political issues.

Japan's liberalisation plan was outlined in June 1960 and put into effect gradually over the following few years. But it was not as revolutionary as it was made to appear. Imports of raw materials were first to be liberalised – meaning that anyone could buy abroad as much as they liked without first obtaining government permission to spend the foreign exchange necessary for their purchases. Next to be liberalised were the products of industries, such as steel, where Japan's own producers were already internationally competitive and therefore able to hold their own against import competition; even if these industries had then to lower domestic prices as their monopoly supply position at home was eliminated. Last to go would be restrictions on imports of the products supplied by Japan's newer infant industries, which were not yet competitive at an international level. Automobiles, computers and heavy machinery came into the sheltered industry category. Norman Macrae of *The Economist* summed up this policy concisely in reporting a conversation he had had with a Japanese bureaucrat. He asked what the Japanese might now import from Britain as a result of trade liberalisation. 'Plobably wooden crogs' was the answer, i.e., something so primitive that the Japanese themselves had stopped making them.

The Iwato boom had three new features. Hitherto there had always been surplus underemployed labour to draw upon during any upswing. In the early 1960s this surplus disappeared and labour finally became scarce. Labour shortages began to cause inflation to accelerate. Liberalisation, however, helped to keep prices in check and profits were squeezed, particularly when activity turned down again. The drive to modernise moved downwards from the large keiretsu companies to small- and medium-sized companies, often helped by their keiretsu client companies. Small- and medium-sized company investment expanded even faster than large companies' investment. Indeed some medium-sized companies became large in their own right and independent from the keiretsu families, e.g. Panasonic, Sony, Honda and Pioneer. They combined state-of-the-art technology with investment funds culled from competing banks. Japan moved decisively into the computer age during the Iwato boom, exploiting the new technology enthusiastically and extensively at a time when American and European business remained cautious and timid in its application.

The boom ended in the usual way. There was a balance of payments and foreign currency crisis in 1961. The traditional deflationary monetary measures were taken. During the Iwato boom, Japan's GNP had grown by 11% in 1959, 12.5% in 1960 and 13.5% in 1961, an increase of 42% in three years. The recession which followed was short and moderate. None of the 42% rise in output was lost. The economy merely grew at a slower rate for a while. By the autumn of 1962, the Japanese economy was up and running again. The rapid recovery was partly due to the expansion in public investment which the National Income Doubling Plan initiated. A second reason was the approaching 1964 Tokyo Olympic Games, which prompted a massive flurry in construction activity. But the major reason was strong growth in export markets in America and Europe.

Transition to excess savings

Throughout the 1960s, the world trade environment remained benign. This was largely because the US had decided to go for growth and damn the consequences for the dollar. During the decade, the US experienced its longest post-war upswing, starting in February 1961 and lasting for 106 months to December 1969. When John F. Kennedy took over the US Presidency from Dwight D. Eisenhower in January 1961, the economy was close to the trough of a recession. Unemployment was high and output stagnant. The Republicans had pursued a conservative policy of balanced budgets. The Democrats were Keynesians. President Kennedy cut taxes to reflate the US economy. After Kennedy's assassination in late 1963, President Lyndon B. Johnson set about creating the 'Great Society'. In the years that followed, the Vietnam War built up towards its

77

peak, which was reached in 1968 when 3.5 m Americans were in the armed forces. The Americans had no intention of paying for the cost of Vietnam by tightening their own belts. Their behaviour in the 1960s was in large measure responsible for the manner in which Japanese growth became dependent on exports for their own sake, rather than a necessity to meet bludgeoning import bills.

The modest upswing in Japanese activity in 1962–4 was never designated a boom nor dignified with a name. Japan moved into current account deficit in 1963–4, in part due to US action to defend the dollar. But the yen was no longer a devaluation candidate. Hence Japan had no difficulty in financing its current account shortfall by attracting capital from abroad. The dollar by this time had become persistently weak and was widely regarded as having become structurally overvalued. So there was no currency crisis forcing Japan to curb GNP growth. Nonetheless, in 1964 the brakes were applied, to head off an acceleration in inflation in the now fully employed economy.

The 1964 deflationary measures were mild. The economy moved into recession in 1965, thanks largely to the unaided operation of the business cycle. The explosive growth in investment during the Iwato boom and following Ikeda's National Income Doubling Plan simply could not be sustained. Capacity was expanded faster than demand could rise to utilise it. The downturn in investment occurred largely of its own accord, although it was accentuated by the drop in construction expenditure after the Tokyo Olympics.

Japan's savings become excessive

The 1965 recession was a watershed. Before it, investment demand was so dynamic that, given its head, it always outran the supply of savings. But 1963–4 were the last years in which inadequate savings resulted in a balance of payments deficit. After 1965, Japanese savings rose faster than investment and persistently exceeded the amount required to finance it. Consequently, the balance of payments moved into surplus. But at first the savings excess was modest. From 1965 to 1970 its current account surplus averaged only around 1% of GDP. Japan has experienced temporary deficits since 1965, as when the 1970s oil price shocks turned the terms of trade sharply against it. But after each such stumbling block, Japan has rapidly bounced back into surplus again.

The emergence of excess savings had two direct consequences. It meant that, whenever world demand growth weakened, slower export growth only caused Japan's trade surplus to diminish and not to disappear. But the reduced trade surplus put downward pressure on

78

Japanese demand causing its GNP growth to slow. Instead of fast growth causing trade deficits, necessitating deflation to correct them, falling trade surpluses caused slow growth, necessitating reflation to correct it.

Secondly, such recessions could no longer be cured by relaxing the monetary squeeze which had hitherto precipitated them. The economy had lost its natural bounce. Positive stimulation became a prior condition for recovery. Monetary ease no longer worked. The problem was not a scarcity of credit but an excess of capacity. Fiscal stimulation was required, meaning government dissaving through budget deficits to offset excess private savings. The policy of balancing the Japanese budget, which had ruled since the 1949 Dodge Plan, was abandoned.

Budget deficits become fashionable

The 1947 Finance Act, which banned the issue of government long-term bonds, and the 1949 Dodge Plan strictures, which further banned short-term bond issues, continued in force up to the 1965 budget. Ikeda, who put absolute priority on economic growth, fell ill and resigned in 1964, shortly after the end of the Tokyo Olympics. He was succeeded by the more cautious Eisaku Sato. As usual the initial budget for fiscal 1965, the year starting in April, was designed to be balanced. But the growing recession caused tax revenues to decline so that during the year the budget started to move into deficit. The government's immediate reaction was to plan emergency measures to reduce public spending. These would have intensified the downturn. Opinion was divided over the wisdom of maintaining the balanced budget policy.

The issue was decided by the stockmarket. There had been a roller-coaster bear market on the Tokyo stock exchange, where the Nikkei index had peaked above 17,000 in July 1961. It fell short of its 1961 peak when it topped out again in May 1963 and by July 1965 it was down by one-third. The final bear trap bankrupted the number two stockbroker, Yamaichi Securities, threatening to cause a financial collapse. The Bank of Japan had no option but to provide unlimited credit to bail out Yamaichi. Fears of recession gained the upper hand. The fiscal conservatives lost and the 1947 law preventing government bond issues was revoked. The government authorised an expanded programme of public works to be financed, for the first time since 1947, by the issue of long-term government bonds. The initial reaction to the problem of excess private savings, when it emerged, was therefore the move to reduced government savings by means of budget deficits. The government remained a net saver, in that its current revenues continued to exceed its current expenditures. But instead of these surpluses covering all of public investment, the government was prepared to borrow from the private sector to cover part of the cost.

The 'Izanami' boom

Despite the changed nature of the 1965 recession, Japan's miraculous growth machine was on the brink of its biggest and best post-war boom. It was called the 'Izanami' boom after the progenitor of the sun goddess Amaterasu. It lasted five years from 1966 to 1970 and in each of these years real GNP rose by 10% or more. It took Japan by 1968 to the position of the free world's second largest economy, exactly 100 years after the Meiji restoration, and made the country, which joined the OECD in 1965, the world's first fully industrialised and modernised Asian economy. The Izanami boom, unlike its predecessors, created no balance of payments or foreign currency crisis to force its termination. It ran full steam ahead largely as a result of exceptionally favourable international conditions. Ironically, Japan's miraculous growth years, spawned by the Korean War rearmament boom, ended in style with the Vietnam War boom.

The US was the linchpin of the Bretton Woods fixed exchange rate system. The dollar was the world's reserve currency. Thus when the US abandoned moderate growth and stability and flooded the world with dollars, both world growth and inflation accelerated. Japanese exports grew by 20% a year over 1966–71. Yearly increases in private investment also ran at 20%. Moreover investment during 1966–71 switched from increasing capacity to labour-saving, as labour shortages emerged as an unaccustomed problem.

The Izanami boom had three new features. First, it occurred following Japanese membership of the OECD. This carried with it an obligation to relax exchange controls over capital movements. Thus capital liberalisation, which produced the same fear of disaster amongst inferiority-conscious Japanese industrialists, was to the Izanami boom what trade liberalisation was to the Iwato boom. Trade liberalisation had been dubbed the 'second coming of the black ships'; capital liberalisation was promptly dubbed the 'second second coming of the black ships'. In response to the first second coming, Japanese companies had drawn together with the Ministry for International Trade & Industry to rationalise industry. The second second coming led to amalgamations and cartels, the better to resist American competition and take-overs. Yawata Steel and Fuji Steel were amalgamated to form New Japan

Steel, a striking reversal of the post-war division of Nippon Steel. The result was the world's largest steel company.

Secondly, during this period the broadening of Japan's industrial base paid off handsomely. Heavy industry remained basic to Japan's exports. Steel, shipbuilding and petrochemicals all expanded strongly during the Izanami boom. But Japanese manufactured goods now started to invade and penetrate world markets. Exports were no longer totally dominated by these energy-guzzling, metal-bashing industries. Instead, processing industries, with a higher added value and a lower import content, came to the fore. To offer one example: Japanese automobile exports totalled 370,000 in 1967 and 2,370,000 in 1971.

Finally the Izanami boom occurred during the years in which the Bretton Woods fixed exchange rate system began to disintegrate. The first sign was the 1967 sterling devaluation. At the time there were popular fears that the yen would also depreciate against the dollar. These were ill founded. The realisation instead dawned that the yen had become seriously undervalued. There was therefore considerable consternation in the international community when, in 1969, the West German Deutschmark was revalued from Dm 4 to the dollar to Dm 3.66, without Japan following suit. As Japan's export surplus bulged ever larger, so the days during which the yen could remain fixed at ¥360 to the dollar were numbered. The Bretton Woods fixed exchange rate system could deal with temporary payments imbalance, but could not cope with persistent structural disequilibria caused by excess and inadequate savings.

End of miraculous growth

Japan's Expo '70, Asia's first world trade fair, marked the crescendo of the Izanami boom. It also marked the end of the miraculous growth years. For the following six years the economy would languish in relative stagnation, though this did not stop the politicians' addiction to growth. As late as June 1972, on the eve of becoming Prime Minister, Kakuei Tanaka published his best-selling book, *A Plan for Rebuilding the Japanese Archipelago*. This envisaged continued 10% a year real GNP growth and an extensive government regional development programme. Like the cartoon character who walks over the edge of a cliff, but does not fall until he looks down, the Japanese miraculous growth machine continued to function in the minds of the people long after it had no visible means of support.

Seen in the perspective of history, Japan's miraculous growth years occurred as a result of unusually favourable domestic and international circumstances. Nobody should belittle the achievements of those years.

They resulted from Japanese thrift, industry, good government and sound business management. They were the product of a unique set of institutions, created largely by the Americans' post-war reforms, which were singularly conducive to growth. Democracy and an equitable income distribution, the growth of a large middle class and a mass consumer market, were all critical factors at home. But they would never have produced such outstanding results without good fortune abroad. Free trade and exchange rate stability under the Bretton Woods liberal system allowed a rapid expansion of exports to pay for crucial imports. The ease with which Japan was allowed to buy Western technology in order to modernise its decrepit and backward industries was also vital. The US defence umbrella saved Japan the burden of its own defence spending. The rapid expansion in world markets kept the growth miracle alive beyond its natural term. Yet only a fool would have believed that such conditions could persist indefinitely. The Prime Minister, Kakuei Tanaka, was not the only one who foolishly held such a belief.

5

Decade of Shocks

The story of the 1970s was one of shocks to the international system. It began with the collapse of the Bretton Woods fixed exchange rate system, continued with the commodity price rise in 1972–3 and the first oil price hike in 1973–4. This led to world recession in 1974–5 and a feeble recovery in 1976–7 which ran out of steam. In 1978 Japan and Germany were forced into fiscal stimulation and 1979–80 experienced the second oil price shock, leading to the 1980–1 recession. The 1970s were an age of stagnation and 'slumpflation', the evil combination of slow or no growth with rapid inflation. In these years the Japanese economy performed worse than it had during the 1950s and 1960s, but better than most countries' (see Chart 7). Japanese living standards continued to improve both absolutely and compared with those elsewhere. Indeed Japan's relative success was more a cause of foreign envy than its absolute success had hitherto been. This was unwarranted. Like other countries in the 1970s, Japan had plenty of problems to contend with.

Problems at home

One was the quality of life. Ever since the Second World War, growth had been given absolute priority with disastrous results for pollution and the environment. Pollution affected health as early as 1953 with an outbreak of 'Minamata' disease, in Minamata village in Kyushu, caused by mercury poisoning in the water. A local chemical company, the Chisso Corporation, made vinyl chloride using mercury in the process and simply dumped its raw waste in the sea. The fish were contaminated and the villagers ate the fish. Yokkaichi asthma followed in 1959, the consequence of sulphur dioxide pollution in the air from the big oil refineries in that area. But cadmium poisoning caused the greatest outcry. It afflicted people living by the Jinzu river close to Tokyo. Cadmium poisoning causes bones to grow brittle, fracture or splinter. It became known as

83

CHART 7: Japanese GNP and OECD GDP Growth 1950–70
Annual percentage growth

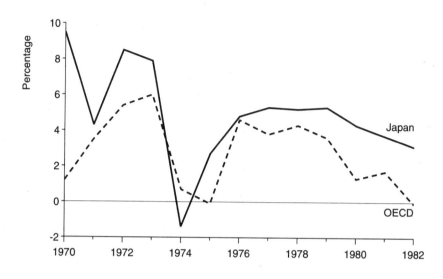

'Itai-Itai' disease, meaning 'it hurts, it hurts', which was surely an understatement. By the mid–1960s environmental pollution had become a major issue in certain parts of the country and instead of scrambling to entice new developments into their areas, local government began positively opposing them.

National politicians were slow to take the pollution issue seriously. They were influenced by big business, which was still reeling from the feared impact of capital liberalisation. The government at first acted half-heartedly. Its Pollution Counter-Measures Basic Law in 1967 was lenient and poorly enforced. It was not until 1970 that firm and effective legislation was enacted to prevent future abuses and to force a clean-up of existing dirty industries. These anti-pollution measures imposed a severe burden on capital-intensive heavy industry, thereby reducing the rate of return available on capital spending, which slowed their growth.

Contending with economic reality

The greatest problem the Japanese had to contend with was coming to terms with slower growth. The underlying reason why growth had inevitably to slow lay in the available rate of return on capital investment. In the immediate aftermath of the war, labour was plentiful and capital

84

scarce. The shortage of capital inflated the returns available from investment. Once reconstruction was completed, the catching up or modernising period began. Backward Japanese industry was then able to exploit the technological progress made in the West during the previous 20–30 years. All growth miracles are achieved by well-educated people catching up with the progress already made by the most advanced nations. Fast-growth economies always come from behind, they never race on ahead.

The high returns on Japanese investment reflected the superior productivity of modern capital equipment compared with the old plant and machinery which the Japanese were replacing. Such high returns explain why so much of the nation's GNP was devoted to capital investment rather than consumption. The profits from investment were shared by the nation at large, through the growth in real incomes which was spread beyond the manufacturing sector. It was this sharing of the rewards which gave fast growth its universal appeal. Everyone collectively united behind the drive for expansion, because everyone individually benefited from it. But when the labour force had been equipped with state-of-the-art plant and machinery, the scope for high returns on further investment diminished. After Japan caught up and became aware of the evil consequences of uncontrolled growth, the pressure for a continued high level of capital spending abated. The economy was no longer able to sustain double-digit GNP growth.

The rate of growth of any country, which already possesses an adequate stock of modern capital equipment, necessarily slows until it equals the rate of further technological advance plus the rate of growth in the labour force available to use modern equipment. Even in the heyday of the industrial revolution, technological progress rarely supported more than 2–3% annual growth in productivity. Labour force growth seldom exceeds 1–2% a year. Consequently, a modern economy, with no large reservoir of underemployed labour in agriculture and distribution, can normally expect no more than a 3–5% underlying annual growth. The amount of new investment required to support 3–5% growth is considerably less than 40% of each year's GNP.

The capital stock of a modern economy is normally worth about three years' GNP, and wears out at a rate of about 5% a year. Thus some 15% of GNP needs to be devoted each year to repairing wear and tear. About half the capital stock is industrial and commercial buildings, plant and equipment. Labour force growth of 2% a year requires further investment of 3% of GNP to equip additional workers with plant and equipment. Existing workers can also be supplied with more and better equipment. But there is a limit to the rate at which this can be achieved. Labour must be organised and trained to use new equipment. Increasing

CHART 8: Japanese and US Investment 1970–82
Percent of GNP

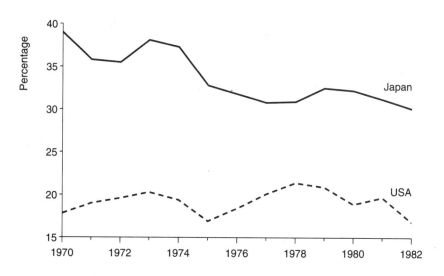

the industrial capital stock to labour ratio by 2% a year requires a further 3% of GNP to be devoted to investment. Finally, additions to social capital are limited by the government's ability to finance them. In all, a modern economy needs to devote at most 30% of its GNP to investment. Moreover, this figure allows for substantial public investment in social capital.

Investment peaked in Japan in 1970 at nearly 40% of GNP, and then moved on to a longer-term declining trend, which did take it back to 30% by 1980 (see Chart 8). Savings, however, which only marginally exceeded investment in 1970, remained close to 40% of GNP through to the mid–1970s. The problem of excess savings, with which Japan has grappled unsuccessfully for over two decades, became a serious one at this time. It has affected Japan's economic development ever since.

Problems abroad

As in other countries, inflation in Japan accelerated in the late 1960s. In 1969 the government responded, for the first time since the 1949 Dodge Plan, by deflating demand to curb rising prices rather than to deal with a balance of payments crisis. Japan's current account surplus was 1% of GNP when the brakes were applied. It had reached such a level only

CHART 9: Japanese and US Current Accounts 1970–82
Percent of GNP

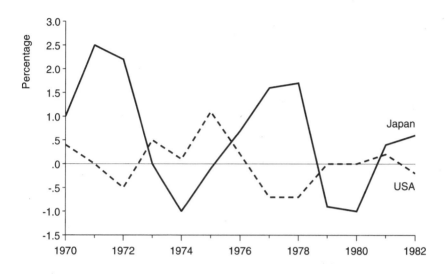

twice before in the post-war period, in 1959 and 1964–5. Both were during recessions. Stringent monetary measures were introduced in September 1969 and sustained for a full year. The results were disastrous. While the measures caused domestic business to slump and restrained domestic inflation, their main impact was to make the large current account surplus even larger. It rose to 2.5% of GNP in 1971–2 (see Chart 9). A wise policy would have been to revalue the yen in 1969 at the same time that the Germans revalued the D-mark. This would have reduced demand by making exports less competitive and imports more attractive. It would also have reduced inflation by making imports cheaper. As it was, Japan's domestic deflation brought down on its own head the wrath of America, under President Nixon.

Japan's actions cannot be singled out as the sole cause of the subsequent collapse in the Bretton Woods fixed exchange rate system. The more fundamental reason was America's refusal to act as the anchor to the system. It fought the Vietnam War without saddling the US taxpayer with its cost. It made no effort to restrain the outflow of American long-term capital, particularly to Europe, despite a balance of payments current account deficit with the rest of the world. If this policy lumbered other countries with increased quantities of dollars in their foreign currency reserves, that was their problem. They could always revalue, or even reflate to ensure that they followed as inflationary a path as the Americans. If US exports became expensive, the solution was for Japan and Germany to take steps to raise the price of their exports to an equal extent. If they were not prepared to do so by revaluation, they could do so by being equally irresponsible in their budgetary and monetary policy.

The simple fact was that the US was not prepared to pursue policies of slow growth and fiscal austerity in order to protect the dollar's exchange rate. Quite the contrary. President Nixon, elected in November 1968, faced re-election in November 1972. The economy was weak in early 1971. He therefore favoured fiscal stimulation, regardless of its effect on the US current account deficit or on capital outflows, indeed he positively encouraged a run on the dollar. Other countries, which had benefited considerably from the Bretton Woods fixed exchange rate system, could save the system themselves. They did not oblige. Foreign capital fled into Germany in May 1971. The Germans were forced to float the D-mark. Flight capital then switched its destination to Belgium and France. The French promptly exchanged dollars for gold with the US Federal Reserve system. The French 'bank robbery' of America's Fort Knox gold forced the US to suspend gold convertibility.

The Nixon shock

This was the so-called Nixon shock. On 15 August 1971, the President announced that foreign central banks could no longer sell dollars for gold at a fixed rate. The world's reserve currency thus became inconvertible into the only asset which central banks trusted. Countries held dollars in the belief that they were as good as gold, but also earned interest. When they could be sold for gold at any time, nobody wanted to sell them. Immediately they became inconvertible, nobody wanted to keep them.

Nixon also imposed a 10% surcharge on imports, which was an underhand method of devaluing; cut foreign aid by 10%; and put a ninety-day freeze on US wages and prices. All this was combined with a tax cut to stimulate American demand. That meant the US would import more and run a larger current account deficit, which could be financed only by other countries holding more, and not fewer, dollars in their reserves.

The Japanese were too shocked to react immediately. The Tokyo stockmarket collapsed. But while Europe closed its foreign exchange markets then re-opened them with floating exchange rates, the Japanese foreign exchange market remained open. Dollars flooded into the yen and the Bank of Japan was forced to buy them in order to prevent the yen

CHART 10: Yen–Dollar Exchange Rate 1970–82
Yen per Dollar

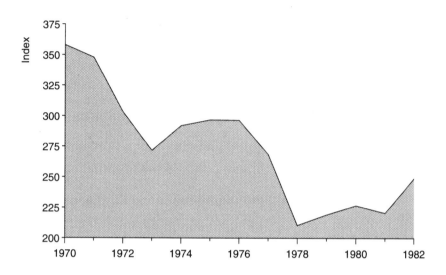

from rising. It had to borrow or print yen to finance its suddenly increased dollar holdings. This powerfully increased liquidity in Japan – but all in vain. On 28 August 1971 the yen was allowed to float and promptly rose (see Chart 10). An effort was made to resurrect the fixed exchange rate system in the December 1971 Smithsonian Agreement, so named because the meeting of finance ministers at which the deal was hammered out, took place appropriately in the Smithsonian Institution in Washington, DC. The deal itself was a museum piece destined to survive only fourteen months. Under the Smithsonian Agreement, the yen was re-pegged at ¥308 to the US dollar, an appreciation of 17% against the ¥360 rate that had lasted for twenty-two years. But the yen rose far less in terms of the weighted average of its value against other major currencies. They had also gone up against the dollar. The yen, for instance, rose only 3% against the German D-mark and 7.7% against sterling and the French franc. Moreover in the Smithsonian Agreement, the US also scrapped its 10% import surcharge. But nonetheless the US was Japan's most important trading partner, so the yen's rise against the dollar mattered and hurt.

With the passage of time it is hard now to appreciate the panic and alarm caused by the yen's modest rise. The change in its value in 1971 was relatively small compared with swings which have occurred

89

subsequently. Between the beginning of 1977 and October 1978 the yen, for instance, rose 70% against the dollar, from ¥290 to ¥170. But it ended 1978 at ¥240, only 40% up. The panic partly reflected fear of the unknown. Not only had the yen exchange rate been fixed for two decades, but during that time the economy had periodically been squeezed to protect its value. A stable exchange rate had been accorded an even higher priority in the short term than fast growth, on the grounds that it was crucial to fast growth in the long term. But the panic was also due to the downturn in the economy, which was already under way thanks to the 1969 monetary tightening. Appreciation in 1971 was seen as re-enforcing the monetary squeeze, and therefore likely to turn recession into depression. These fears were compounded by the fact that the recession in 1970–1 was not confined to Japan. There was a synchronised downturn in all major economies.

The policy response in Japan during this period was founded upon hysteria. Nobody could comprehend that the miraculous growth machine had been raced to destruction in the Izanami boom. Having tightened monetary policy instead of appreciating during 1969, the government proceeded to pull out all the stops to get the economy back on its fast growth track. The result of foreign exchange market intervention in defence of the dollar, not only in Japan but also in Germany and other continental European countries, was to produce rapid monetary growth.

The US under Nixon continued to behave with total irresponsibility towards the international community. It is well known that to make a devaluation stick and correct an external trade deficit, it is necessary to restrain home demand to free resources for increased exports and import substitution. But far from adopting policies of fiscal restraint and monetary stringency, the Nixon administration focused its attention solely on the November 1972 Presidential Election. It became more, not less, profligate. Taxes were cut, spending increased and interest rates lowered. Far from declining, the US trade deficit soared. The US continued to pump dollars into the rest of the world. Between the end of 1970 and early 1973, international liquidity doubled.

Despite the appreciation in the yen, the Japanese current account surplus continued to expand rapidly. Superficially the reason was the powerful growth in world demand in 1972–3, produced by the worldwide increase in money growth. The breakdown of the Bretton Woods system was followed by the first major synchronised world boom in which, as all economies were expanding simultaneously, the world upswing in demand was of record proportions.

Tanaka plans to rebuild the Japanese archipelago

The vast monetary stimulus delivered to hold the yen down did not restart the miraculous growth machine, as it would have done in the 1950s and early 1960s. It was therefore re-enforced by fiscal profligacy, that is government dissaving. Although the balanced budget policy had been abandoned in 1965, issues of government bonds remained modest up to 1970. But then all restraint was abandoned. In October 1971, the Sato government announced an unprecedented ¥165 bn tax cut. In December 1971, following the Smithsonian Agreement the government went further. The initial 1972 budget included a 22% increase in government consumption and 32% in public investment. Not only were public works to be expanded substantially, but also social security expenditures were raised. When Sato left office in July 1972, he was followed by Kakuei Tanaka, complete with an ambitious plan to rebuild the Japanese archipelago. This was predicated upon resumed 10% a year GNP growth. Tanaka's vast government-sponsored redevelopment plan captured the imagination of the nation. He was seen as a man to get things done.

To be fair to Japan, Tanaka's policies fitted with the demands other countries were making. As Japan's structural payments surplus emerged, international pressure broadened from issues concerning individual categories of exports, such as textiles, to those concerning trade in general and macro-economic policy. In 1972, even the OECD called upon Japan to introduce an expansionary 1973 budget. Japanese fiscal and monetary reflation was seen as the solution to the trade surplus problem. Pressure continued on the dollar during 1972. But despite the year that had passed since the Nixon shock and the yen's appreciation, the Japanese current account surplus showed no sign of shrinking. Tanaka therefore introduced a supplementary budget in October 1972, pushing public works spending even higher.

Evil of asset price inflation

Tanaka's first regular budget, for 1973, built on Sato's 1972 excesses by pushing government spending up a further 25% and investment up nearly 30%. The effects of fiscal and monetary excesses were not what had been expected. They did less to accelerate growth and more to accelerate inflation. They also produced an evil new phenomenon – asset price inflation – which was to return under similar circumstances in the late 1980s, when Japan once again made money cheap and plentiful to help bail out the dollar.

Japan: The Coming Collapse

CHART 11: Tokyo Share Price Index 1971–82
Nikkei Dow Index

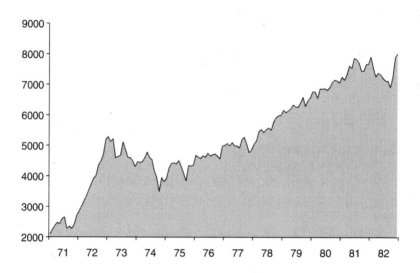

The collapse in the propensity to invest meant that when loans became plentiful and cheap, there was a rush to borrow in order to speculate on land and on the stockmarket. The land rush was encouraged by the Tanaka plan and there was a scramble to buy property in areas scheduled for development. Property speculation was not confined to real estate companies, but extended to trading, construction and investment companies, banks and to individuals. Manufacturers lost interest in making textiles and machine tools and started instead to devote their financial resources to making money out of speculation. Nor was this confined to property. Companies started to borrow in order to speculate in the shares of other companies. Moreover since capital gains from stockmarket speculation were included with trading earnings in company profits, the rise in stockmarket prices itself pushed up company profit which in turn accelerated the stockmarket rise. Between March and December 1972 the Japanese stockmarket rose 66% (see Chart 11). Nobody could have earned that much as quickly by investing in new plant and equipment.

Japan's ambitious measures to stimulate the economy, coupled with its well-publicised trade concessions, could not prevent the collapse of the Smithsonian rescue attempt for fixed exchange rates. On 13 February 1973 the dollar was devalued by 10% against IMF Special Deposit Receipts – SDRs – which are a basket of foreign currencies, and all the major currencies including the yen thereupon floated. The yen promptly climbed to ¥280 by July 1973. But although Japanese (and German) stimulation could not save the dollar, it did succeed in grossly over-heating the economy. The 1970–1 recession reached bottom at the time of the Nixon shock and real GNP growth accelerated back to 10% in the year to the middle of 1973. But this was a different kind of growth. Instead of output and capacity rising at the same rate and therefore leaving the pressure of demand little changed, the increase in output was produced by using up existing spare capacity until the industry was running flat out. The pressure of demand rose considerably and led to accelerating inflation. The miraculous growth machine could no longer deliver 10% a year GNP growth, and the effort to make it do so produced chronic overheating.

Like the Jimmu boom nearly two decades earlier, by the summer of 1973 shortages and bottle-necks were throttling Japanese growth. Steel and plastics were scarce. Power stations could not meet all the demand for electricity. There was even a water shortage as the result of a drought. Petrochemical plants were pushed beyond their limits causing a number of explosions and accidents. This was not all. The synchronised world boom of 1972–3 caused world-wide shortages of raw materials. Initially, these were concentrated in construction materials, cement, wood, steel and plaster, but shortages soon spread to paper and plastics. Abnormal weather conditions simultaneously hit world food production, reducing supplies of wheat, soybeans, coffee, sugar and cotton. To make matters worse, Richard Nixon restricted grain exports in order to bring US food prices down. Real shortages produced a scramble for supplies, and speculative buying and hoarding made the shortages seem worse and pushed prices even higher. Japanese companies, whose excess liquidity had been employed speculating on land and stockmarket shares, switched to speculative food and raw material purchases and hoarding.

In 1972–3 commodity prices world-wide increased dramatically. Consequently every country imported world inflation to add to their home-made inflation. Japanese home-made inflation was worse than most other countries', so the effect of adding world inflation to it was disastrous (see Chart 12). By March 1973 the Japanese government was becoming alarmed, yet it failed to take any vigorous steps to deal with the problem. Restrictions on finance for real estate deals was the only half-hearted attempt to attack the excessive liquidity in the system.

The Economic Planning Agency sponsored a 'Law to Prevent Attempts to Corner Markets and Hold Goods off the Market', which did more to alert smaller and medium-sized companies to the possibilities of making a killing, than it did to restrain the larger companies which had

CHART 12: Japanese and OECD Consumer Price Inflation 1970–82
Annual percentage change

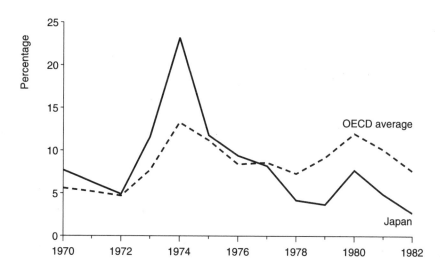

already got in on the act. Large companies had always worked hand-in-glove with the leading politicians and the bureaucrats. The government would make a display of doing something by passing Acts – but none would ever be effectively implemented. That was the way Japanese politics worked, or so they had come to believe.

First oil price hike

Then came the first oil shock. The Yom Kippur War erupted on 6 October 1973, when Egypt and Syria unexpectedly attacked Israel. The Organisation of Arab Petroleum Exporting Countries (OAPEC) was quick to respond; first, it cut supplies to anyone who did not support the Arab cause, then it increased oil prices fivefold. The effect on Japan seemed catastrophic. Japan imported 99% of its oil from the Middle East and depended on oil for 90% of its energy supplies.

Panic and chaos followed the oil price hike. The orderly behaviour of the Japanese collapsed in the crisis. The ethics of group above self were abruptly replaced by 'everyone for himself'. Panic buying created real shortages of any item which was rumoured to be short supply. Shops were cleared of all their supplies of toilet paper and detergents. There were runs on banks and saving institutions. Producers capitalised on this

94

situation by deliberately withholding supplies to precipitate panic buying and thus obtained inflated prices and profits. Oil companies formed price rings. Other companies operated illegal cartels. Collectively they rushed to exploit the novel situation of a sellers' market for almost anything they supplied. Companies which had been doing their utmost to cut each other's throats in the intensely competitive buyer's market, which had been a feature of the previous two decades, suddenly found that they had a common interest in fleecing the consumer instead. To hell with anti-monopoly and anti-cartel laws, this was the chance of a lifetime. For some months it seemed as if the companies were right. The government did nothing to discipline or punish them. But that was to come later. For the moment, the government itself was at a loss what to do.

The oil price rise was price-inflationary but demand-deflationary. It increased inflation directly, while, by taking money out of Japanese pockets and transferring it to Arab oil sheikhs, it cut Japanese real incomes so that consumer spending collapsed. The oil shock caught the Japanese economy on the wrong foot and pushed it further in the direction it was already going.

Consumer price inflation reached 26% in the year to March 1974. Wage demands in the spring 1974 wage round, called shunto, were therefore outrageous. Not merely were workers used to their share of company profits, but also the harmony between workers and employers had been broken by the evidence of the way that big businesses exploited the shortage situation and the consumer. Companies were ill placed to resist workers' demands for inflationary wage increases. Workers were simply exploiting their bargaining power regardless of the consequences, in the same way that companies had exploited the consumer in a sellers' market.

In the days of miraculous growth, sharing expanded profits with workers raised real living standards generally. But sharing windfall speculative gains was altogether different. These were once-off profits which had no lasting basis in increased capacity, sales and productivity. They were bound to evaporate, while the wage increases would stick, permanently raising labour costs. It was inevitable that these extra costs would be passed on in prices or offset by reduced employment, once the windfall gains ceased.

Big industry becomes the scapegoat

To their surprise, companies discovered that the government would not turn a blind eye to their profiteering. Instead, they were singled out as the scapegoats for an inflation which was caused, more than anything, by the

95

government's own fiscal and monetary profligacy. In February 1974, officials of the Fair Trade Commission raided the offices of petroleum-refining companies and prosecution followed of senior executives accused of operating an illegal price cartel. Similar raids followed on general trading companies and detergent producers. Shortly afterwards there was uproar when the Diet debated inflation. The opposition parties demanded that companies be punished and taxpayers get their cut from excessive profits made at consumers' expense. The opposition parties forced the government to pass a Special Temporary Corporate Profits Tax Law, which imposed a tax on windfall and abnormal profits. Industry was forced to pay out its excess profits a second time to the tax man.

The oil price increase destroyed Tanaka's ambitious plans for continued double-digit growth. Controlling inflation became the number one priority. Both fiscal and monetary policy were tightened. In December 1973 the Bank of Japan raised its official discount rate by 2% to a record 9%. In addition, 'window guidance' was used to place special credit restrictions on problem industries such as real estate agents, construction and general trading companies. Price controls were introduced on key products, from toilet paper and liquefied petroleum gas to vinyl chloride. The 1974 budget was stringent, halting or delaying the grandiose public spending plans incorporated in the 1972 and 1973 budgets.

All systems stop

Suddenly it was all systems stop. Corporations were facing high costs for energy, raw materials and wages, exacerbated by the yen's weakness which followed the oil price rise and the lurch into balance of payments deficit which it occasioned. They found that they could no longer pass on these costs in higher prices as their markets at home and abroad collapsed. Land prices, hoarded raw material prices and stockmarket shares crashed as the economy moved into recession. Eagerly anticipated speculative profits became onerous realised losses. Production was cut back and although statistically unemployment did not rise much, there was a sharp increase in concealed unemployment through short-time working and enforced 'holidays'. Real GNP fell in Japan in 1975 for the first time since the immediate post-war period. The growth machine was well and truly torpedoed and Tanaka went down with his ship. He took office as Japan's most popular Prime Minister with 62% public support (a figure not surpassed until Toshiki Kaifu in 1990). He left office in November 1974 as Japan's most unpopular Prime Minister with only 12% public support (subsequently beaten by Takeshita and Uno in 1989).

Hitching a lift on the US locomotive

Real GNP recovered briefly in 1976, even spurted, but then settled back to rise at a sedate pace which the government was unable to accelerate. Whereas growth had averaged 11% a year in the 1960s, it barely achieved 5% a year in the second half of the 1970s. The situation would have been worse, but for exports. The oil price shock turned the terms of trade against Japan. Between 1973 and 1976 Japanese import prices rose by 130%, while export prices rose by 50%. Relative to export prices, import prices rose by a quarter. Japan had to increase exports by a quarter in volume terms to pay for an unchanged volume of imports. In 1974 and 1975 there was no way that Japanese exports could grow so fast. Japan was not alone in suffering a recession and its foreign markets were also collapsing. Moreover the fall in the volume of imports, as the economy moved into recession, did not offset the rise in import prices. Japan, like other industrial countries, plunged into balance of payments deficit. Between 1972 and 1974 Japan's current account slumped from a surplus equal to 2% of GNP to a deficit of 1%. It recovered to balance in 1975, as a result of the collapse in the volume of imports and not to any recovery in exports.

Nonetheless, from late 1975 onwards Japanese exports started to grow strongly once more. Alarmed by the depth of the oil crisis recession, the US and Britain reflated too soon and too much. Japan and Germany, by contrast, reflated too little and too late. The Japanese, therefore, were able to take advantage of the upturn in US activity. Their companies, as usual, moved aggressively to export when their home markets stagnated. In this they were helped by the yen's weakness. During 1973 it had risen to ¥265 to the US dollar, but in 1974–6 it moved back down to ¥300 where it remained for nearly three years. The result was that in 1976 Japan moved back into payments surplus and this surplus continued to rise through to 1978. The US, meanwhile, moved from a surplus in 1975 to a modest deficit in 1978. Both Japan and Germany were seen as hitching a free ride on US expansion. The US was called the 'locomotive economy', because it was dragging the rest of the world forward.

From 1976 onwards, Japan was severely criticised as a free-rider at all international meetings and particularly at the new annual summit meetings of the leaders of the Group of Seven advanced countries. In late 1977, it was forced to agree a 7% growth target for the following year and the 1978 Bonn summit spent much time debating whether this target could be met. Starting in early 1985, Japanese fiscal policy became expansionary. Tanaka had been severely criticised for the big budget deficits of the early 1970s. But under pressure from abroad, his more conservative successors ran even larger ones (see Chart 13).

97

CHART 13: Japanese and US Budget Balances 1970–82
Percent of GNP

The stimulatory policy pursued from 1975 to 1978 caused the budget deficit to soar. The nature of the budget deficits also changed. While public works spending was decisively checked after the oil crisis, social security spending continued to rise sharply. When the time came in the 1980s for the deficit to be brought back under control, the hardest kind of expenditure to cut was the highest, while the easiest, public investment, was dangerously low.

Second oil price shock

As the 1970s approached their end, it seemed as if things were at last returning to normal. Excess capacity was gradually reduced and investment was recovering. Growth accelerated and the balance of payments surplus started to diminish. Inflation had been brought down to a respectable level and it was possible to start thinking once more about cutting the size of the budget deficit. But at this point fate again intervened. The Iranian revolution and the Iraq–Iran War cut oil supplies. In 1979–80 oil prices trebled; the world economy was hit by the second oil price shock in a decade.

98

6

Supply Siders and Savers

The 1980s were marked by exchange and financial market turbulence. The early years of the decade were dominated by the second oil price hike, the epilogue to the 1970s. The Japanese economy performed far better than it did following the first oil price rise and better than any other major economy. In the middle years of the decade, Japan was let off the hook by President Reagan's supply-side economics; its economy again hitched a lift from rapid US demand growth. But in 1985 the dollar peaked and by 1987 its value had halved against the yen. The US stopped pulling the world forward. Threatened with trade warfare, Japan tackled the symptoms of its structural trade surplus with the palliative of cyclical reflation. Its budget deficit was still worryingly large, so the burden of reflation was thrown upon easy money. By the late 1980s the economy was awash with credit, cheaper and more plentiful than ever before. This produced the 'bubble' economy, which burst in 1990 revealing many a scandal.

Better the second time round

Japan was far better placed in 1979 when the second oil price rise occurred than it was before the first. At the Bonn summit in 1978, Japan and Germany had been persuaded to stimulate their economies to help keep world economic expansion going. In that year Japan achieved nearly 6% GNP growth, despite the fact that exports rose less than 1% in volume while imports climbed 8%. The reduction in Japan's current account surplus knocked nearly 1% off the expansion in GNP, instead of contributing towards it. At the 1979 economic summit, Japan was no longer in the dock. So by mid-year the government felt it was safe to apply both fiscal and monetary brakes to curb rising inflation. Designed to tackle the deficit, which had risen to 4.6% of GNP during the 1970s, the budget

99

CHART 14: Japanese and OECD Consumer Price Inflation 1980–90
Annual percentage change

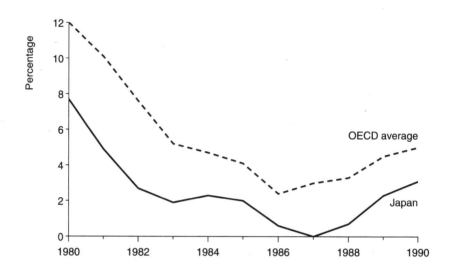

was the most severe in eighteen years. This timely deflation prepared the economy to meet the second oil price increase.

The second price hike was less severe than the first. Between 1972 and 1974 oil prices quintupled; between 1978 and 1980 they little more than doubled. But their starting level was much higher in 1978, and consequently the effect on Japanese import prices was almost as bad. Higher oil costs were largely absorbed by lower profits and reduced real wages the second time round, instead of being passed on in higher prices (see Chart 14). In the two years following the 1973 oil price rise, wholesale prices, consumer prices and hourly earnings all rose by around 40%. In the two years following the second oil price rise, wholesale prices rose 22%, consumer prices 14% and earnings 13%. The yen exchange rate fell briefly and then recovered.

In 1972–4 Japanese inflation was almost as bad as Britain's; it peaked at 25%. In 1978–80 it was better than Germany's, staying below 10%. By absorbing the costs of higher oil prices in lower wages and profits, Japanese exports became more competitive. The worsening terms of trade still forced the Japanese current account balance into the red. But in volume terms, the trade balance improved strongly. As a result, instead of activity collapsing and the economy moving into a recession, growth merely slowed down (see Chart 15).

CHART 15: Japanese GNP and OECD GDP Growth 1980–90
Annual percentage growth

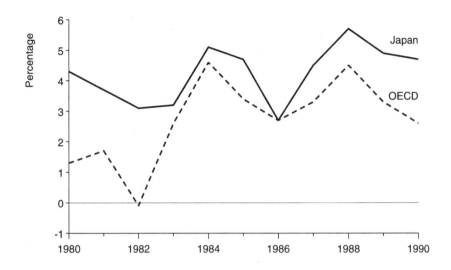

Trade friction

Other countries did not admire Japan's superior performance, and particularly disliked the Japanese invasion of their markets. Japanese car exports, for example, rose by half in the twelve months to April 1980, while US and British vehicle production fell by a third. Europe and the US threatened to shut out Japanese cars, unless Japan 'voluntarily' shut them in. The principle of voluntary export restraint was conceded and, from May 1981 onwards, the Japanese imposed a limit on the number of vehicles which could be exported to the US. Inevitably the Japanese car industry moved up-market. It immediately started selling fewer but more expensive cars, thereby continuing to increase its export earnings. This did not deter pressure for similar action on other products and, by early 1982, the Japanese claimed that one-third of their exports to the US and Europe were subject to some form of voluntary restraint. Exports still rose. Japan pushed the Americans and Europeans out of Third World markets. So the foreign attack switched to Japan's closed import market.

By December 1981, the Japanese Trade Minister, Toshio Komoto, was warning that the country was on the 'verge of a trade war'. Three annual instalments of GATT round tariff reductions, due over 1982–4, were brought forward to 1 April 1982 – but this was not enough. Fearing trouble at the June 1982 Versailles summit, the Japanese offered a further package of trade liberalisation measures. Tranquillisation might be a better term. The package included tariff cuts on 119 items from April 1983 and the abolition of tariffs on another ninety-six; the list ran from chocolate biscuits to power stations. Import procedures, said the Japanese, would be simplified and accelerated. Restrictive practices on the distribution of imports would be discouraged. An ombudsman would be appointed to settle trade grievances and foreigners would have a say in future standards. Fine words, but the fine print mattered more. The liberalisation measures did little to accelerate the growth of imports. So foreign criticism changed its focus, from trade barriers at Japan's frontiers to the unfair way the domestic economy worked.

Reaganomics

Ronald Reagan's election to the Presidency brought supply-side policies to the White House in 1981. Reaganomics came to the rescue of hard-pressed Japan, as the new Administration embarked on tax cuts. Supply-siders claimed they would encourage faster growth and higher savings and so increase tax revenues. Together with spending cuts, the Administration reckoned that it would balance the Federal budget by 1983–4. Like most Americans, the supply-siders forgot about foreigners and ignored the effects of tax cuts on the dollar and the US balance of payments.

This was a fatal mistake. The reform lowered the after-tax cost borrowing, and increased the demand for credit. The Federal Reserve, under its powerful chairman, Paul Volcker, moved interest rates higher to limit money supply growth and combat inflation. Reagan's easy tax policy was combined with Volcker's tighter money policy. This attracted an inflow of foreign capital, not least from Japan where exchange controls had been eliminated in 1980. The dollar soared (see Chart 16); between the third quarter of 1980 and its peak in the first quarter of 1985, it rose by 60% on average against other currencies (but only 20% against the yen). US manufactures were priced out of world markets, and foreign imports flooded in. Between 1981 and 1985, the US current account went from a surplus of $7bn, or 0.2% of GNP, to a deficit of $122bn, 3% of GNP. Growth had been optimistically forecast at 5% a year. Domestic demand rose by a little under 4% and, thanks to the deteriorating trade balance, GNP growth fell short of 3%.

One-quarter of extra spending by Americans between 1981 and 1985 went on additional imports. A quarter of the income generated by this spending was earned by foreigners. Tax revenue on this income was lost

CHART 16: Yen–Dollar Exchange Rate 1980–92
Yen per Dollar

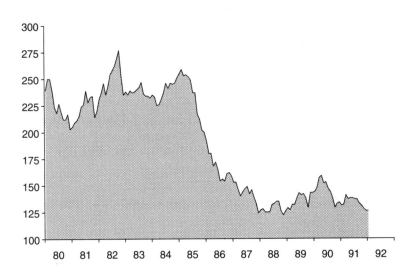

CHART 17: Japanese and US Budget Balances 1980–90
Percent of GNP

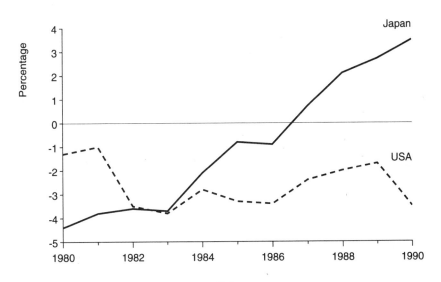

abroad. It went to the German and Japanese governments, whose exports were boosted by the dollar's strength. The US Internal Revenue lost out. Instead of disappearing, the US Federal budget deficit expanded from $74 bn, or 2.8% of GNP, in 1980–1 to $212 bn, or 5.3%, in 1984–5. If the German and Japanese governments had spent their windfall tax gains, all would have been well. Demand in Germany and Japan would have been boosted, leading to higher imports to match their higher exports. America's current account would have deteriorated less, output and incomes would have grown faster, and tax revenues would have been more buoyant. But the Japanese and German budget deficits yawned wide in the early 1980s. America's fiscal profligacy enabled both to embrace stringency with impunity (see Chart 17). Booming exports offset the deflationary impact of public spending cuts.

Reagan's supply-side tax reductions distorted the US economy. The overvalued dollar hit American manufacturers' sales, thus cancelling the cut in the after-tax cost of borrowed money. Industrialists were reluctant to investment in new capacity. But the service sector, unaffected by foreign competition, was helped by the strong dollar. Investment in such things as office buildings, shopping malls, hotels and leisure complexes boomed. These did little to generate extra exports or to reduce imports. America's ability to service and repay debts it incurred by its trade deficit was not increased.

In macro-economic terms, Reagan's measures caused a serious shortfall of domestic savings compared with investment. Service industries invested more. Individuals borrowed more. Personal savings declined. The ratio of household savings to disposable household income dropped from 7.7% in 1981 to 4.5% in 1985. The rise in the budget deficit increased government dissaving. National savings as a whole fell from 18.8% of GNP to 15.8%. Inadequate US savings provide an outlet for excessive German and Japanese savings, through the deterioration in the US current account balance. In these same four years, the Japanese current account surplus rose from $5 bn or 0.4% of GNP to $50 bn or 3.7% (see Chart 18). Domestic demand rose 3% a year and real GNP, thanks to export-led growth, by 4% a year – the mirror image of demand and growth rates experienced in the US.

The Yasu-Ron dog-and-pony show

The deterioration in the US payments balance occurred as the American economy was recovering from the double-dip 1980–2 recession. Demand and activity at home was expanding. Political pressure for increased trade protection remained subdued. The Japanese were asked to

CHART 18: Japanese and US Current Accounts 1980–91
Percent of GNP

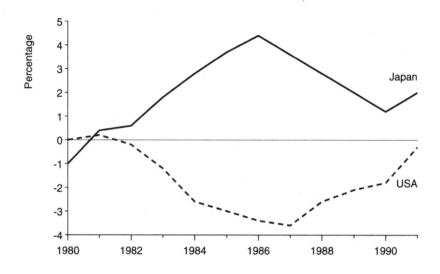

reform the working of their domestic economy, but were able to fob off foreigners with unkept promises. Indeed the longevity of Japanese Prime Ministers depended upon their ability to deflect foreign criticism. Yasuhiro Nakasone was a master of the art of saying much and doing little. After becoming Prime Minister in November 1982, he struck up a most friendly relationship with Ronald Reagan. The Yasu-Ron dog-and-pony show was on the road.

Nakasone was at heart a reformer, which lent credence to the promises he could not keep. But a gulf existed between his rhetoric abroad and reality at home. One example was the Maekawa Report, privately commissioned in October 1984 by Nakasone from a seventeen-strong team of the great and good (and aged), led by the former Bank of Japan Governor, Haruo Meakawa. While full of Establishment figures, it had no formal status within the consultative structure of the Liberal Democratic party. Titled the Advisory Group on Economic Structural Adjustment for International Harmony, its objective was to bypass the conservative bureaucrats who customarily advised LDP policy committees. Its first report, in April 1985, was worthy, wordy and insipid. It called in general terms for 'Japan to make a historical transformation in its traditional policies on economic management and the nation's life-style', with the object of 'steadily reducing the nation's current account imbalance to one consistent with international harmony'. Its recommendations, however, were no more than broad generalisations and pious hopes. Its purpose was to secure a breathing space for the Japanese from the trade protectionist retaliation, which the US Congress had begun to threaten. While the US economy was recovering and the dollar was strong, this was all that seemed to be needed. When the dollar peaked and collapsed, times changed. The second Maekawa Report, presented to the Prime Minister in April 1987, reflected this change. It did come up with a fairly comprehensive list of detailed recommendations, which then required further study within the LDP's formal policy-making bodies. But to be fair to the Japanese government, efforts were made in the second half of the 1980s to change the workings of the economy. Tax reforms were introduced in 1987, and Takeshita lost the premiership in 1989 in part because he pushed a 3% sales tax throughout the Diet.

Financial deregulation was another area in which serious, if slow, progress towards reform was made. This began in the 1970s and already encompassed the dismantling of inward and outward restrictions over international capital movements. Free capital flows from Japan were a major contributor to the dollar's strength in 1981–5. Domestically, the Japanese financial markets remained highly regulated and rigorously compartmentalised through most of the decade.

Low interest and poor returns at home, said the Americans, explained why Japanese capital flowed abroad, weakening the yen and strengthening the dollar. The yen was consequently undervalued and Japanese exports unfairly cheap. When President Reagan visited Japan in November 1983, Nakasone agreed to the formation of an ad hoc 'yen-dollar exchange issues' group to agree how and when Japan should liberalise its financial markets. This was as far as Ron and Yasu themselves took the matter. But on America's side, the issue fell into Vice-President George Bush's bailiwick, and something did get done. An agreement was reached in 1984 between the Japanese Vice-Minister for Finance, Tomomitsu Oba and Beryl Sprinkel, the US Treasury Under Secretary, on capital market reforms. In the event, the progress made towards financial deregulation contributed substantially to the speculative crisis which overtook Japan in the late 1980s.

Endaka

'Endaka' or 'yendaka', as it is sometimes written, refers to the period of yen strength and dollar weakness which began in March 1985 after the dollar peaked at ¥260. During the summer and autumn, the dollar moved gently downwards. Then Finance Ministers of the US, Japan,

Germany, France and Britain – the Group of Five (G5) major economies – meeting in the Plaza Hotel in New York in September, agreed to
co-operate in a 'managed and orderly depreciation of the dollar'. In view
of the alarming growth in the US budget and trade deficits, private
investors were already nervous. So when the G5, in a blaze of publicity,
announced their decision, the dollar's depreciation became anything but
orderly. By February 1987, its value against the yen had almost halved to
¥140.

The yen's rapid rise caused panic amongst Japanese businessmen and
exporters. In 1986 the US current account deficit, in volume terms,
stopped rising and started to decline. The stimulus which rising exports
had given to the Japanese economy was withdrawn. Making profits by
making things became extremely hard. Growth abruptly slowed and
fears of recession spread throughout the country. The government responded with further *ad hoc* fiscal packages. But since each year's
regular budget was immensely tough, interim measures merely reduced
the degree of fiscal deflation to which the economy was subject. The
main burden of reflation was placed on monetary expansion.

Throughout 1986 and into 1987 the dollar headed down. The US
authorities could not care less. The 1985–6 collapse in world oil prices
checked any increase in inflation. No bottom could be seen to the abyss
into which the currency was plunging. Japan was not alone in fearing
that the dollar's fall might go too far. Meeting in the Louvre in Paris in
February 1987, Finance Ministers decided that the time had come to
prop it up. The dollar, they said, had already fallen 'within ranges
broadly consistent with underlying economic fundamentals'. How they
reached this startling conclusion is a mystery. To make depreciation
work in eliminating an external payments deficit, it is necessary to release
resources at home by reducing domestic demand. The Americans had
not done so, and Congress had taken limited action to bring the budget
deficit under control. The improvement in trade volumes, therefore, was
modest and not sufficient to offset the deterioration in America's terms of
trade caused by the dollar's fall, i.e., import prices rose faster than import
volume declined so that the import bill became larger. The US current
account deficit consequently widened to $145 bn in 1986 and $162 bn in
1987.

Foreign private investors were reluctant to lend the US enough to plug
this payments gap. They required the bribe of higher US interest rates to
do so. Without this, they did not believe the G5 could halt the dollar's
fall. The Federal Reserve Board, however, decided interest rate policy
on purely domestic considerations, and had no intention of raising rates
because of external pressure to do so. When private investors boycotted

CHART 19: Japanese Broad Money and Nominal GNP 1980–91
Annual percentage change

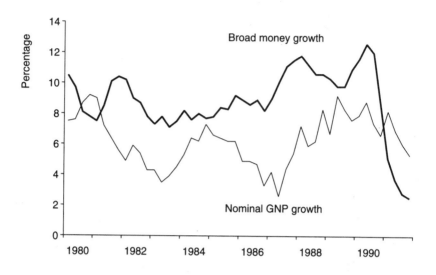

the dollar, believing it was still overvalued, central bankers set out to prove them wrong. They intervened on a massive scale to support the dollar; from February to October 1987 they bought $100 bn on the world's foreign exchange markets, spending the equivalent billions of their own yen, D-marks, francs and pounds to do so. The US twin deficits were thus largely financed by Japanese, German, French and British government borrowing.

Crash of 1987

Government borrowing provides the reserve base on which bankers are able to expand credit. Official intervention in support of the dollar in 1987 substantially increased the money supply growth in Europe and Japan (see Chart 19). It gave the Americans scope to neglect rather than correct their problems. Had the dollar's fall continued, the US would have been forced to raise interest rates or tackle its budget deficit sooner. The consequences were disastrous. Stockmarket shares and property prices had been rising since the early 1980s. At the end of 1986 markets were reasonably priced. But then monetary excesses in 1987 fuelled speculation: stockmarkets boomed and property prices soared. Between December 1986 and August 1987, share prices on Wall Street climbed

CHART 20: Tokyo Share Price Index 1980–92
Nikkei Dow Index

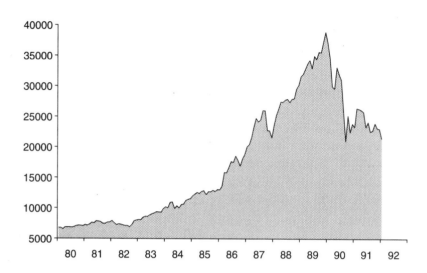

43%, to a peak not seen again until early 1991. Tokyo climbed 42% through to October (see Chart 20). Inflation generally began to accelerate, spurred by a rebound in world oil prices from their 1986 low. By early autumn, central bankers were getting scared. Led by the Bundesbank, they raised interest rates to curb speculative excesses. The US Federal Reserve was forced to follow suit. Bond markets collapsed and bond yields rose. The gap between the return on long US Treasury bills and earnings on overvalued shares widened. Investors took fright and on 19 October 1987 the bubble burst. Wall Street crashed, dragging stockmarkets in the rest of the world down in its wake. Tokyo fell 15% in a single day.

Japan's role in the 1987 crash is of some passing interest. It demonstrates the close interconnection which now exists between the world's capital markets. At the 1986 summit, Japan was the whipping-boy, blamed for destabilising the international economy by running so large a balance of payments surplus. To forestall further criticism at the Venice summit in 1987, the government announced a ¥6 trn package of public spending increases and tax cuts, equivalent to a 2% boost to GNP growth. But Japan was still struggling to cut its budget deficit. Fortunately, as part of so-called 'Administrative Reforms', which was a euphemism for measures to cut public spending and balance the budget, it had embarked on the privatisation of Nippon Telephone & Telegraph. The costs of the reflationary package, therefore, could be clawed back by the sale of the next tranche of NTT shares.

The first tranche of 1,950,000 shares had been sold in February 1987. The offer price was ¥1.2 m per share (over $8000), which was 130 times the company's earnings. The average price/earning (P/E) ratio on the Tokyo market was then 34. It would seem that the NTT shares were grossly overpriced. Nonetheless, 8 m Japanese applied to buy them, promising to shell out ¥2.34 trn or $16 bn in the process. Mrs Watanabe, other Japanese housewives and most major institutional investors who scrambled to buy, felt it was their patriotic duty to do so. They also reckoned that the price must go up. The Finance Ministry and the major brokers would lose too much face if NTT shares did not go immediately to a premium. Up they went with a vengeance. By April 1986 the shares were trading at ¥3.2 m each, a profit of 160% in two months for anyone who managed to get in at the ground floor, i.e., stockbrokers' favourite customers. This price valued NTT as a whole at $340 bn, which made it worth more than the shares in all German companies, than the combined foreign debts of Brazil, Mexico and Argentina, or the combined yearly GNPs of Australia, New Zealand, Portugal and Greece. NTT's P/E ratio went over 300.

The next NTT tranche was scheduled for sale on 9 November 1987. Its issue price was ¥2.55 m ($18,000). The amount of cash needed to be put up for its purchase was ¥5.7 trn, or $35 bn, enough to cover almost all the cost of the July fiscal package. In October, Japanese investors went liquid to fill up their war chests in anticipation. The dollar looked uncertain, so the best way to build up cash was to bring money home from the US, which is what happened. Nicholas Brady, now US Treasury Secretary, was then Chairman of the New York investment bankers Dillon, Reed & Co. He was asked by President Reagan to head a study into the crash and what caused it. In April 1988 he told a meeting of pension fund managers: 'People ask me: "What was it that blew it off on the 19th October – was it the twin deficits, was it Rostenkowski [tax] legislation, what was it?" I don't think it was any of those things that really was the trigger. The real trigger was that the Japanese came in for their own reasons and sold an enormous amount of US government bonds and drove the thirty-year government bond up through 10%. And when it got through 10%, that got a lot of people thinking, "Gee, that's four times the return you get on equity. Here we go, inflation again." That to me is what really started the 19th – a worry by the Japanese about the US currency.'

Although the Japanese pulled the trigger, they didn't load the gun.

The October 1987 crash was a direct consequence of central banks meddling with markets to support the dollar. But its severity evoked folk-memories of 1929. People feared that it presaged a 1930s-style depression, and economists fed those fears with gloomy forecasts. Governments forgot their fears of inflation, as dangers of recession loomed larger. With markets tumbling around the world, there was only one thing to do: all relaxed their efforts to restrain money supply growth.

Gloomy predictions proved groundless. The slow-burn recovery from the 1980–2 recession was about to get its second wind. Hitherto the upswing had been driven by falling savings and rising consumption. The recovery in investment had been feeble. The early 1980s recession had left an excess of idle plant and equipment in its wake. Unemployment remained high and labour plentiful. It was not until the fifth year of the recovery that capacity utilisation rates reached levels at which it paid to invest in expansion. Belatedly, investment boomed, sustaining and reinforcing the upswing just when forecasters said it would end. 1988 turned out a real humdinger. Japan's GNP rose 6%; Britain and America notched up 4.5% growth; sluggards France and Germany managed 4% apiece. It was the second-fastest growth year in the 1980s.

Japan's great monetary binge

The US and Europeans soon recognised their mistake. They tightened monetary policy and raised interest rates in early 1988. Japan was the exception. Its current account surplus had climbed to $87 bn in 1987. Pressure for trade retaliation intensified. The US Congress, with the Presidential Election due in November, was in a nasty mood. In April 1988, it passed an Omnibus Trade Bill, including the notorious clause 'Super 301'. This clause required the President to impose sanctions against countries guilty of running large bilateral trade surpluses with the US due to unfair trade practices. (Running a large surplus with the US was regarded by most Congressmen as proof positive of unfair trading.) The President signed it into law in August 1988.

Worsening trade friction persuaded the Japanese to maintain their cheap and easy monetary policy a year longer than any other country. The Bank of Japan did not move to raise its official discount rate from its record post-war low of 2.5% until May 1989. The results for growth and the balance of payments were highly gratifying. As the US economy slowed down, the Japanese economy boomed. America's real GNP growth dropped to 2.5% in 1989 and under 1% in 1990. Japan's growth accelerated from 4.9% to 5.4%. Better still, the Japanese current account surplus shrank to $36 bn in 1990, or 1% of GNP, while the US deficit fell to $90 bn.

The boom seemed to solve Japan's problems: savings fell; investment rose; output rose rapidly; and the payments surplus shrank. Japan was back on the fast-growth track. Between 1987 and 1990 it changed from guard's van (caboose) to locomotive economy. Domestic demand rose 6% on average over these three years, but 1% of this spilt over into higher imports helping other countries to expand. Japanese output rose on average by 5%. Unfortunately the expansion was unsoundly based. It was caused by asset price inflation. Share prices on the Tokyo stockmarket rose by 120% in the two years following the October 1987 crash. The Nikkei index climbed from its post-crash low of 17,387 to a peak of 38,915 at the end of December 1989. The rise in property prices was almost as steep, with residential and commercial property values doubling between 1986 and 1989.

Rising share and property prices made the one-third of Japanese who owned everything effortlessly better off; they saw no point in saving out of income. The two-thirds who owned little also saw no point in saving; they could never save enough to buy their own homes. The Japanese consumer went on a spending spree. Personal savings declined as personal wealth increased. Household net savings dropped from 16.1% of disposable income in 1986 to 13.8% in 1990. Companies also went out and spent with abandon. Total investment rose by nearly 40% in real terms between 1987 and 1990; investment in plant and equipment rose by nearly 50% in three years. The share of total investment in GDP increased from 31% to 37%. The share of plant and equipment investment rose from 18% to 23%.

Capital spending increased sharply because money was almost costless to borrow. Companies also made fat profits on their stockmarket and land speculation. Investment projects were decided on their desirability, without a thought being given to how they would be financed. Money was no constraint as far as production managers and personnel departments were concerned.

Increased investment was initially a damage-control exercise. The strong yen made it imperative for Japanese manufacturers to move up-market, to manufacture goods which sold because they were technologically the most advanced available, almost regardless of price. Then, as the boom gathered momentum, labour became scarce. Cheap capital was used to replace labour. Finally, a quarter of all new capital spending was an alternative to higher wages. New dormitories, swimming pools and sports arenas were built for young workers; fleets of new company cars were purchased for senior executives. The productivity of capital fell. Even so, Japan's investment boom added to capacity which, if not used to supply the home market, will certainly be switched to increasing exports once again.

The speculative bubble burst early in 1990. The Tokyo stockmarket ended the year with share prices 40% lower. At the worst point during the year, 1 October 1990, the Nikkei index was down to 20,221, almost half its December 1989 peak level. Property prices weakened, but only modestly. Even after interest rates started rising in May 1989, and particularly through 1990 when the stockmarket crashed, the easy investment spending went on. It took a long time before the message got through that money had become expensive and scarce. So investment continued to rise long after the conditions which supported it had changed. Domestic demand growth did not slow down significantly until 1991. When it did, the old problem of excess savings re-appeared. The Japanese balance of payments surplus started rapidly to expand once more. Despite Gulf War support payments of $9 bn, Japan's current account surplus rose to $73 bn in 1991, 2% of GNP. By the end of the year it was running at an annual rate of $120 bn.

PART II

Neo-Feudal Corporatism

7

A Nation of Tax Cheats

So far I have described *what* happened to Japan after the Second World War. It is now time to explain *why* things happened. Why do the Japanese save so much? Politically, can they do anything about it? Will they be forced to change by other countries?

Economists have tried to discover why the Japanese save so much. No simple answer has been found. The view taken here is that there is no single reason, or even a few simple ones. The collective behaviour of millions of people is not that of sheep, driven by a single sheepdog. High saving is the sum of millions of individual decisions, not just by people, but by politicians and businessmen, since governments and companies also save. Each decision to save rather than spend may be made for any of a number of reasons. High savings are likely to be the result of many factors – historical, institutional, psychological, moral and even accidental – each of which has a bias encouraging people to save rather than spend.

The Japanese are not sheep, but they could be lemmings, driven by some innate compulsion to their own destruction. It is normally wrong to apply a single personal attribute to an entire nation. But ethnically the Japanese are nearly all the same, unlike other nations which are mostly a mongrel mixture of many different tribes and races. The ethnic uniformity of the Japanese could be associated with a genetic tendency to seek the long-term security which savings offer, rather than immediate satisfaction from spending all one's income. It is more likely, however, that the shared history of past tribulations and natural disasters, such as earthquakes, encourages thrift. Then again, possibly Confucian virtues of simplicity and frugality are deeply ingrained in the nation's psyche. While not fervently religious, most Japanese are Buddhist, blended with their indigenous religion, Shintoism, the Japanese nature and hero cult. They are the only advanced high-income country with a Buddhist background.

If there is anything in such theories, the government can't easily change things – in which case, the nation is heading inexorably for trouble. The view here, however, is that the Japanese save a lot for basically the same reason that people in communist countries did. They were forced to save, because they could not buy the things they wanted. The analogy with communism is clear. In a capitalist free market economy, wants and needs raise prices, producing profits for those who privately supply what is required. The ballot box democratically determines the supply of public sector goods and services. In the communist system, supply and prices were fixed by fiat. People queued or did without. Russians and east Europeans were unable to buy material goods such as cars, washing machines, fridges, telephones and other consumer durables. Often they had to wait years before obtaining such items and, when able to do so, paid exorbitant prices for them. Consequently, people accumulated large cash balances which they were unable to spend. This was demonstrated dramatically following German unification. East Germans were given spendable D-marks in exchange for their unspendable Ostmarks and gained access to an unlimited supply of reasonably priced products. East German spending on west German and imported products soared. The west German economy boomed and Germany as a whole went into balance of payments deficit.

Shortages persisted in a centrally planned economy because nobody had the incentive or ability to correct them. The government was under little pressure to admit its shortcomings. By contrast, the Japanese consumer in material terms is amongst the most affluent in the world. His unsatisfied wants are different. They are for things which improve the quality of life: a better home, main sewerage, more parks, golf courses and leisure facilities, better roads, less crowded trains and so forth. As with material goods under the communist system, there is no fundamental reason which prevents the Japanese from obtaining such things. Instead, regulations and restrictions prevent the pricing system from allocating resources efficiently. High saving results from many small forces all pushing in the same direction, to deny the individual what he wants.

The tax system, which is the subject of this chapter, encourages savings both in general and in detail. Japanese public spending and taxes are low by international standards. The state does not provide social amenities on the scale which people have a right to expect. More money is left in the individual's pocket out of which to save. Taxes are monstrously complex, making the economic system subject to detailed bureaucratic control and intervention in all aspects of its operation. The difference from communist controls is that Japanese intervention is not centrally planned. It reflects different special interest groups competing to obtain sectional advantages at the expense of the nation at large. Taxes are consequently unfair and inefficient, so people cheat. Conspicuous consumption attracts the tax man's attention. So they must hide their ill-gotten gains. Taxes encourage the misuse of land, contributing to the shortage of living space. They encourage corporate savings out of retained earnings. In short, the inefficiency of the system prevents the authorities from raising more revenue with which to supply what the individual wants.

The Japanese post-war tax system was designed by the American occupation authorities, SCAP, in 1949. As soon as they went, the Japanese tinkered about with it. Then, from the early 1950s to the late 1980s, the system remained broadly the same. Political battles to change it began over a decade ago, in the late 1970s. They cost three Prime Ministers their jobs before anything was accomplished. It will be argued here that mighty efforts produced a mouse. The Japanese tax system remains in as bad a mess as ever.

Low taxes

Japanese taxes collect relatively little revenue. When OECD tax league tables are examined, Denmark, Sweden and Norway win gold, silver and bronze medals respectively. Scandinavian governments regularly take around two-thirds of their citizens' incomes. Until recently, Japan always came last. In 1978 its tax take was less than a quarter of incomes. But it rose during the following decade, to reach one-third of incomes in 1988. This put Japan into fifteenth place in the tax league, out of seventeen OECD countries. It might be supposed that, as low taxes go with low government spending, the Japanese are left to provide more for themselves and their family. They must save hard for their old age, for their children's education, for illness, the risk of unemployment, and so forth. Unfortunately, the league table reveals that Switzerland comes sixteenth and the US comes last, with lower taxes than Japan. The Swiss also save a lot, but Americans save little. One sees little relationship in the table between tax levels and savings rates.

The way the Japanese are taxed is also unusual. Over 70% of revenues come from taxes on personal incomes and company profits, well above the OECD norm. Only four countries tax companies more severely than the Japanese, and all are at the top of the tax league. Japan levies the highest taxes on capital, owing to a harsh and effective inheritance tax. Taxes on spending, however, are low. Until 1989, Japan levied no general consumption tax or value added tax. Instead, it imposed a variety of commodity taxes on specific goods and services, originally regarded as luxuries, as well as the usual excise duties on alcohol, tobacco and petrol. To complete the picture, local authorities levy minuscule poll taxes and there are annual levies on the ownership of property and land.

Country	% Taxes	Tax rank	% Savings	Savings rank
Denmark	65	1	16	16
Sweden	63	2	18	13
Norway	57	3	23	7
Netherlands	53	4	23	6
France	51	5	21	9
Belgium	49	6	19	12
Austria	49	7	25	3
Germany	45	8	25	4
Britain	44	9	16	15
Finland	43	10	24	5
Greece	41	11	17	14
Italy	40	12	21	10
Canada	40	13	20	11
Australia	36	14	22	8
Japan	34	15	34	1
Switzerland	32	16	33	2
United States	31	17	15	17

Table 2   Taxes and Savings, 1988

Although the revenue collected from personal incomes is modest, until recently tax rates were savage. The starting point was low and the top marginal rate amongst the highest in the world. In the late 1980s, when the highest US Federal income tax rate was 28% and the top British rate was 40%, the highest Japanese rate was 86%. At the same time, the Japanese effective corporation tax rate was nearly 53%, compared with 40% in the US and 35% in Britain. The Japanese tax system is inefficient and harsh; its penal tax rates collect peanuts, because most people don't pay them.

Blame the Americans

The cranky way in which Japan tries to extract taxes from its citizens results from a chapter of accidents. One could say that it began with a feather. Ancient man in Asia and the Middle East picked one up, dipped it in dye or blood, and started to make marks on the nearest cave wall. By chance, the ancient Asian dipped the blunt end in the ink and painted pictures. The Middle Eastern caveman used the sharp end and drew sketches. As a result, different forms of writing developed in the Orient and Occident. The Greeks perfected a phonetic alphabet in which twenty-six characters stand for sounds. The Chinese painted thousands of pictures, each standing for different things; in time these pictures became stylised symbols.

The Japanese imported Chinese writing in the fifth or sixth century AD. It took thousands of Chinese kanji characters, standing for nouns, verb roots and adjectives. Like words in a language, nobody knows precisely how many kanji characters there are. Each is highly complex, made up of a dozen or more brush-strokes. Certainly there were far too many for the poorly educated women to remember. So the Japanese invented a separate writing system called katakana, which was phonetic, based on an alphabet of forty-six letters, representing all the basic sounds in the Japanese language. It was a better and simpler system. The letters were written with straight strokes and sharp angles, like capitals such as N, K and T. Children begin to read and write it. But it would have been beneath man's dignity to use it, so a third system of forty-six letters was invented for general use, called hiragana. Its letters are rounded, like S, U and C. Katakana came to be used in telex and tele-grams, because of its simplicity. It is also used to translate phonetically the foreign words and names which have crept into the Japanese lan-guage. The word 'television' will always be written in katakana. Today the Japanese use all three systems simultaneously. A scientific textbook is littered with katakana, for foreign words, hiragana for ordinary Japanese words, and kanji where appropriate. Moreover, the grammar used in written Japanese differs from that used in ordinary speech. Writing even the most simple message is thus fearsomely complicated. Having decided what to say, it is then necessary to consider how to write it. Then for each word or expression the choice must be made between kanji, katakana and hiragana. Most Japanese draft written material several times before they are satisfied that they have expressed their meaning in the correct form – which, like tummy language, conveys meaning.

Each writing system has its advantages and drawbacks. To speak, one must learn thousands of words. Europeans and Americans then find it comparatively easy to read and write. But they can communicate in writing only to somebody who speaks the same language. If they want to communicate in a foreign language, they must learn thousands more words. Chinese and Japanese writing involves a further great feat of memory. But once it is mastered, it can be used to communicate with people who speak different dialects, or even different languages. The vast Chinese empire of old, with its millions of people, could never have been controlled from Beijing but for this superior means of communications.

A major drawback to Chinese and Japanese writing emerged in the nineteenth century, when the typewriter was invented. The original American Remington typewriter had fifty-two keys, twenty-six for capitals and twenty-six for lower-case letters. An experienced stenographer could nonetheless type a letter faster than it could be written by hand. With the addition of carbon paper, ten copies could be made simultaneously. A simple Japanese typewriter was out of the question. Mechanical typewriters were manufactured. They were massive, rather like church organs, with serried tiers of keyboards and numerous shift keys. Not only were such monstrosities impossibly expensive for widespread use, but typing with them was infinitely slower than hand-writing. Even a trained typist took ages to find the right kanji key. So Japan failed to benefit from the typewriter age. Copying documents remained difficult and slow. Consequently, Japanese book-keeping remained Dickensian. Centralised accounting was impractical. Banks and the postal savings system continued to use handwritten ledgers, maintained at local branch level, until the advent of the photocopier and computer. To this day, Japanese offices are incredibly inefficient with the abacus still in use. Almost everything is handwritten, then the photocopier takes over.

The computer belatedly brought Japan into the typewriter age. The operator simply types sentences using either hiragana or katakana alphabets. At the press of a button, the computer screen shows a menu of kanji characters for each word. The operator then selects the appropriate one, or tries again. It is like a spell-check on a British or American computer. Sometimes the operator uses the English phonetic alphabet to write Japanese words and obtains the Japanese translation in return.

Another consequence of Chinese and Japanese writing is that people cannot sign their names. Signatures require that a few letters, although written badly, remain recognisable if not readable. But even small variations in Japanese characters produce different words. The Japanese therefore use personal 'chops', on which the characters for their names are carved. They stamp documents with these chops, instead of signing them, in much the same way as seals and sealing wax are used on legal documents.

Further problems arose from Japan's feudal past. Like the Welsh, many Japanese have the same names. Tanaka, Suzuki and Watanabe are the Japanese equivalents of Evans, Williams and Jones. This is because a century ago ordinary Japanese were forbidden family names. Only 10% of the population, the daimios and samurai, were allowed names.

But following the Meiji restoration, when land ownership was introduced, this was found to be inconvenient. Everybody was therefore
allowed to choose names for themselves. But being Japanese, they all
took the same name, that of their village. Indeed, there are so few Japanese
family names, that ready-made chops can be bought from racks in street
corner shops. I purchased chops carrying the names of Tanaka and
Takeshita in Tokyo recently, with the help of a Singaporean who reads
only Chinese; she couldn't find Kaifu.

Family names are not the only problem. A visitor to Japan will usually
ask at his hotel for a local map. On examining it, something unusual
immediately strikes him. Except for a few major roads in big cities, given
names for the benefit of foreigners, Japanese streets don't have names.
Only areas have names. Under the Shogunate, people were forbidden to
move from the villages in which they were born. So nobody needed
names or maps to find their way around. By now the astute reader should
have guessed what comes next. Buildings in Japan are numbered hier-
archically, according to when they were built, not spatially, according to
where they are located. Number 1 Nihonbashi is the first building put up
in that area. Number 2 is the second. It could be next door or a quarter of
a mile away. Fortunately, the Japanese do not go to the absurd extreme of
re-numbering all buildings when one is pulled down and another put in
its place. Still, a Japanese postman has a job for life. This system turns
many taxi rides into major exploration expeditions. As soon as one moves
out of the centre of a city, the driver stops at street corners to seek local
directions, which are frequently misleading. Finally, although irrelevant to this argument, the Japanese also have a funny way of measuring
age. A child is aged one the day he is born. All children born the same
year become two the next New Year's Day, and so on. Thus a baby born a
minute to midnight on New Year's eve, is two years old one minute later.

Not surprisingly, the use of bank cheques never caught on. Until the
credit card, Japan remained almost entirely a cash-using society. Most
purchases, even big ticket items such as cars and washing machines, were
made with cash. Electricity bills, taxes and the like were paid with cash.
Most people are themselves paid in cash. While the credit card is now
widely used, for many it is mainly fed into holes in the wall which eat
plastic and spit paper.

All this seemingly escaped the notice of the experts who designed the
post-war Japanese tax system. For four months from April to July 1949,
seven Americans, led by Professor Carl A. Shoup, visited Japan to investigate its old tax system, which was on the point of collapsing. The
Shoup mission report, produced in August 1949, set out a new system
which has formed the basis of Japanese taxation ever since.

The Americans have disliked indirect taxes ever since the Boston tea party. So it was hardly surprising that the Shoup proposals envisaged that the greater part of tax revenues would come from taxes on incomes and profits rather than on spending. Progressive income tax systems, in which the proportion of tax increases the higher the taxpayer's income, are generally regarded as more equitable than indirect taxes, which bear heaviest on people with low incomes. But they suffer from two defects compared with taxes on spending. There are many more people who have income to tax than there are shops from which to collect spending taxes. Also income taxes work only where transactions leave some record or mark in their wake, or taxpayers are unbelievably honest. Neither is the case in Japan's cash-using society.

To be fair to Shoup, he did propose a VAT on the lines of that now in operation in most European countries. This was designated to finance local government expenditure. The rest of the Shoup proposals were for a broadly based neutral system, in which tax rates were low and exemptions few and modest. Overall, it was a brilliant effort. Shoup gave Japan the sort of tax system which the 1980s supply-sider reformers in Britain, the US, New Zealand and elsewhere took as their ideal. Moreover, he did so with notable speed. All Shoup's proposals were accepted by the American occupation authority, SCAP, and were enacted by the Japanese puppet government in 1950. The system went smoothly into operation, except for the local VAT whose introduction was postponed.

The tax system Shoup invented and the Americans imposed was revolutionary. No Asian country had ever had a modern tax system. Never before had the bulk of taxation fallen on incomes rather than spending. Never before had any experienced progressive taxation. Never before had so many people been expected to pay taxes directly to the government. Never before had an Asian country, using Chinese character writing and cash for most purchases, faced a tax system so reliant on written records to determine tax liabilities.

The Americans left Japan in 1952. As soon as they were gone, the Japanese started to change taxes to their taste. Shoup's splendid system was distorted to serve political ends: politicians bought favours for their supporters by offering many and varied reliefs and allowances; bureaucrats meddled with taxes to regulate activity and to steer industrial development along chosen lines. It took Shoup and his colleagues five months, or about 700 man-hours, to give Japan a tax system which was simple, practical, elegant and fair. Millions of Japanese man-hours have subsequently been spent making it complex, impractical, grotesque and inequitable. The task of unravelling the mess they created has only just begun.

The income tax maze

Shoup's simple income tax was massacred. His system lumped all kinds of income, including capital gains, from all sources together, provided a few simple personal reliefs and allowances and taxed what was left on a simple sliding scale with few steps and a modest top tax rate. The Japanese replaced Shoup's system with what amounts to sixteen different systems, depending on the type of income and the tier of government at which it is taxed. Ordinary income was split up into ten different sorts, ranging from employment income; pensions; business income; interest and dividends; capital gains; income from growing timber; or obtained from gambling. Each receives its own set of allowances and deductions. Business expenses were defined differently for each type of income. Taxable income is calculated separately for each type of income by deducting the relevant reliefs and allowances. The individual totals are then all lumped together again, to give 'ordinary taxable income'. Personal allowances are deducted from this total and a sliding rate tax scale applied. Until 1989 the general income tax scale had fifteen steps on which the marginal tax rate rose from 10.5% to 70%. This calculation produces the income tax liability to the national government. The same income is then subject to prefectural and municipal tax. Prefectural tax has three steps of 2%, 3% and 4% rates; municipal income tax goes up in seven steps from 3% to 12%. The steps, reliefs and allowances for municipal income tax are different from those for prefectural income tax, and both differ from those applicable to national tax.

Three types of income are not consolidated into this system: occasional income such as from prizes and gambling; retirement income; and timber income. They each receive special tax treatment. The tax on timber income, for example, is assessed by applying the ordinary progressive income tax rates to one-fifth of the income and then multiplying the answer by five. The taxpayer can elect to have dividend and interest income taxed separately from ordinary taxable income. He then pays a flat 35% tax rate on it. This obviously appeals to people paying a higher marginal tax rate.

The Japanese tax unit is the individual, not the family or the household, except for dividend income. So this schedular approach encourages the taxpayer to shift income from himself to his relatives, and from one category to another, to maximise reliefs and minimise rates. Deductions for itemised expenses from business income are exceedingly generous. By contrast, only mean and low standard deductions are allowed for employment income. Corporate status, by which employment income can be converted into business income, can be easily obtained. A limited company needs only two shareholders with a paid up capital of ¥10,000 (about $75, or half the cost of a cab ride from Narita International Airport to the centre of Tokyo). Partnerships and unlimited companies need no paid-up capital. Consequently, all small shopkeepers, professional men, and virtually anybody self-employed, set themselves up as companies, which allows them not only to deduct generous business expenses, but also to pay employment income to themselves, their wives and other family members. They then obtain standard deductions on each of these incomes. Finally, the progressive income tax scale is applied separately to each of the family's earned incomes. Not surprisingly, business expenses tend to be large. Played properly, the game allows most small companies to pay no corporation tax at all. In 1985 over half of all companies in Japan made 'losses'.

The 'Maruyu' system

Until 1988, the income tax system included a specific savings incentive, with interest income being favourably treated. The taxpayer, as already mentioned, could elect to pay a maximum 35% rate on it, but more likely paid nothing at all. This was because of the 'Maruyu' system, which gave tax exemption to interest on a range of small savings deposits. Each person could hold up to ¥3 m ($23,000 at ¥130 = $1) on deposit with a bank without interest upon it being taxed. He could also legally hold one postal savings system deposit, maximum size ¥3 m, on which interest was also tax free. He could save a further ¥5 m in funds dedicated to the purchase of shares in the company he worked for, and ¥500,000 in a postal savings system plan for house purchase. In all, he could legally hold up to ¥14.5 m (over $100,000) in interest tax-free accounts.

The maximum size of a postal Maruyu account was ¥3 m. Since no tax was payable on it, there was no obligation to report interest income from it. The rule was simply that a person could only hold one tax-free postal savings deposit. But there was no way of enforcing it. Using chops and false names, a person could open Maruyu accounts at many different branches. Nobody checked his true identity. Accounting was done separately in each branch, so he could even use his own name if he liked. In 1987 there were 23,673 postal savings offices and nearly 20,000 of them conducted banking business. The Japanese postal savings system was the world's largest 'bank' with ¥300 trn ($2300 bn) in deposits. Japan's biggest commercial bank, Dai-Ichi Kangyo, has only 425 branches. The postal system has more branches and bigger deposits than all sixty-five regional banks put together. It has almost as large personal deposits as the thirteen city banks combined. Despite the law saying nobody could have

126

more than one tax-free postal savings account, Japan's 124 m population held 400 m of them.

But it is a mistake to think that multiple deposits were used primarily to avoid tax on investment income. Postal savings offered miniscule interest rates to savers. The amount of tax avoided was less than the depositor lost by not pooling all his savings in a single large deposit with one major institution. The main aim of multiple deposits was to hide cash saved out of undeclared income.

Hiding ill-gotten gains

One method which the authorities employ to track down tax fraud is to look for examples of ostentatious consumption. One year they traced the owners of some luxury yachts. They found several belonging to Buddhist monks who were supposed to be too poor to pay income tax. In consequence, the tax dodger has a problem. He dare not spend his elicit gains too openly. He must therefore find somewhere safe to hide his hoarded cash. The special tax treatment of small savings has ended with the abolition of the Maruyu accounts. But the use of postal savings accounts as a bolt-hole for illicit income continues. The only small dent in it was caused by the asset price explosion in 1985–9. In the late 1980s, the normally frugal Japanese went on a spending spree. They were told it was their patriotic duty to buy expensive and exotic imports. They could always explain that the money came from some successful securities speculation, which was effectively tax free. Once everybody started spending, nobody could be nailed for ostentatious consumption. But this spree ended with the 1990 stockmarket collapse. The Japanese have therefore gone back to their old tricks, cheating the tax man and saving the proceeds.

Most politicians have a vested interest in tax evasion. The funds collected by the postal savings system provide cheap finance for the government's public works programmes. Ministers decide who gets it. Some 18,000 local postmasters' jobs are passed down from father to son, many have been since 1870. These postmasters are powerful individuals, closely connected with LDP politicians. Many parliamentarians belong to the 'yuseizoku' or 'postal family', meaning that they support post office interests against rival interests, being rewarded in various ways for their loyalty. After all, local postmasters have a shrewd idea who has money salted away in many different accounts. They can be relied on to extract a fair proportion in political contributions for their parliamentary friends. They can also help to persuade electors how to vote.

Reform Japanese-style

The Finance Ministry is the only department which is interested in making people pay their taxes. But its efforts to do so are often blocked. The postal savings system comes under its own minister and is independent from the Finance Ministry. In Japan, no minister can tell any other what to do. Even the Prime Minister cannot lay down the law. In 1982 the National Tax Agency, which is part of the Finance Ministry, wanted to investigate the ownership of savings deposits. But the Minister of Posts & Telecommunications thwarted its efforts by making it illegal for post offices to divulge such information.

After being prevented from discovering the ownership of deposits, the Finance Ministry proposed that everybody be issued a green card, which would have to be used whenever a deposit was made, to identify the depositor correctly. The deposit would be marked on the green card. The idea, however, was shot down in flames. More recently, the Ministry of Finance tax commission has proposed identification numbers to be used in all financial transactions, including securities transactions. Each account would then be identified by both name and number. This proposal is also likely to fail.

As with everything Japanese, the conflict between the ministries was resolved by a compromise. From 1 April 1988 the Maruyu system was abolished. In its place, a 20% withholding tax was imposed on interest payments from postal savings accounts. This was designed to remove the tax bias in favour of savings and to raise extra revenues. But as the withholding tax preserved the anonymity of depositors, the postal savings system remains a safe bolt-hole for tax cheats.

The tax that nobody pays

Shoup proposed a wealth tax, despite opposition from wealthy businessmen. It was declared unworkable and scrapped. Capital gains are counted as part of income and taxed accordingly. But to encourage savers to provide cheap finance for industry, the Japanese made an exception of gains on stockmarket securities. Only the regular punter was liable to tax. He was defined as anyone who entered more than thirty share transactions a year or bought and sold more than 120,000 company shares. This capital gains tax remained in force until 1989, collecting virtually no revenue. There were no more than a handful of regular punters in Japan. In most years, fewer than 100 people reported capital gains to the tax authorities. That was not surprising. There is nothing in Japanese law which obliges a nominee shareholder to reveal the name of the principal for whom he acts. It was not a stockbroker's job to establish the bona fides of a customer, provided he paid up as required. Anyone could use as many false names as he wished in which to open accounts. No questions were asked. People in Japan are not traced through their names and addresses, but through the network of who knows whom. Big stockbrokers even helped rich and important clients to open numerous accounts in their many branches. In doing so, they risked being legally powerless if a client defaulted. But getting people to honour debts in Japan is not generally litigious. Yakuza gangsters handle debt collection cheaply, efficiently and with despatch, sometimes of the debtor. The most effective reform would be to hire the yakuza to collect taxes!

The lack of an effective tax on stockmarket gains encourages savings. Dividend incomes are highly taxed. Individual Japanese prefer companies to plough back retained earnings into investment. They get their reward from faster growth and hence the rise in the company's share price. This is one reason why price-earnings ratios are higher on the Tokyo stockmarket than elsewhere. Japanese companies customarily pay out only about 25–30% of their annual earnings as dividends, compared with up to 80% for some British or American companies. For the individual, the temptation is to spend dividends, but to hold on to shares which show capital gains.

Few people were ever caught evading capital gains tax. As a *Japan Economic Journal* article in 1988 observed: 'The number of tax evasion cases related to share trading for fiscal 1987 ballooned to twenty-three from three the previous year.' But to suppose that this crime was rare and unimportant would be a mistake. The quote was from an article discussing the prosecution of a former businessman, Isao Nakaseko, for failing to report ¥2.7bn of capital gains over 1983 to 1986. i.e., before the rampant bull market of the later 1980s. At ¥130 to the US dollar, this was a cool $21m, possibly too large a sum to be easily hidden or spent. He used 404 share-trading accounts with thirty-one stockbrokers to cover his tracks. Nakaseko had extensive political connections. His arrest in early 1988, preceding the Recruit Cosmos scandal by only a few months, might have become the hottest political issue, had the Recruit Cosmos affair not come to light.

Politicians did nothing to change or seriously enforce capital gains tax on share transactions, because they were often the beneficiaries. Illicit capital gains were an important source of funds for them, as Recruit Cosmos revealed. In its aftermath the system had to be cleaned up. But again the solution ducked the main issue. As part of the 1989 tax reform, declared gains from securities transactions were subject to a 26% tax. But the taxpayer was given the option of a 1% withholding tax on the total value of any shares he sold. Most people will opt for this withholding tax. It is cheaper on capital gains in excess of 4%. More to the point, it allows the taxpayer to conceal his activities. The anonymity necessary for political corruption is preserved. The new system will do little to reduce savings.

Taxing companies

Shoup's corporate tax system was simple. A maximum rate of 35% was imposed on every company's net income, regardless of its size or the nature of its business. Companies could deduct normal depreciation of capital assets from taxable income. Land and other assets were to be revalued periodically and companies charged capital gains tax on any appreciation in their value. This system was neutral in its impact. But the Japanese authorities wanted one which they could use to control the development of the economy. In the early 1950s, they raised the general corporation tax rate to 42%. A split tax rate, lower on dividend payments than on retained earnings, was also imposed. This was designed to boost the stockmarket. Companies were further subject to local prefectural and municipal income tax. Allowing for the proportion of earnings distributed, the effective corporation tax rate in the late 1980s worked out at 53%.

High tax rates were not applied to all companies. Small companies paid lower rates. From 1953 to the mid 1960s, income from manufacturing petrochemicals and from exports was tax exempt. Large allowances encouraged investment. Favoured companies could deduct money from taxable income, if they put it into special funds, e.g. for future bonus payments, risky activities, bad debts, losses on returned goods, price fluctuation, and drought. These tax-free reserves encouraged companies directly to save. All told, special reliefs and allowances reduced corporate tax revenues by a tenth in the early 1970s. Finally, land and other asset revaluations were discontinued. Firms pay capital gains tax only when they sell land and realise their gains. Individual share holdings, however, are revalued whenever a company deals in any of the shares which it already holds. Such transactions establish the new price for its old holdings. This problem is circumvented by the use of special 'tokkin' funds which hold shares on behalf of companies. The effect of this system is to lock up vast tracts of unused land, surplus to companies' requirements. It is also another factor which increases Japanese price-earnings ratios.

Up to the mid–1970s, these special reliefs were combined with a steady reduction in the corporate tax rate. The tax burden on major companies therefore declined. But when the budget moved into substantial deficit following the first oil shock, companies became the government's easiest target. Corporate tax rates were steadily raised. Many reliefs were abolished and others reduced. Not all the myriad of relief and allowances were scrapped. Special measures remained to aid energy saving, pollution control and research and development. But by 1987, the losses from special allowances, deductions and tax credits had been halved to around 5% of corporate tax revenues. The incentive for companies to save was reduced; it has not been eliminated.

Taxing the dead

Shoup introduced a lifetime gifts and bequests tax. The tax payable on any new gift or legacy depended on how much the taxpayer had received in previous years. This tax was scrapped and replaced by a monster which only the Japanese could have devised. With impeccable logic, they proceeded from erroneous assumptions to an absurd conclusion. The tax levied on any legacy, they argued, ought to depend upon the wealth of the recipient. The richer he was, the more he should pay. But it was found that families got together to agree that dad's money should go to its poorest members. They shared it with the others after the tax had been paid.

The present system, introduced in 1958, was designed to defeat this dishonesty. When anyone dies, his estate is notionally divided up amongst all his surviving relatives. Every relative is attributed a statutory share, which varies according to their number and the closeness of their relationship with the deceased. The hypothetical tax payable by each statutory beneficiary is then calculated on a sliding scale. The total tax due on the estate is the sum of all the individual tax bills. The average tax rate produced by this calculation is then applied to the real beneficiaries, whoever they are and however much they receive.

Gifts are taxed in the hands of the recipient. Gifts tax is an annual tax on the amount received in a year. Gifts within three years of death count as part of the estate of the deceased. Gifts to a politician running for public office are exempt from taxation, even though he may keep them personally. The gifts tax presents no problems. The Japanese are an ungenerous lot, as far as the taxman knows; not really. But since cash holdings can be easily hidden, gifts tax is easily avoided.

Inheritance tax is a different matter. Most wealth left on death consists of real estate. Unlike company securities and cash, ownership cannot easily be hidden. Given soaring land and house prices during the late 1980s, quite ordinary people can leave a fortune. It is not uncommon for a small house near Tokyo or Osaka to be valued at $2.5 m. A small paddy field in Tokyo – and there are plenty of them – could be worth as much. Some relief is given by valuing houses, for probate purposes, as much as 50% below what they would fetch on the open market. Nonetheless the inheritance tax is penal and for most people unavoidable. Moreover, it must normally be paid within six months.

Only the very rich get out of paying. They hide behind trusts or negotiate large loans on the security of their property and 'lose' the loot one way or another. They fiddle the company books. These options are not open to the average salary earner. He can avoid leaving his property at death by selling it. But capital gains on the sale of land or buildings are subject to tax. Long-term gains on property held for more than ten years are taxed relatively lightly. Short-term gains, on the other hand, are clobbered. The gain is either charged a minimum of 52% or taxed at 110% of the individual's top marginal tax rate, whichever produces the bigger tax bill.

The 1989 tax reform package did a little to lighten the burden of inheritance tax by doubling allowances. But at the same time probate valuations were raised to 70% of market value. Between 1979 and 1989 the value of estates left at death rose fivefold. Even though it is hard to evade inheritance tax, everybody tries his best to do so. Out of 11,247 cases audited in 1989, 98.6% involved incorrect returns. In one case the survivors of an 85–year-old Tokyo lawyer were caught trying to avoid ¥623 m in tax payments. Securities certificates and savings pass books were discovered in wardrobes, and gold and platinum were uncovered in a hospital run by one of his heirs.

How not to tax spending

Shoup's value added tax was never introduced – shopkeepers were against it. Local income tax took its place. Nonetheless, indirect taxes accounted for around a quarter of Japanese tax revenues in the late 1980s. Spending taxes displayed all the usual characteristics of complexity, severity and random incidence beloved of Japanese politicians and bureaucrats. Commodity taxes were levied as a percentage of the manufacturers' or retailers' selling price on a list of items running over two pages just to classify them. Rates varied not only from item to item, but according to the price and quality of each. Commodity tax was originally designed to apply only to luxuries, but most of the things so taxed would no longer be regarded as such. The list included the obvious: fur coats; precious stones; cars; motor boats; and yachts. It also included refrigerators; air-conditioners; desk lamps; TVs; radios; carpets; furniture; clocks;

watches; washing machines; hang-gliders; cosmetics; soft drinks; coffee; cocoa; and tea. Golf balls were taxed, tennis balls were not; water-skis were taxed, snow-skis were not. Tax rates ranged from 5% to 30%. Commodity taxes were supplemented by a range of more specific taxes. The usual ones included excise duties on alcoholic drinks; tobacco; petrol; and car registration fees. But there were also specific taxes on sugar; playing cards; theatre tickets; pachinko (pin-ball) machines; hotel rooms and meals; and bathing at public baths.

The beauty of this jumble of taxes, categories and rates was that details could be adjusted as political favours to producer interest groups, or manipulated to restrict imports and favour home-produced goods. An example of the former came to light in 1986, when two Diet members were prosecuted for taking bribes from the Yarn Twisters Association. Sakonshiro Inamura, an LDP Nakasone faction member, received ¥5 m and Fumio Yokote of the Social Democratic party ¥2 m. The trouble was that both tried to bribe MITI officials to do the Yarn Twisters a favour. This was to re-classify certain of their products into lower tax brackets. Bureaucrats are not supposed to be bent, at least not until they move out of the Civil Service. Shugo Inoue, the Yarn Twisters' chief, was an ex-MITI official.

The manipulation of excise duties on alcohol to discourage imports of Scotch whisky is well known and documented. Imported Scotch, by definition, must be premium-grade stuff. Home-made sake must be hooch. So top-grade sake was taxed at ¥570 per litre, while imported Scotch paid ¥2098. Second-class, i.e. home-made, 'whisky' paid ¥296 a litre. By the time the rival beverages reached the corner shop or bar, these differentials had been multiplied several times over.

Tax reform battle

Little social stigma is attached to tax cheating. What annoys many Japanese is that they have less opportunity than others to do so. Big companies and their employees have little scope for tax evasion: employees have their income tax deducted at source; big firms must keep proper books. All other Japanese cheat by hiding from the taxman the real size of their incomes. It is estimated that employees generally declare only 90% of their true incomes. Doctors, lawyers, small businessmen, artists, musicians and the like are suspected of declaring only 60% of their incomes, while farmers declare only 40%. These percentages, 90–60–40, are so widely quoted that they have entered Japanese folklore as 'ku-ro-yo'. Serious efforts are made to catch tax dodgers. In the year ended March 1988, the National Tax Administration Agency traced no fewer than 168,962 offenders, who between them had under-declared ¥724 bn in income, or an average of ¥4.5 m each. This exceeded the average ¥3.7 m earned by salaried workers during that year.

Topping the list of fifteen worst offenders were pachinko parlour owners, understating their income on average by ¥38 m. Pachinko is a pin-ball game, to which many Japanese are addicted. The use of small change makes it easy to hide takings. Many parlours are run by local yakuza gangs and most have close ties with local politicians. Second on the list were hospitals, while medical practitioners and gynaecologists took the last two places. Undertakers came sixth, two places above bar owners. Land dealers, moneylenders, fish merchants, and motel operators all had places. If caught, escape is unusual; 95% of the 1987–8 haul were prosecuted and convicted.

But there is an easy way out. Anybody or company that suspects the taxman is on to them, can admit having made a mistaken tax return and pay a voluntary tax payment to correct it. Traditionally, when such payments were made, no further questions were asked. It was under this system that the big four Japanese securities houses in 1991 attempted to atone for their sins in compensating large clients for share trading losses. They had treated these payments as business expenses and deducted them from their taxable incomes. But in this instance the tax officials deliberately leaked to the press what they knew, causing the securities scandal.

Pressure for reform mounted from the late 1970s, when the government needed to increase its revenues to eliminate its budget deficit. It did so by leaving the unindexed progressive income tax system unchanged, and by raising corporations tax further. Both the tax bias against incomes and the big company and its employees and in favour of spending and the small shopkeeper, businessman and farmer were increased. Consequently the government's ability to obtain extra revenues from its grossly unfair tax system approached its limit. The obvious solution was to impose a new sales tax. The first attempt to do so was made in the late 1970s. The Prime Minister, Masayoshi Ohira, announced plans to introduce a value added tax. Whatever this did to please big business and its employees, it caused a howl of rage from all the LDP's other supporters. VAT, in itself, was not bad. What mattered was that, in collecting it, the tax authorities were bound to find out most shopkeepers' and small businessmen's true incomes.

VAT normally works on an invoice system. The tax is applied at every stage of manufacture and sale and to services. Companies charge the tax on their sales and pay it on their purchases. They hand over the difference to the government. But to get back the tax they have paid, they must produce purchase invoices to back up their claims. Each company has an incentive to demand a proper invoice for everything it buys. Every company is therefore forced to provide a proper bill for everything it sells. The system is self-policing. Only the final consumer is unable to reclaim tax and does not demand a bill. But the shopkeeper must still produce invoices showing what he has sold. VAT forces companies to keep proper accounts. A paper record must be kept of all transactions. This was the last thing tax dodgers wanted. The tax was not feared because it would shift the burden of taxes from income to spending, but because it would shift it from tax payers to tax dodgers.

Ohira fought a bitter battle in the LDP and Diet to introduce a VAT. He called an election in 1980 to appeal to the country, but died during the campaign. The matter was then shelved until 1987, when the Prime Minister, Yasuhiro Nakasone, again proposed tax reform. His efforts were also defeated. Third time lucky, his successor Noboru Takeshita succeeded in 1988 – but only because he changed the proposed VAT into a sales tax, collected in a different way.

The sales tax, which came in on 1 April 1989, is levied on the basis of business accounts. Big companies are assessed on the basis of their accounts, the same ones that they rig for corporations tax payments. They profit from the system, since they pay over the tax they collect only twice a year. In the meantime, they have the use themselves of the tax revenues. Companies with an annual turnover of less than ¥500 m (i.e. 96% of all companies) are simply assumed to have paid VAT on purchases equal to 80% of their sales. They pay the 3% tax on the remaining 20%. Few companies' value-added, that is labour costs plus profits, are as low as 20% of their sales – which means that most pay less tax than they should. But they charge their customers all the tax and make a profit on the deal. They were even helped to do so. Anti-cartel legislation was suspended for two years, to allow smaller businesses collectively to agree on the new higher prices they would charge. The smallest companies, with annual sales of ¥30 m or less, are exempt from the tax; they still charge it to their customers.

Takeshita's 1988 tax reforms also included deep cuts in individual income taxes. The number of tax rates was reduced to five, running from 10% to 50%. The number of local tax rates was also reduced. Tax allowances and deductions were simplified and increased. The employees' tax burden was cut, but by no more than it needed to adjust for inflation. Corporations tax was reduced, but only to 37.5% on retentions in fiscal 1990. In fiscal 1991, part of the corporations tax cuts have been put back, to help pay for Japan's $9 bn Gulf War contribution.

Conclusions

Despite the immense political battle fought to reform taxes in the 1980s, the results have been meagre. The balance of taxation has not changed. The additional revenue the sales tax collected hardly replaced those lost by the abolition of commodity taxes and the reduction of other indirect taxes. In 1988, 36% of tax revenues came from personal income tax, 35% from corporations and 25% from spending taxes. In 1991, 41% of revenues came from personal incomes; only 31% from corporations; and the share from spending taxes went down to 24%, instead of going up. The new tax itself did nothing to eliminate tax cheating. Instead it provided additional profits to businessmen, shopkeepers and the self-employed, at the expense of the consumer in general. The monstrous income tax system was not changed. The elimination of the Maruyu system was engineered in a way which preserved anonymity for postal savings depositors. Similarly, the tax on stockmarket gains preserved the anonymity of speculators. Farmers still receive privileged tax treatment. Nothing has happened to encourage the release of more land for development. Nothing has been done to prevent tax cheating from continuing. The system is no better placed today to raise additional revenues than it was in the early 1980s. It is no less unfair.

After 1989, pressure for tax reform waned. Buoyant tax revenues due to the booming economy pushed the budget into a healthy surplus. The need to raise additional tax revenues from higher tax rates seemingly disappeared. But as with the balance of payments, the bubble economy merely obscured, rather than cured, the tax problem. As the economy slows down, tax revenues will fall and the need for tax reform will again become pressing. The political battle will soon be resumed and more bloodily than ever before.

8

Public Squalor

Private affluence and public squalor was a phrase originally coined to describe the results of low taxes in the USA. It applies even more so to Japan, whose consumers are the most affluent in the world. Their tiny homes are packed with all the latest and best consumer goods. Every Japanese home has a washing machine, fridge and colour TV; nine-in-ten have cameras; eight have bicycles and sewing machines; seven have cars; six have air-conditioners, stereos, videos and microwave ovens; one-in-three have golf clubs and one-in-five have pianos. Amongst all this clutter of material possession, two-thirds live with aged relatives, or vice versa. Only a third of British family homes include three generations, a quarter of American and a tenth of Scandinavian. In Japan, there is no room in which to put more goodies, grannies or even kiddies. Space is at a premium. For example, I discovered a device in a Japanese home which I have not seen anywhere else in the world. The top of the lavatory cistern was a wash-hand basin. When the toilet was flushed, the basin automatically filled. After you had washed your hands, the waste water emptied into the cistern below. This saved both space and water.

Affluence is not confined to adults. Japanese children are amongst the world's most pampered. A 1990 government survey of 695,000 children aged four to nine found that half had their own televisions, radios and tape-recorders, and one-third had their own telephones. But the only parks many ever saw were in picture books and most had never picked a wild flower in their lives. In Tokyo, mother nature is a kept woman.

This sad little story says much of what the Japanese want and can't get. They want decent public amenities. Sewerage is always cited first in this context. Fewer than half of Japanese homes have main drainage. Many are connected to septic tanks. Almost 40% do not have flush toilets. Some have daily sewerage collection. Only 20% of electricity cables are buried below ground in Tokyo, compared with 100% in London and Paris. There are few parks in Japanese cities. The total area of Tokyo's public parks is 25 m sq. yds; some 12 m people live in Tokyo, so each has about 2 sq. yds of parkland – not enough room in which to swing a cat. By comparison, London's 7 m inhabitants share over 200 m sq. yds of parkland, giving each about 30 sq. yds. But there is actually a lot more open space in Tokyo than in London. There are 360 m sq. yds of paddy fields. Around 100,000 farmers between them own seven times as much land, which mostly they don't use, than the other 6,900,000 have available to use.

Many Japanese city workers commute long distances to work. They stand in grossly overcrowded trains, in which two people stand for every one who gets a seat, for three or more hours every day. The average Japanese salary-earner spends a whole month each year travelling in these conditions. Women who commute are often molested in the crush of bodies. Newspaper and magazine articles give advice to women on how to hold handbags to protect themselves. They neither wear nor use stiletto-heeled shoes, a lethal weapon at close range. On the homeward journey, it is not uncommon for someone to vomit. The high-speed road system is anything but. How could it be? There are only 5 yds of road per car in Japan. A third of that is not paved. The new Narita International Airport is 50 miles from the centre of Tokyo. Arriving early Sunday evening, the drive in can take three to four hours, even when the driver does not get lost. Much has been written about public squalor in Japan. Urban squalor is the price paid for small government and low taxes. The subject of this chapter is why Japanese government has remained so small and what is now happening to change it.

Public spending can be divided between current spending, collectively to provide goods and services such as the police, defence forces, public education and health services; capital spending to build roads, railways, ports and provide parks; and social security, which involves transfer payments such as sickness and unemployment benefits and old-age pensions. The amount a government can spend on these things is limited by the revenue it can raise from taxation and social security contributions, and by the amount it is willing and able to borrow. At no time since the war has Japan raised enough tax revenues adequately to cover all three forms of public spending.

During the miraculous growth years, revenue rose rapidly owing to the fast income growth. Tax buoyancy could have been used to increase the share of public spending in GNP. Instead, tax rates were regularly reduced. So until the mid–1960s, public spending remained relatively stable at a little below 20% of GDP. Nonetheless, as real GDP rose at a double-digit annual rate, public spending also increased rapidly. Infrastructure spending was given priority. Ports, roads, water conservation, electricity supplies and the like received the lion's share of the available resources. The bullet train was a crowning achievement of this period. Social security, on the other hand, was neglected. With so much to be done, sacrifices were required of all and the provision of a decent welfare system had to wait its turn. All the nation's energies were devoted to rebuilding and modernising the economy. The Japanese considered themselves too poor for the state to look after the individual.

Surrogate social security

This meanness was part of an unwritten social contract. In return for low taxes, the individual was expected to look after himself by either saving or working. Work was readily available, even for the old. Although the industrial sector was superbly efficient and productive by international standards, the services sector was deliberately sheltered and dismally inefficient. Massive over-employment existed in the service sector and still does. Four people fill up your car at a petrol station: one puts in the fuel, a second cleans the windscreen, a third empties all the ashtrays and trash, and the fourth takes your money; all bow politely as you leave. Old men trim lawns to perfection, not actually with nail scissors but almost as carefully. Thousands of small family-run stores dominate retail distribution, protected by law from competition from big and efficient supermarkets. The consumer pays the costs in inflated prices. In the miraculous growth years, service sector inefficiency was the Japanese surrogate welfare system. It meant that almost everybody was able to contribute something in return for the money they were paid. Nobody wanted to receive charity from the state. The social role of the service sector still explains Japanese resistance to its reform.

Balanced budgets

The government could have borrowed to provide welfare cover. But following the 1949 Dodge Stabilisation Plan, it was obliged by law to balance its budget without recourse to borrowing. The balanced budget in these years meant that the whole of private savings was channelled into financing investment. It was the copious supply of cheap capital for industry which allowed Japan to rebuild its shattered economy and catch up with the West so rapidly. The sacrifices seemed well worth it at the time. Low taxes meant high savings; high saving financed high investment, which produced more jobs and rapid growth.

The mid–1960s was a watershed in Japan's post-war development. A variety of forces converged to force changes upon the economy. Growth slowed down in the 1965 recession, because industries' demand for capital to invest had finally become satiated. Surplus savings had emerged. Consequently, when the brakes were taken off, lower interest rates and easier credit failed to ignite the economy. Profits and incomes continued to be squeezed and tax revenues declined. The balanced budget policy demanded that the government choose between cutting spending or raising taxes, action which would have deepened the recession. A small budget deficit is no problem, provided it increases public sector debt at no faster rate than nominal GDP is rising. The burden of debt is then unchanged. It also makes sense to borrow to finance part of public investment. The increase in financial debt is matched by an increase in the nation's physical assets. To finance all public works spending out of taxes means that today's taxpayers pay for benefits tomorrow's taxpayers enjoy. They may reasonably be expected to shoulder some part of the cost, in the form of debt interest. Limiting investment to what can be covered out of current taxes inevitably distorts the economy. It puts the growth in public investment in a straitjacket, while spurring private investment with ample and cheap credit. Provided that the return on public sector investment is comparable with that obtainable from private sector investment, there is no reason why it should not be a claim on private savings. Indeed, when there is excess private savings, which would otherwise produce bothersome balance of payments surpluses, it makes sense to borrow to eliminate public squalor.

After much debate, the government decided to accept this logic. In 1965 it rescinded the Dodge law forbidding bond issues, thus allowing it to run a budget deficit. Borrowing, however, was restricted to cover only capital expenditure. The government was still obliged to pay for all its current spending out of taxation. It started to issue what were known as 'construction bonds'. During the following decade, it ran modest deficits each year, ranging from 0.5% to 2% of GDP. Nonetheless its gross debts climbed from zero in 1965 to over 11% of GDP by 1974. Government dissaving, through budget deficits, offset the excess of private savings, allowing fast growth to continue into the early 1970s. But because this borrowing offset slower revenue growth rather than higher public spending, it did little to deal with the problem of public squalor.

But times were changing. The older of the post-war generations were willing to accept surrogate social security. The family system remained strong. People expected to look after each other, rather than for the state to provide. But as workers migrated from the country to the towns, family ties were weakened. Moreover the younger of the post-war generations, who struggled single-mindedly to rebuild and modernise Japan's economy, expected some reward for their labours. Once Japan had caught up with other advanced economies, as it did in the late 1960s, people were no longer willing to worship growth as the only god. They demanded a welfare system on a par with those of other advanced economies. They objected to the poor quality of life, including industrial pollution, in Japan's burgeoning metropolises. Above all, the urban Japanese salary-earner wanted a fairer deal from government.

The ruling Liberal Democrats were slow to recognise these problems. Consequently public support for the government steadily declined. The LDP's share of the popular vote dropped from 58% in the 1958 General Election to 47% in 1972. Local government, particularly in urban areas, fell into the hands of the Socialists and other parties. They went ahead with their own local welfare systems. By the early 1970s it looked as if the LDP's monopoly of government could be broken. Something had to be done.

The Prime Minister, Kakuei Tanaka, was the man to do it. He attacked on two fronts. Under his plan for 'Rebuilding the Japanese Archipelago', Tanaka launched a massive public works programme and also greatly improved the welfare system. The state pension up to 1973 provided a retirement income equal to only 20% of average earnings, which was insufficient for anyone to live on in their old age. Moreover, to obtain the maximum benefit, the pensioner had to have contributed to the scheme over many years. Medical insurance covered only 50% of an individual's costs. Unemployment benefits were insignificantly small. Tanaka raised pensions to 43% of final earnings and indexed them to inflation. Moreover the ratio between earnings and pensions continued to be improved so that, by 1985, it had risen to 83% of average income, a very generous rate. Medical insurance was increased to cover 70% of costs, with free care for the aged and greater help for expensive or protracted treatment. The definition of medical expenses was also widened to include such things as home nursing care. Since 1973, Japan has had as generous a welfare system as the major European countries. At first, the costs of improved pensions was modest. Individuals had to build up the requisite number of contributions to obtain the full benefits. There were few pensioners relative to the numbers of workers contributing to the scheme. But from a small base, social security expenditure increased rapidly; with a rapidly ageing population it is now set to rise sharply.

Means and ends

Tanaka's plan was a splendid dream, but predicated upon continued 10% a year GDP growth. It collided with reality. The first oil price hike and the 1974–5 recession led to the collapse of Japan's miraculous growth machine. Modern welfare and ambitious public works, based on annual 10% growth, could not be financed from tax revenues generated by growth at barely half this rate. Something had to give: initially it was the budget, which moved into considerable deficit. As in the mid–1960s, the government was loath to raise taxes or cut spending for fear of slowing growth further. A special law was therefore enacted allowing the government for one year to borrow by issuing 'deficit' financing bonds, to pay for the excess of current spending over current revenues. This special law was renewed year after year. From 1975 onwards, the whole of the central government's capital spending was covered by the issue of construction bonds, to which were added rapidly rising sales of deficit financing bonds. In 1979, total bond issues paid for a third of central government expenditure and amounted to over 6% of GDP. More bonds were issued than could be bought by state pension funds. In consequence, the public sector also moved into a substantial deficit, which reached 4.4% of GDP in 1979. Central government gross debt trebled between 1975 and 1979 to a third of GDP. Net public sector debt also rose, but more modestly.

Budget arithmetic

The way a government does its budgetary arithmetic affects how much it feels it can borrow and spend. Government-run pension funds occupy an ambiguous place in public finance. Contributions are collected by the state from employers and employees, but for the sole benefit of employees when they retire. The money thus belongs to the personal sector and the government is merely the agent which runs schemes on its citizens' behalf; it does not itself own the money it collects. The same is true of unemployment and health insurance contributions. Most countries therefore keep separate such receipts and expenditures in special social security accounts. Where the citizens' entitlements are related to the amount of money they pay into the fund, and this is invested for them by the state, the schemes are said to be 'funded'. If there are lots of young workers and few old-age pensioners, more money is collected each year than is paid out. The schemes thus run surpluses.

Countries which separate social security funds from their regular budget accounts regard such surpluses as available to finance budget deficits. This is the Japanese system. The government's 'gross' debts include the social security fund surpluses which it borrows. As social security funds are managed by the government, some countries treat social security surpluses as reducing their budget deficits rather than financing them. Government debt is then 'net' of its borrowing from such funds.

Some countries, notably Britain and Australia, operate unfunded or 'pay-as-you-go' pension funds. This means contributions count towards general tax receipts and expenditure is part of general government spending. Any current surplus is automatically used to finance other government spending. Both the budget deficit and the level of government debt are thereby reduced. Under funded systems, the money saved by today's contributors should be available, when they retire, to pay for their pensions. Under pay-as-you-go systems, tomorrow's contributors have to pay for tomorrow's pensions with higher taxes.

Funded schemes are transparent, because they show the size of the bill which future taxpayers must shoulder. It is easy to calculate how much personal taxes or contributions will have to rise to meet it. On a pay-as-you-go scheme, the future costs are hidden, other than when actuaries are set to work to estimate them. But their reports receive scant attention. The lack of transparency in unfunded schemes allows the British government to say it has a budget surplus, when it has not. It therefore feels under less pressure to increase taxes or contributions in anticipation of future pension claims.

The Japanese and other governments, which run funded pension schemes, admit that they are in budget deficit when they borrow from their own schemes. When this borrowing becomes substantial, they feel obliged to raise taxes or cut other government spending to reduce it. Hence governments running funded pension schemes are invariably more tight-fisted. In 1991, by British definitions, Japan had a public sector surplus equal to 3.5% of GNP. But by Japanese definitions, excluding the social security surplus, the central government had a deficit equal to 1% of GNP. Japanese fiscal policy is driven by this figure, meaning that the Finance Ministry struggles to cut spending to eliminate this deficit.

Japan financed almost all its budget deficits between 1965 and 1974 out of pension fund borrowing. Thereafter budget deficits exceeded pension fund surpluses and net borrowing from the private sector increased sharply. The rapid growth in government debt in the late 1970s led to the abortive attempt by the Prime Minister, Masayoshi Ohira, to introduce a sales tax in 1979. His aim was to eliminate deficit bond issues by 1985 by raising more tax. Since he could not do so from taxing income more severely, he tried taxing spending. Following his death, the attempt was abandoned. Eliminating deficit bond issues nonetheless remained the first priority of budgetary policy throughout the 1980s, even though the target date for its achievement floated forward to 1990.

When tax reform was abandoned, there was no alternative but to reduce the budget deficit by the most stringent control over public spending growth. Social security expenditure could not easily be checked, although in 1985 contributions were raised and benefits restricted. Moreover, as long as the budget remained in deficit, public sector debt rose and the cost of servicing it took an increasing share of tax revenues. By 1990, gross public sector debt had reached 70% of GDP and debt interest accounted for a fifth of central government expenditure. Under these circumstances, general government spending, including public works spending and grants to local government, was the only area in which severe restraint could be applied. Central government public works were cut in each year from 1983 to 1986. Local government spending was held in tight check. For five years from 1983 to 1987 no increases at all were budgeted for general expenditure. While under the programme of administrative reform, a start was made on privatising Nippon Telephone & Telegraph and the loss-making Japan National Railways.

To sum up, while tax revenues were booming in the 1950s and 1960s, priority was given to cutting tax rates. But since spending on social security was negligible, there remained plenty of funds for public investment. In the 1970s, slower growth reduced the buoyancy of tax revenues, but the improved fully funded social security system at first generated substantial surpluses. The government borrowed these to finance large general budget deficits. In the 1980s, the burden of social security spending began rising and it was foreseen that it would continue to rise dramatically because of the ageing population. The government became alarmed by the size of, and growth in, public sector gross debt. It therefore set out to eliminate its budget deficit. In the process it starved public investment of funds. For the 1990s it plans to heavily increase public investment, but at the same time it does not want to run big budget deficits again. But unless the tax system is reformed, it can't raise the money to pay for its ambitious public works programme. There is one way out of this dilemma.

Oh FILP

When the Japanese talk about their 'budget', they usually mean what is more accurately called the 'general account budget'. This is the common pool into which almost all tax revenues go and from which almost all government bills are paid. This budget includes both current and capital spending, and was the one which the Japanese government was obliged to balance under the Dodge Stabilisation Plan. But a substantial amount of government spending is omitted from the general account budget and included instead in an off-budget account called the 'Fiscal Investment & Loans Program'. FILP was invented in 1952 to circumvent the Dodge Plan balanced-budget law. Hitherto, postal savings deposits and state pension fund surpluses had helped to finance budget deficits. These funds did not dry up when the budget was balanced, but accumulated in the government's hands. It had to decide what to do with them and FILP was the answer. Balancing the budget was thus partly achieved by changing the way the government did its accounts, by pushing some public spending off-budget and instead through FILP.

FILP spending is financed entirely by borrowing. Until recently, all government pension schemes surpluses went into FILP, together with insurance policy payments from the general public to the postal system. Ordinary postal savings deposits, on the other hand, all went to the Trust Fund Bureau, run by the Ministry of Finance, and were used to buy government bonds. After the bond issue had been sold out, any money left also went to FILP.

FILP makes cheap loans or grants to a large range of public enterprises and agencies, local government or public corporations. Most of the money is then spent on further public works, but part is passed on to the private sector in support of worthy causes. FILP's money goes to many institutions. The state-owned Japan Development Bank and the Export-Import Bank of Japan are fed from it. Many other funds receive FILP help, such as the Housing Loan Corporation; Small Business Finance Corporation; Agriculture, Forestry & Fisheries Finance Corporation; Hokkaido-Tohoku Development Corporation; and the Japan Finance Corporation for Municipal Enterprises. Public corporations such as Nippon Telephone & Telegraph and Japan National Railways before privatisation received funds from FILP. Many key local services are run by public enterprises rather than by local authorities. In 1983 there were 3800 separate water supply corporations and over 1000 sewerage enterprises. Hospitals, slaughterhouses, markets, housing site preparation, toll roads, parking lots, local transport, electricity and gas supplies, and sightseeing facilities, are all run to some extent by local public enterprises. Their number totalled 8753 in 1983. Their budgets are separate from local authority budgets and much of their current revenue is from charges. But much of their capital expenditure is financed by grants or cheap loans through FILP. In other words FILP is the vehicle through which the government directs savings to needy and worthy borrowers. This helps the bureaucrats to manipulate the development of the economy and also provides another slush fund, through which politicians can provide favours for their supporters.

In the early 1950s, some 80% of FILP money went to the two state banks and local authorities. Almost all went to help big industry finance reconstruction and expansion. Big business invested cheap money, grew rapidly and made profits. These profits were used to pay good incomes to lifetime employees and, given the severity of income tax, to supply the many and varied perks that they enjoyed. When the capital needs of big industry declined with the end of the miraculous growth years, the pattern changed. Today, the bulk of FILP money goes on public housing and amenities, social welfare, education, small-scale industry, farming and roads. A significant proportion goes to LDP supporters, and the remainder goes on improving the nation's social capital. FILP is important in that its expenditure regularly equals the central government's own spending.

FILP partly explains how the government could boost public spending with its ¥6 trn 1987 package without unbalancing the budget. Only ¥1 trn came from increased on-budget spending. FILP spending rose by ¥4 trn and the final ¥1 trn went in tax cuts. The revenue lost from these cuts, however, was clawed back by the abolition of the Maruyu system of tax exemption for small savings. FILP has a crucial role to play in the promised ¥430 trn expansion in public works spending over the next ten years. But FILP is also the Achilles' heel of public finance in Japan.

Both of FILPs revenue sources – the postal saving system and pension fund surpluses – are at present buoyant. Banks are being forced by lack of capital reserves to restrict the growth in their lending, which means that they are no longer aggressively competing for deposits. Instead, they are offering lower interest rates than can be obtained on postal savings deposits, which are consequently being flooded with money. This explains why, when President Bush visited Japan in January 1992, the Prime Minister, Kiichi Miyazawa, was able to promise him that public spending in Japan would be boosted, while at the same time the proposed rise in budgetary expenditure for fiscal 1992 was miserly. The extra spending could readily be financed from the funds flowing through postal savings into FILP.

In the longer term this source of funds will dry up. The role of postal savings in tax evasion has already been explained. It is the bolt-hole for ill-gotten gains. As long as people can stash away money anonymously in postal savings, tax dodging will continue and direct personal taxation will remain unfair and inefficient. But if this loop-hole is closed, by depositor identification numbers or in some other way, funds will be withdrawn from postal savings and FILP will be deprived of a major source of cheap money. Postal savings are under attack from another quarter. As financial liberalisation proceeds, it will become necessary to eliminate the privileged treatment postal savings receive compared with bank deposits. Public sector pension fund surpluses are also set to decline. So as FILP's needs increase, so its revenues are likely to decline. The Japanese budgetary dilemma will then re-emerge.

Unfair shares

The level of Japanese public spending is not the only issue. Its distribution between urban and rural Japan is also distorted. Japan has three tiers of government: the central or national government; forty-seven municipalities, of which the Tokyo metropolitan government is the largest; and some 3300 municipalities, ranging in size from Osaka to a tiny little village in the Aichi prefecture. Local government is supposed to be financially autonomous. The central government, in theory, can interfere only to prevent anyone cooking the books or when localities make a muck of running their own finances (up to a third of all prefectures did so in the late 1970s). Local government spends twice as much as the central government, but the central government collects twice as much tax revenue; it therefore passes half of this over to local government.

The rules determining how much money the central government hands over to each local authority are complex. A few minor taxes, such as vehicle excise duties, are collected nationally but the proceeds are handed straight to local authorities. In addition, the central government is legally obliged to give local authorities a third of the revenue it collects from income, corporate and liquor taxes. This money is divided between them according to means and needs of each. It can be spent in any way that a local government wishes. The aim, however, is that the services supplied by local governments, whether rich or poor, should be of an equal standard. Where means exceed needs, the local authority gets nothing, but nor does it have to surrender its excess revenues.

Next, there are obligatory payments to local governments for specific purposes. This money must be spent on the things for which it's been given. Central government pays for part or all of the services which each local authority provides on its behalf. It foots the entire bill for local election expenses, and half the salary bill for the teachers employed by local government.

Finally, the central government is free to allocate further money at its own discretion to pay for new roads, hospitals, schools, bridges, parks, housing for the poor and so forth. It does so on a cost-sharing basis, bearing a higher share the greater the priority it attaches to any project. Hospitals may get a 70% grant, whereas swimming pools would rank for only 30%. Roughly speaking, tax allocations account for about half of central government transfers to local government, obligatory and discretionary payments each account for about a quarter.

There are obvious consequences of this system. Local fiscal autonomy is a myth. The government holds the purse-strings and consequently has considerable power over local authorities. The tax allocation system automatically gives the lion's share to rural areas. In 1981, for example, the four richest cities – Tokyo, Aichi, Kanagawa and Osaka – received little or nothing. Tokyo's local tax revenue per head was assessed at ¥159,000 and its standard needs were put at ¥133,000 per head; it was given nothing. Aichi also received nothing, despite tax revenue of only ¥83,000 per head; its needs were put at ¥79,000. Kanagawa received ¥129 per head and Osaka ¥2881. These four richest urban areas were left with sums ranging from ¥71,000 to ¥159,000 per head to spend. At the other end of the scale, the four poorest local authorities – Okinawa, Kochi, Shimane and Tottori – received fat hand-outs. Okinawa was given a further ¥83,000 per head, making its income up to ¥115,000, more than rich Kanagawa's ¥75,000. The other three authorities had their income made up to between ¥154,000 and ¥160,000. One of the four poorest authorities, Shimane, ended up with more money per head to spend than any of the four richest. Three of the four richest authorities ended up with less money per head to spend than any of the four poorest.

The tax revenues which paid for local tax allocations came overwhelmingly from the salary-earner and his employer in the big cities. It was given overwhelmingly to the farmer and small shopkeeper in the countryside, who cheated on paying taxes. Rural areas enjoyed the same or better standard of public amenities, without suffering the disadvantages of urban life. Although Japanese textbooks on public finance tell us that other central government hand-outs are fairly distributed, they are in fact a pork barrel from which LDP politicians compete to get as much as they can for their own, mostly rural, constituents. The size of disbursements to local government, the over-representation of rural areas in the Diet, the greater strength of the LDP in the countryside than in the towns, combine to starve urban areas of amenities and public services. The division between central and local government finance contributes to urban squalor and to the salary-earner's feelings of unfairness: he pays the tax bill and the farmer picks up the benefits.

9

Managed Money

In communist control economies, money was of secondary importance. It acted as a unit of account, but its role as medium of exchange was restricted. Bureaucrats decided what was produced and the price at which it was sold. Who made what and how income was shared was dictated by officials, not determined by markets. Japan's post-war financial system worked in a similar way, except lending was controlled rather than spending. The financial chaos of the immediate post-war years ended in the early 1950s, when the Japanese established a fragmented, tightly regulated and internationally isolated financial system. It was deliberately designed to prevent a free market in savings. If the funds to finance investment had been allocated by market forces, interest rates would have risen to cripplingly high levels. The Japanese government judged rightly that high interest rates were not necessary to persuade people to be thrifty. They would save a large part of their income, however low the returns they received. It was therefore able to ration credit, directing funds exclusively to priority borrowers at officially dictated low rates, without the supply of savings drying up. The saver was fleeced, but he did not take umbrage. That was a part of an unwritten social compact between the government, industry and rural Japan. Tax-paying big industry thrived on the flow of cheap money from tax-dodging small farmers and businessmen.

This dirigiste system was highly successful. It was made possible by the fact that 90% of Japanese savings were deposited with 'bricks-and-mortar' institutions, rather than transferred from savers to borrowers through markets. Bricks-and-mortar intermediaries are banks, postal savings offices, insurance companies and the like, which daily open their doors to borrowers and lenders. They act as principals, borrowing and lending in their own names at set rates for given periods. The rates they pay depositors and charge borrowers depend more on the period and type of the deposit or loan than on the status of the depositor or borrower. A prospective borrower either gets a loan or he doesn't. The disappointed borrower cannot get one by offering to pay a higher rate of interest than the successful borrower.

Markets act as agents, bringing borrowers and lenders together. The rates at which money is borrowed and lent, or the price at which stocks and bonds are bought and sold, are determined by supply and demand under the free play of market forces. The lender, not the intermediary, decides who borrows his money. The borrower can usually obtain the money he wants but may have to pay through the nose for it. If the borrower defaults, the lender loses, not the market. Markets never become insolvent, although stockbrokers do. Yamaichi Securities would have gone under in 1965 had not the Bank of Japan come to its rescue. Markets offer the lender the best available rate, together with some risk of losing his money. Bricks-and-mortar institutions offer lower rates but no risk. Controlling bricks-and-mortar institutions' borrowing and lending rates is easy; controlling free market prices is impossible.

Divide and rule

The pre–1973 Japanese financial system was regulated by compart-mentalisation. All financial intermediaries were categorised by the type of business they were allowed to do; they were not allowed to do any other kind of business but their own. Competition between different categories of institutions was eliminated. No newcomers were allowed to enter the market and compete with existing institutions. Categories were decided according to the ways in which institutions borrowed and the purposes for which they lent. The Ministry of Finance, the Bank of Japan and the Ministry of Posts & Telecommunications dictated the rates which financial intermediaries paid or charged for funds. Most lending and borrowing rates, except for postal savings rates, were set at fixed margins over the Bank of Japan's official discount rate.

Institutions such as banks or stockbrokers could compete with other banks and stockbrokers only by offering more, if not better, services to their clients. City banks in the early 1970s charged 3.5% more on average on their loans than they paid on average for their deposits. In addition, depositors faced extortionate charges for money transfers.

Guaranteed fat margins led to inefficiency. Big banks' profits were eroded by the high costs of operating too many small branches, even though opening new branches was strictly regulated. Instead, rival banks, stockbrokers and insurance companies put armies of sales ladies, known as gaikoin, on to the streets, selling their wares and soliciting deposits. Fuji Bank alone employes 15,000 gaikoin. Nomura Securities' post-war success came about from putting piggy-banks into millions of Japanese homes. Its collectors called regularly to empty them, investing the funds in securities on the savers' behalf. It still has a house-to-house sales force of 2500 women, selling the company's fixed-income investment trusts. But today telephone sales are more important. Every year, the National Tax Bureau publishes local lists of the largest taxpayers. The aim is to expose blatant tax dodgers to public opprobrium and the effect is to show local politicians where best to solicit contributions. Brokers and banks base their telephone sales compaigns on these lists, with housewives, who run family finances in Japan, as the target. Every home has to be visited, particularly following the traditional twice-yearly bonus payments. These can amount to as much as four months' regular salary. There is little doubt that intense moral pressure was brought to bear on Japanese housewives to be frugal and cautious, to guard against uncertainty and to provide for the future, which must have been a factor in the high level of Japanese personal savings.

The inefficiency which eroded big banks' earnings was not an option for the thousands of small banks and credit co-operatives, which lacked the economies of scale the big boys enjoyed. Little banks needed fat margins between deposit and lending rates to cover their higher costs. Lower margins would mean their extinction, which is why the authorities set them so wide. The system was deliberately designed to protect the weakest from the strongest.

Only a few financial markets were allowed. The bond and equity markets had existed for years, and were allowed to continue. But the bond market was extremely narrow. Between 1950 and 1965 the central government balanced its budget and paid off old bonds. There was therefore no significant secondary central government bond market. Local government and public corporations issued bonds on a limited scale. Few large companies were willing to issue debentures (another name for bonds) because they had easy access to cheap loans from their banks. Few small companies could issue debentures, they were too risky a proposition. The bond market was dominated by issues of bank debentures.

There were virtually no short-term money markets. Companies were not allowed to issue commercial paper or certificates of deposit. A kind of short-term market existed on the back of the secondary bond market. It was called the gensaki market. Companies that owned bonds could sell them together with a re-purchase agreement, called a 'repo', under which they undertook to buy them back again at a stated price three months later. The price difference between selling and buying back was the gensaki interest rate. The gensaki market provided an outlet for surplus liquidity. But during the years of miraculous growth, when money was scarce, few companies had much to spare. The market was therefore small and illiquid, but it was a real market, in that the gensaki interest rates were determined by supply and demand.

The only other short-term money market of significance was an overnight or call money market, through which banks with surplus deposits could lend to other banks which were temporarily short of funds. Although short term in principle, in practice such loans were renewed time and again over extended periods. Only banks could deal in this market. Call money rates were set by the Bank of Japan at a small premium over the Bank of Japan's official discount rate, so it was not a free market but a clearing house for surplus bank funds.

Little guys matter

The commercial banking system in Japan forms a pyramid. At its base are some 3700 agricultural co-operative societies and 1750 fishery co-ops, mostly with only one branch each. They borrow from local farmers and fishermen, and lend part back to their members, putting what's left into the giant Norinchukin national agricultural bank. There are another 414 credit co-operatives assembled under the wing of the National Federation of Credit Co-ops and 47 labour credit associations which operate under their own National Federation. These provide the same services for small businessmen, shopkeepers or union members. The deposits collected by this raft of tiny banks amount to an eighth of all bank deposits. Economically, they are insignificant and hence normally ignored. Politically, they are of major importance. A large number of people are involved in their operations and most of them form the bedrock rural support for the Liberal Democratic party. The formation and proliferation after the war of these myriad small banks was sponsored by the American occupation authorities to encourage savings and to break the concentration of financial power which existed under the old zaibatsu system. Whatever their success in these directions, the small banks, like the postal savings system, help to shift the political balance from town to country. In small towns, co-op managers are big men. Like postmasters, they have the power to deliver contributions and votes to local politicians; they expect and receive favours in return.

The most important favour, which must be given to retain their support, is their protection from annihilation by market competition. A rural politician, who loses the support of his local postmaster and farming co-op manager, risks saying goodbye to public office. He will be replaced by a rival willing to heed their needs. The Diet is dominated by members whose concerns are necessarily parochial for their political survival. In this way the Americans reduced Japanese democracy to its lowest common denominator, rather than raising it to its highest common multiple.

Next in size are 445 larger Shinkin credit associations and seventy-one Sogo mutual savings and loans operations. Sogo banks were mainly limited to lending to companies with fewer than 300 employees. These are followed by sixty-three regional banks and thirteen major city banks. The city banks are descended from big pre-war banks, which were at the centre of the zaibatsu industrial conglomerates. These were the banks bailed out by the government after the war, when the zaibatsu were disbanded. They developed into keiretsu banks, at the centre of their own related families of companies. City banks each have a nationwide system of branches, through which they collect small savings deposits. Together, they account for half of all bank deposits. The commercial banking structure is completed by three long-term credit banks and seven trust banks.

Big banks and big business

Before 1973, city and regional banks were allowed only to collect current and interest-bearing time deposits to a maximum maturity of two years. They were not allowed to obtain longer-term finance or to sell bank debentures. Their lending was limited to short-term loans at variable interest rates. City banks' loan clients were mostly big business in urban Japan. Lending to smaller businesses accounted for less than a third of their activities and until recently, consumer loans were virtually non-existent. Loans for house purchase were dominated by Public Housing Corporations, which received their money from FILP, a government agency. Employers also made housing loans to their employees. Consumer credit was available, but through disreputable loan sharks, called sarakin, who charged usurious interest rates on unsecured credit; annual interest often exceeded 100%. Strong-arm tactics were employed to collect debts, often leading to the suicide of the debtor. Not unsurprisingly, the amount of credit provided by sarakin was limited, because few Japanese wished to fall into their clutches.

City banks provided trade credits and working capital to members of their own keiretsu families. Most loans, although technically short term, were regularly rolled over. Overdraft facilities, which borrowers draw upon according to their immediate needs, were unobtainable. Instead, bank loans were made on condition that a part of the funds advanced was held in non-interest-bearing current accounts with the lending banks. This raised the cost of borrowing above the nominal rate at which loans were made. Varying the amount of the loan which had to be deposited back with the banks was a way banks could vary the interest rates which clients actually paid without breaking the rules. Companies were forced to accept this system because there were no short-term money markets in which to place a temporary surplus of funds and from which to meet a temporary shortage.

The relationship between banks and members of their keiretsu families was frequently incestuous. Each big company had its 'main' bank. Banks owned large stakes in their client companies, which also owned stakes in the banks, and board membership overlapped. These cross-holdings protected companies from take-over bids. Banks could be relied upon to bail out any big company in danger of going under. That was a part of the favours a company received in return for keeping its spare cash in the bank. Banks had intimate inside knowledge of what was going on within client companies and could often intervene early to stop bad situations from getting out of hand.

When the Sanko Steamship Company went into bankruptcy in August 1985, with post-war record debts of ¥520 bn, it was because, unusual amongst large companies, it had no main banker to bail it out. The banking fraternity was therefore shaken when the Daishowa Paper Company in March 1986 repaid Sumitomo ¥23.5 bn and sacked it as its main banker. Daishowa had been rescued from bankruptcy in the early 1980s by Sumitomo.

Regional banks competed for deposits with city banks. They borrowed on the same terms. They lent to small and local businesses. But whereas the city banks regularly lent out more money than they collected in deposits, regional banks regularly collected more money locally than they were able to lend. The regional banks' surplus funds were lent to the city banks through the call money market. There was thereby a flow of funds from the countryside to the towns, from small rural depositors to big industrial borrowers. Since both regional and city banks borrowed deposits at the same rates, somewhat below the Bank of Japan's official discount rate, the city banks had to pay a premium over ODR to regional banks for any funds they obtained through the call market. Such borrowing raised the cost of city bank funds. Given that the margin between their deposit and lending rates was fixed, the increased cost of funds reduced city banks' profits.

The three long-term credit banks are the Industrial Bank of Japan (IBJ), the Long Term Credit Bank (LTCB) and the Nippon Credit Bank (NCB), which were founded at the turn of the century as state-owned

banks to finance Japan's growing industries. After the Dodge Stabilisation Plan cut off subsidies to industry, which these state banks distributed, they were privatised. Long-term credit banks are not allowed to
take short-term deposits. Their funds come from the sale of three-to
five-year bank debentures or from large long-term deposits. They traditionally lent long-term at fixed rates to industry for fixed capital investment. Unlike the city banks, the long-term credit banks are not part of the
keiretsu system, but will lend to any company. IBJ has 90% of the largest
200 companies as clients. City and regional banks were thus segregated
from long-term credit banks by both the nature of their borrowing and of
their lending.

Money mismanagers

The seven trust banks managed private pension fund money, ran investment trusts and sold trust certificates. They were obliged to invest the
greater part of their funds in bonds. After the government started running large budget deficits, this meant that much of private pension fund
money ended up in central government bond trust accounts. The trust
banks are mostly subsidiaries of stockbroking companies and competed
with life insurance companies for pension fund business. The life funds
generally went after the individual, selling him personal insurance and
pension plans, whereas the trust funds went after private sector companies' pension fund money. Fund management in Japan was another
way in which the individual saver was cheated. With-profits insurance
policies were unknown. The saver was offered a guaranteed low return.
This was partly because trusts and life funds were only allowed to pay
policy-holder's dividends out of the interest income. Capital gains have
to be placed in special reserves. So trusts and life funds, investing most
of their money in bonds, failed to benefit from equity bull markets. Even
investment trusts active in equity markets, regularly under-performed
the Nikkei index. Trust fund managers and staff usually came from their
parent securities companies, to which they returned after two or three
years. Their loyalties were elsewhere; they were not rewarded individually by results, but operated as teams. The securities houses used
to stuff their related trusts with any over-priced shares they could not get
rid of elsewhere. Trusts also 'churned' their portfolios of securities,
buying and selling large chunks of shares for no other purpose than to
enhance the broking commissions earned by their parents. Trusts would
normally deal only through their parent brokers. Brokers customarily
earned three times as much from transacting their subsidiary trust funds'

business, than from the management fees the funds themselves received. (In January 1992 such exclusive dealing was banned.)

Churning and cheating the individual was often blatant. In 1986 Koji Wakabayashi inherited the Wakabayashi Real Estate Company from his father. He sold some of the property and placed funds with New Japan Securities, Japan's fifth largest stockbrokers, requesting that the money be kept in liquid assets. New Japan Securities persuaded him that it would lend him any cash he needed, and he would do better allowing them to run a margin account for him. He agreed. Then, according to *The Economist*:

> Between September 1987 and January 1989, 1163 trades were executed, for a total of ¥13.9 bn (about $100 m) in the two accounts. On top of ¥185.5 m in commissions, New Japan charged ¥21.8 m in margin interest. Turnover was hectic. On average a given shareholding was held for 21 days, and none was held for more than one year. About 46% of all shares bought were held for less than one week. The Tokyo stockmarket was going up during this period. Not so WRE's capital. By the time the two accounts were closed in January 1989, more than a year before the market began falling, it had lost ¥122.8 m.

To complete the banking picture, one city bank, the Bank of Tokyo, formerly the Yokohama Specie Bank, was given a monopoly of foreign currency transactions, which were rigorously restricted through a system of foreign exchange controls. Japanese savers were not allowed to lend abroad in order to obtain the higher interest rates offered in other countries. Japanese borrowers, prevented from getting loans at home because of the government's controls, could not tap foreign markets for credit. Almost the only foreign exchange transactions that a Japanese company or individual could enter into were those directly related to exporting and importing. Funds earned abroad had to be converted into yen without delay. Permission was required to spend foreign currencies. Japan's domestic financial system was cut off from the rest of the world's.

Riggers and rampers

The final division was between commercial banking and stockbroking. Article 65 of the Japanese Securities & Exchange Act is an imitation of the US Glass-Steagall Act, which prohibits banks from underwriting and transacting securities business and stockbrokers from taking deposits and doing banking business. Stockbroking is dominated by the big four: Nomura, Daiwa, Nikko and Yamaichi Securities. There are a further 200 small stockbrokers, but many are owned by the bigger brokers. Stockbrokers make their money in two main ways. High and legally fixed commission rates are charged on all share sales and purchases. Fees range from 1.25% on trades up to ¥1 m ($7700) to 0.25% plus a flat fee of ¥1.25 m ($9600) on trades above ¥1 bn. Fees are also obtained from underwriting new issues, whereby the underwriter is paid to take any of the stock in the new issue for which other buyers cannot be found. It is up to the underwriter to find buyers. By pitching the issue price too low, the stockbroker can guarantee to sell all of a new issue. Buyers are guaranteed a capital gain, often as much as 40% or 50%, when the new stock opens for trading. They clamour to buy shares at the issue price. The securities houses, which can decide who gets the newly issued shares, customarily gave them to favoured clients. In return, the favoured clients were expected to rig or ramp the market, by taking dud shares, when their brokers asked them to do so.

The Recruit Cosmos scandal involved the allocation of unlisted shares to politicians before they were brought to market. It was the company, not the brokers, who arranged this shares-for-favours deal. Following the Recruit Cosmos scandal, the system of underpricing new issues came under attack. The securities companies could not ignore public criticism. They promised to reform their ways and, as a sign of good intentions, started to price new issues of their own shares close to market rates, thereby doing themselves a favour.

Companies did not greatly object to getting less than the full value of the new shares they issued. They could thereafter expect the brokers to support the price of their shares on the market. Market rigging was so commonplace that relative share values bore little or no relation to corporate performance. The game began with company accounts, a parent company reporting its own accounts separately and at a different time from those of its subsidiary companies. It was not only able to cook its books by offloading inventories or recalling loans, but also had considerable flexibility in the accounting system it used. It was able to show, within limits, whatever level of profitability it wished. Moreover, to prevent awkward questions being asked by shareholders at an annual meeting, it employed sokaiya hirelings. These gangsters shouted down or physically threatened any shareholder wanting to ask an embarrassing question and moved blocking motions of praise for the directors. Companies were expected to employ sokaiya for protection from their shareholders; if they did not, the sokaiya still turned up, but disrupted the meeting instead.

Bank shares were a classic case of market rigging. Until the mid–1980s all thirteen city bank shares were the same price and paid exactly the same dividends per share. The price remained stable for long periods. Nobody could buy a significant number of bank shares without the bank's blessing, since it could refuse to register the new owner. About every three years, the banks all raised new capital at the same time. They did so exclusively from their existing shareholders. Each sent out the same offer letter on the same day. But to ensure that the money came cheap, the bank's shares inexplicably rose like a rocket just before the new issues were announced. Seiji kabu, or political shares, were another blatant example of market rigging; these were shares, usually of smaller companies, which took off for no particular reason then crashed back again to where they had been. This mostly happened just before an election. Politicians needed funds and stockbrokers needed political influence. So the brokers tipped off the politicians in advance what shares they planned to ramp. They also lent them the money to buy into the market at the bottom. The politicians always got out at the top, earning fat capital gains which, needless to say, were never reported to the tax authorities. Everybody looked out for seiji kabu, jumping on to any stock which rumour had it was about to be ramped. Many jumped too late and were burnt – but that was the idea.

Month-to-month the major brokers decided which shares to push up. They then issued a flood of research material showing why so-and-so company was undervalued and a good buy. Pharmaceutical companies, on the verge of discovering new miracle drugs, were a perennial favourite. During October 1991 the shares of Meiji Milk Products Company rose 45% in four days following reports that the firm had developed a new substance that completely kills cells infected with the AIDS virus. Insider trading was commonplace. A company thought nothing of releasing price-sensitive information to its stockbroker and major shareholders in advance of its general release. Analysts and journalists frequently received tip-offs. That was the way the system was expected to work. Information permeated outwards from the centre with those closest to it having the best chance of making a killing. At the end of the chain was the ordinary punter. After the fun started, stockbrokers' armies of sales ladies set out to visit or telephone punters everywhere, telling them the latest hot tip or flavour of the month. Naturally, the brokers informed their most favoured clients which shares had been selected for this treatment. They, in return, remained loyal to their brokers transacting all their business with them. They could also be persuaded to hang on or buy into a falling market, in return for future favours. When the big four brokers together handled two-thirds of all turnover on the Tokyo stock exchange they were in an unassailable position to manage the market.

Insider trading was illegal in Japan. But the law was so broadly written that it was never tested in the courts. The system had its merits. In return for the lucrative business they did, stockbrokers were expected to step in at their own loss and support the market in any crisis. The Ministry of Finance called in all the major brokers during the October 1987 world stockmarket crash, telling them to stop Tokyo's fall. They did. The Tokyo market fell less than any other and was first to recover. By 1990, however, the authorities were unable to exercise as great control.

Ministerial rivalry

All the boxes into which different financial institutions were placed have now been described. The question which must next be considered is how interest rates were determined and credit controlled. This seemingly arcane subject again takes us to the root of Japan's political problems. No one government ministry controls the entire financial system. The Ministry of Finance, operating through the Bank of Japan (which must do its bidding), controls most banks, insurance companies and stockbrokers. The Ministry of Trade & Industry controls consumer credit, sarakin, and latterly the 'non-bank banks' which emerged during the 1980s. The Ministry of Posts & Telecommunications controls the postal savings system. This division makes for problems in both running and reforming the system. Theoretically, differences between ministries go to the Cabinet and Prime Minister for resolution. But under Japan's consensus system, the Cabinet does not settle differences, it endorses agreements. If a problem is taken to Cabinet, it is simply referred back for further consideration by the ministers involved. Action requires agreement, and agreement requires compromise and concessions. Ministers often prefer inaction and the status quo to compromise.

It does not even stop there. Within the Ministry of Finance there are different bureaux, each with its own bailiwick. These bureaux not only regulate their own little bits of the system, they also represent their parochial interests within the Ministry. A disagreement between the head of the banking bureau and the head of the securities or international finance bureau is expected to be settled by negotiations between them. Each will seek concessions in return for agreeing to give up anything. Seldom will the Vice-Minister step in to impose a settlement. The result is that change takes years. This is why reform of the financial system has been so protracted.

Within its own sphere of influence, the Ministry of Finance and its agent, the Bank of Japan, operate by moral blackmail rather than legalistically. This is partly because of the concentration of business in the banking and securities industries in the hands of a few large banks and brokers. It is also the result of the system of 'administrative guidance'. Japanese laws are usually general and vague. Power under them is delegated to bureaucrats, who exercise it in the most detailed manner. Banks and brokers must refer every major decision and most minor ones to the relevant divisions in Ministry or Bank for approval. This is given or refused by kacho or divisional managers within the Ministry. Even the size of signs on banks' rural branches must be sanctioned by Ministry of Finance officials. All the kacho's decisions and orders are given orally. They are often vague and ambiguous, as is the Japanese style. This gives the big banks and brokers some latitude in deciding what they can actually get away with. It also enables the regulators to decide, in the light of subsequent events, whether the banks and brokers did as they were told. The Nomuragate scandal was partly due to brokers compensating big customers for stockmarket losses in a way they believed that the Finance Ministry privately permitted. When this compensation became public knowledge, the officials promptly denied having sanctioned it.

There is no book of rules to show how administrative guidance is operated. Nothing is written down and codified. The rule book exists only in the minds of the kacho, who make new rules and change old ones at whim. They grant permission to one broker or bank to do something which they deny to another. They speed or delay decisions for months. Their unwritten orders cannot be legally enforced – they do not need to be. If a bank or broker transgresses an oral instruction, it can expect to be punished by bureaucratic obstruction the next time it wants to do something. There is thus little difference between the Japanese kacho and the Soviet commissar.

The regulator is not, however, the bogeyman he seems. Rules are generally applied to ensure competitors in each sector do not cheat one another, the better to cheat everyone else. The regulator pursues the narrow producer interests of the sector he regulates, at the expense of the public interest. He has reason to do so. Most top officials retire early to take plum jobs with companies they have regulated or with their trade associations. This system is called amakuari, meaning 'descent from Heaven'. Most major companies want senior ex-ministry officials on their boards. The ex-official knows best how to interpret administrative guidance. He has a wide range of contacts with former colleagues, some of whom have benefited from his patronage. A favour given earns a favour in return.

This system has many drawbacks. Japanese ministries are small and poorly staffed. The Finance Ministry keeps close tabs on the big boys. But it mostly leaves the myriad of smaller banks and brokers to their own devices. They have a habit of getting up to no good. Many of the scandals which followed the 1990 Tokyo stockmarket collapse resulted from inadequate supervision of small to medium-sized companies and banks. Moreover officials are less able to enforce their will on the small fry. Recently, to the Ministry's immense embarrassment, its wishes were challenged. In August 1986 its inspectors, checking the books of a medium-sized bank, the Daiichi Sogo Bank, found that it had lent ¥30 bn ($600 m) to a property development company, Mogami Kosan. This was three times its limit for loans to a single client. The inspectors demanded that this lending be reduced and that the bank report progress every three months. Instead the loans rose to ¥80 bn. The bank President, Chihiro Kobayashi, was investigated by the Tokyo public prosecutor about his connections with Mogami Kosan, but no charges were brought. The Finance Ministry demanded Kobayashi's resignation. He refused, saying his bank had not been charged with breaking any banking law. The Ministry's bluff was called.

A Job for the Bank

The Bank of Japan had considerably more power over major banks than simple moral persuasion. During the miraculous growth years, the city banks were not able to finance all their lending from their own deposits or by using the call money market. They were regularly 'overlent' and made good the shortfall by borrowing from the Bank of Japan. This was the linchpin of the credit rationing system. Such borrowing was done at the Bank's official discount rate. Commercial banks' deposit and lending rates were fixed at set margins above and below the ODR. The Bank could therefore influence interest rates directly by changing its ODR. But a more effective way of controlling bank lending was to vary the amount that the banks could borrow at the Bank of Japan's discount window. When this was reduced, banks had to borrow more expensively on the call money market. Their profit margins were consequently squeezed. The Bank's ability to squeeze profit margins gave it a hold over the big city banks.

The Bank in its heyday used its hold over the banks to issue the most detailed instructions. It held quarterly meetings with city banks to dictate the extent to which they could expand credit during the following three months. It was in daily contact over the details of bank lending. It issued instructions, called 'window guidance', setting out which sectors, even which individual companies, were to be favoured or starved of credit. The sanction behind such guidance was reduced access to the discount window. The 1990 squeeze on property loans was the result of 'window guidance'. Its legal foundation is no more than undefined powers, under Article 25 of the Bank of Japan law, to maintain and foster the credit system. The 'window guidance' system was scrapped in July 1991.

The operations of the postal savings system have already been described. The interest rates they pay on deposits is set independently by the Ministry of Posts & Telecommunications. They are 'stickier' than those offered by the banks. The Postal Minister is loath to lower postal savings deposit rates, because his job is to protect the interests of small savers. But equally, he is rarely keen to raise deposit rates, because the postal system lends the money it collects to the Ministry of Finance. It pays as little as possible for post office funds. Postal savings rates lag bank interest rates on the way up and on the way down, causing some funds to be switched one way or the other between banks and postal savings. This was not a serious problem while interest rates were relatively stable and low. It became more serious in the early 1970s, when the Ministry of Finance wanted to cut interest rates during a recession. The Postal Minister refused. Fearing that a switch of deposits from banks to the postal system would restrict bank lending, the Ministry of Finance could not go it alone. The recession was over before the Postal Minister gave way, and interest rates were lowered just in time to give an inflationary shove to the 1972–3 boom.

Limited liberalisation

The fragmented, regulated, isolated and crooked Japanese financial system performed magnificently during the high growth years. But its successful operation was predicated on four conditions: savings had to be scarce in order to be effectively rationed; bricks-and-mortar intermediation had to dominate the system, so that interest rates could be regulated; transactions with foreigners had to be rigorously restricted to limit access to freer markets; bureaucrats had to know best which industries and activities required privileged treatment.

All these conditions have been invalidated since the mid–1970s. Events have forced change on the system even if politicians have resisted change rather than encouraged it. The story of deregulation illustrates how limited liberalisation in one small corner of the financial system ineluctably led to more liberalisation elsewhere. The more that was done, the greater the pressure to do even more. It is this inherent momentum which will lead, over the next few years, to completely free financial markets in Japan.

Change was necessitated by the slowdown in Japanese growth following the 1973–4 oil shock. Private investment collapsed, while personal savings soared. Savings became excessive instead of scarce. At home, interest rate regulation was undermined by a relative decline in banking business and rise in the extent to which savings were channelled through markets to final borrowers instead. Abroad, a large current account surplus turned Japan into a capital-exporting nation. It could no longer isolate its domestic financial markets from the rest of the world. Slower growth caused big companies to reduce capital spending. They began to make enough profit to finance their investment programmes from their own resources and no longer needed to borrow from their banks. At the same time, the government started to run large budget deficits. Its borrowing needs replaced the companies'. But governments do not borrow directly from banks. They borrow by issuing bonds, which are market instruments. Budget deficits thus increase market intermediation at the expense of bricks-and-mortar intermediation.

This process was at first resisted. When the government began issuing construction bonds in 1965, it had forced banks, stockbrokers and insurance companies to form a syndicate which was obliged to take up a share of its new bond issues. New bonds were forced on the syndicate at higher prices and hence lower interest rates than those which could be obtained on old bonds traded in the secondary bond market. Stockbrokers could sell their new government bonds to clients only at a loss. Banks were forced to hold their new bonds for a year. The Bank of Japan then bought them at face value, saving the banks from capital losses. But during the year in which they were forced to hold the bonds they earned less from them than they could have obtained elsewhere. The Bank of Japan financed its purchases of bonds by printing money. Thus, with a year's lag, finance for part of the government's budget deficit came from the rise in the money supply. This helped to limit the growth in the secondary market for government bonds.

This system worked well through the late 1960s and early 1970s, when government bond issues were small. When new issues expanded in the late 1970s, it could not stand the strain. By the late 1970s government bond issues had more than doubled, rising to ¥12.3 trn in 1979. The syndicate's share of new issues had also been increased. In 1978 it was forced to take 97% of the ¥9.5 trn bonds issued. Banks were landed with ¥6.9 trn, which made a sharp dent in their earnings. Stockbrokers, however, were happy. From 1975 to 1978 interest rates fell and bond prices rose. Although they were forced to buy a growing quantity of over-priced bonds, they were paid underwriting fees for doing so. Moreover the bonds could ultimately be sold at a profit. The size and importance of the secondary bond market increased dramatically.

Between 1978 and 1979 the budget deficit increased sharply. The economy boomed; money became scarce again; inflation accelerated; interest rates turned upwards; and bond prices started falling. Then the second oil price shock hit Japan. Secondary bond market interest rates soared from 4.25% in early 1979 to a peak of 10.25% in mid–1980 as bond prices crashed. The government could no longer dump all of its over-priced loss-making bonds on stockbrokers and banks. Nor could the Bank of Japan buy them all back without losing control over the money supply. The only answer was to sell some of the new bonds directly on the open market. The government then had to take whatever price it could get for them and lost control over market interest rates. It was forced to set rates on the bonds it obliged the syndicate to buy close to market rates, as otherwise it would have bankrupted syndicate members. To limit the damage, it forced more bonds on its own Trust Fund Bureau, which got its funds from the postal savings system. The Trust Fund's share of new government bond issues was increased from 3% in 1978 to 35% by 1982. The Trust Fund needed more money from postal savings deposits. But the sticky postal savings deposit rates lagged behind as bank deposit rates rose and post offices collected fewer deposits. This forced the postal system to offer extremely attractive terms on its teigaku deposits. These offered the saver a fixed rate for ten years, but after six months he was allowed to withdraw his money without any penalty. Teigaku deposit interest was raised to 10%, which proved widely popular. They awoke the small savers' appetite for higher rewards than those to which they had been accustomed. The share of postal savings in personal savings rose sharply at the expense of bank deposits, which offered only 6% on two-year deposits. The government still got its money from the banks, but indirectly. By introducing teigaku deposits, it lost the ability to force savers to accept artificially low short-term interest rates.

Thanks to the expansion in government bond issues, by 1980 the Japanese bond market had become the second largest in the world. Moreover, since most bonds had a maturity of five years or less when first issued, there was soon a large volume of bonds on the market with only a short life remaining. Companies with excess liquidity therefore started withdrawing deposits from banks, where they earned only low regulated interest rates, and used the money to buy short dated bonds. Those needing temporary finance, raised money by using their bonds in 'repo' operations on the gensaki market. This provided regional banks with an alternative outlet for their spare cash. They were no longer forced to lend it to the city banks at regulated low rates on the overnight call market.

The squeeze on city banks became intense: they not only lost deposits to the postal savings system, but also lost companies' spare cash. They needed to borrow more from the regional banks, but were able to borrow less. In April 1979, the authorities were forced to rescue the banks from this plight, by deregulating call market interest rates thus allowing the city banks to compete for regional banks' surplus funds. In May 1989 they gave banks permission to issue certificates of deposit, which created a CD market. In October they deregulated bill discount rates, and removed restrictions on city banks' operations in the gensaki market in April 1981. All these developments reduced the government's grip on interest rates. A parallel set of market-determined long and short rates emerged. But the damage was limited. A minimum size was set on such things as CD issues, so that only the big boys could play. Small savers still had little alternative but to put most of their money into banks, postal savings and insurance policies at artificially low rates. But at least the postal savings ten-year deposits offered a decent return. By 1980 about 15% of the big banks' borrowing was done in the deregulated wholesale money markets. The remaining 85% was at low regulated rates.

At the same time, external pressures were opening Japanese financial markets to the world. Japan's post-war exchange control system was modelled on Britain's. All capital transactions with the rest of the world required prior exchange control approval. Foreign investment in Japan was largely prohibited. Foreign banks could operate in Japan, but only within strictly defined limits, and they could not compete with Japanese banks for domestic business. Following the breakdown in the Bretton Woods fixed exchange rate system, Japanese exchange controls were used during the 1970s to influence the yen's exchange rate. When the currency was affected by upward pressure, controls over foreign capital inflows were tightened and restrictions on outflows were eased. When the yen came under downward pressure, controls on inflows were eased and on outflows tightened again. Finally in December 1980, following the second oil shock, Japan took the plunge and scrapped most foreign exchange controls. Instead of every transaction being banned, unless specifically approved in advance, all transactions were freed, unless specifically restricted. This step marked the culmination in the first stage of liberalisation, and was to have the most profound consequences during the following decade.

10

Invading World Financial Markets

The first phase of financial liberalisation was driven by domestic pressures arising from large budget deficits. The next phase was driven by external pressure. When the 1980s began, capital could move freely for the first time since 1914 between the world's most important financial centres, New York, London, Tokyo and Frankfurt. Moreover it could do so on a scale and at a speed never before experienced. The global marketplace for money had arrived. It produced a fundamental change in the way the international economy functioned. Hitherto, countries with large trade deficits suffered downward pressure on their currencies. Henceforth, countries from which there were large capital outflows suffered weak currencies, leading to large balance of payments current account surpluses. Instead of trade deficits causing currencies to weaken, weak currencies caused trade balances to strengthen.

In the early 1980s, Japan's excess savings began to flow abroad on an increasing scale. It was easier for Japanese institutions to take money out of Japan and lend it on the unrestricted markets in New York and London, than it was for foreign institutions to lend in Tokyo. Although it was easier for the Japanese to borrow abroad as well, money was cheaper at home. After the death in 1980 of the Prime Minister, Masayoshi Ohira, the LDP abandoned his sales tax proposals. Unable to increase tax revenues, the government started to reduce its budget deficit by spending less. Fiscal policy became severely restrictive. Monetary policy consequently had to be easy, so as not unnecessarily to depress home demand.

By chance, as the Japanese jumped on to one end of the policy seesaw, the Americans jumped on to the other. President Reagan introduced his supply-side tax cuts causing the US Federal budget to move into deep deficit. This fiscal stimulation in the US had to be offset by tough monetary policy to prevent the economy from overheating. So when money became plentiful and cheap in Japan, it became scarce and dear in America.

Capital outflows from Japan increased rapidly after exchange controls were lifted. By the mid-1980s Japan had become the world's largest capital exporter. Big banks, trust funds and pension funds immediately started buying substantial amounts of foreign securities, mostly bonds, because of the much higher yield that they offered. The banks, having lost much of their customary business of lending to big Japanese companies, switched an increasing share of the cheap funds they collected into lending to big foreign governments, particularly the US government. Their holdings of foreign securities quadrupled between 1980 and 1984. By 1985 Japanese city banks had up to a third of their total assets invested abroad (Fuji Bank had 42%) and about a quarter of their earnings came from their foreign operations.

The growth in foreign investment by trust banks and life insurance funds was phenomenal. Life funds' holdings of foreign securities increased sixfold. Companies such as Nippon Life became dominant bond buyers at the US government's three-monthly Treasury bill auctions. Starting almost from scratch, trust and life funds were given permission to invest abroad up to 20% of any new money they collected, up to a limit of 10% of all the funds they held. These limits were later increased. They had an incentive to go to their limits. In 1981, US ten-year Treasury bonds offered 7% more than Japanese government ten-year bonds, and while this gap shrank to 4% in 1983, by early 1985 it had widened again to almost 6%. As has already been explained, life funds can distribute only income. Capital gains go into reserves, and so do losses. During three decades to 1980, life funds built up massive reserves, and were prepared to risk foreign exchange losses. The higher yields available from abroad enabled them to compete with other savings institutions for cheap funds. Moreover, a yield gap of 5.5% over ten years was more than enough to compensate for a 40% fall in the dollar against the yen over the same period. Whenever they failed to invest 20% of their new money overseas in one period, they could not carry the unused portion to the next. They therefore invested abroad up to this limit.

But the main impact abroad from the relaxation in Japan's exchange controls, was the invasion of the international financial markets by Japanese brokers and bankers. Not content merely with channelling excess savings into foreign currency assets, Japanese bankers and brokers poured into the Euro-currency markets underwriting new issues, market making and trading and foreign exchange dealing. By 1983, Japanese banks were doing more foreign currency lending in London than either British or US banks. On the whole, the Japanese invaders set up their own operations overseas. But there were exceptions.

Banks in part bought their way into the US. Fuji Bank was quick off the mark, paying in 1981 $425 m for two subsidiaries of Walter E. Heller, a Chicago-based finance company, obtaining seventy US branches in the process. In the same year Mitsui Bank bought the Manufacturers' Bank for $166 m and in 1983 Mitsubishi Bank bought the Bank of California for $260 m.

The Japanese were operating from a basis of strength. Brokerage houses had greater placing power – that is the ability to find buyers for new issues – than their foreign rivals. Large Japanese companies, stuffed with funds, could be relied upon to divvy up when asked to. Japanese banks, with no obligation to hold significant reserves against their overseas operations, were able to cut margins between their borrowing and lending rates to the bone. In some instances Japanese banks were prepared to make no money at all on some deals, which became known as 'hara-kiri' loans. The Japanese put great store on establishing and maintaining close business ties. They were able to conduct securities business abroad in competition with brokers, who in turn could do banking business. It was worth paying something learning the trade in preparation for the time when the barriers between banking and broking at home would collapse.

Japanese companies loved their new freedom to borrow abroad. At home their options were limited. They could borrow from city banks at regulated short rates, or from long-term credit banks at regulated and fixed long rates. But big companies were as creditworthy as the banks from which they were borrowing. So if they competed for funds in the markets with the banks, they could obtain similar rates and avoid the banks' mark-ups. At home that was difficult. Long-term corporate bond issues took two months at least to arrange. All the terms had to be fixed well in advance, followed by lengthy consultations with the Ministry of Finance covering such things as the use to which the funds could be put. After one bond issue, no more could follow until several further months had elapsed. Short-term borrowing by sales of commercial paper, bills rather than bonds, involved putting up collateral. Banks had to stand behind the company with loan guarantees, for which they charged fat fees. Moreover, markets were narrow so that borrowing was possible only on bad terms.

Things were different on the international Euro-markets. These markets require some explanation. The best analogy is with two Japanese tourists in London, one just arrived with plenty of yen, the other short of cash before going home. The first lends some yen to the second. This is a Euro-currency transaction, because it involves foreign currency lending and borrowing outside the country whose currency is used. The tourists could be of any nationality. An Australian arriving in London from Tokyo might also have surplus yen. They don't have to be tourists. They merely have to lend or borrow currency or bank deposits outside the country which issues it. Euro-bonds are the equivalent of domestic bonds, Euro-deposits are short-term loans. A Japanese company can appoint an underwriter, agree terms and issue a Euro-yen bond in a single day. It can issue another the next day. It can issue a Euro-dollar bond if it likes, then swap the dollars into yen. It can take or place Euro-yen three or six months' deposits with a simple telephone call to its broker. It needs no collateral or bank guarantee. All it requires is that it has the requisite credit rating to undertake such transactions. Better still, it pays competitively low London commission rates to its broker, not fixed and exorbitantly high Japanese ones. It can do all this without bothering to consult any government ministry. That is what dealing in free markets means. It also shows that when a regulated system competes against a liberal one it loses.

Large Japanese companies, their big banks and stockbrokers, picked up their bags in the 1980s and took their business abroad. An important and substantial part of Japan's financial system thereby escapes Japanese regulation, without falling foul in free-wheeling London of anybody else's. This created a loose cannon on the world's capital market decks, which duly wrought havoc.

The other side of the story was different. The trickle of foreign money into Japan hardly changed after exchange controls were scrapped. More to the point, foreign banks and brokers faced an almost impossible task in trying to grab a share of the action in Japan's rigidly regulated domestic markets. They could not get their snouts into the trough of cheap small deposits, and the markets in which they could operate were often narrow. The close relationships between banks, brokers and their clients, cemented by substantial cross-holdings of each other's shares, meant that few major companies were willing to give business to foreigners. Finally, foreigners were unused to operating in a system where almost every decision and deal must first be cleared with the relevant bureaucrats in the Bank of Japan or the Ministry of Finance. Americans were used to being controlled by rule-books everyone could read, not by an unwritten code existing only in the minds of bureaucrats and former bureaucrats.

These developments had both macro- and micro-economic effects. The flood of lending from Japan regularly exceeded the surpluses earned on current account, thereby helping to depress the yen and adding to the dollar's strength. The yen hit a peak of ¥190 to the US dollar in late 1978, just as Japan was moving into current account deficit.

It fell 40% to a low of ¥260 by early 1985. US costs and prices also rose faster than Japanese and the real value of the yen against the dollar was halved. This made Japanese exports extremely cheap or profitable and was the mechanism by which Japan's surplus savings were translated into a rapidly rising trade surplus. The yen need not have fallen so far. The outflow could have been reduced by raising Japanese interest rates closer to US levels. But if that had been done, export growth would have slowed down and the Japanese recovery would have aborted.

At the micro-economic level, US manufacturers clamoured for action to be taken against the unfair advantage Japanese exporters obtained from the weak yen and cheap money. American and British bankers and brokers clamoured for their governments to pressure Japan into opening its markets wider. President Reagan, when he visited Japan in November 1983, bullied the Prime Minister, Yasuhiro Nakasone, into bilateral talks on the yen/dollar exchange rate issue. The threat was that the US would close its markets to Japanese financial institutions, unless Japan opened up. It was a potent threat, since it put big Japanese banks and brokers on the gaijins' (i.e., foreigners') side. The major brokers have considerable clout with leading politicians, supplying money for favours in ways described above. Japanese bankers were desperate not to be shut out of underwriting in London. In May 1984 a joint US–Japanese working group brought out its first report, containing an action programme of the measures the Japanese promised to take.

The principle conceded by the Japanese was that, since their regulated domestic financial system could not compete with liberal Western markets under free trade in money, step by cautious step they would completely liberalise at home. The action programme set out a timetable for the first cautious steps, the main measures of which were as follows:

- The regulation of all deposit interest rates would be progressively abandoned. To begin with, rates on large and long-term deposits would be freed from control, and then gradually the minimum size and maturities would be reduced. Ultimately all control over interest rates on small savings with banks and post offices would go, but this step would be left to last and was not included in the timetable.
- New financial markets would be opened and the regulations governing the use of existing markets eased. As with interest-rate deregulation, only the biggest and best institutions could participate at first in large block transactions with limited maturities. But progressively these restrictions would be relaxed.
- The rule restricting forward exchange transactions only to trade-

related deals was dropped (April 1984). Henceforth Japanese investors in foreign securities could cover their exchange risk.
- Foreign brokers (including subsidiaries 50% owned by banks) were
allowed to become members of the Tokyo stock exchange (from Feb.
1986).
- Foreign banks were allowed into trust banking (also from Feb. 1986).
- Foreigners were allowed to lead manage Euro-yen issues.

The effect of these changes on foreign banks' and brokers' ability to
compete in Japanese financial markets was limited, yet they acted as a
catalyst. Japanese trust funds had now to look to their laurels and stop
performing so miserably. The standard of stockmarket analysis markedly improved. Some of the worst share rigging behaviour had to change.
But the most significant fact was the growing momentum given to interest-rate deregulation, the consequences of which were felt during the
following phase.

II

The Ticking Financial Time-Bomb

Liberalisation and deregulation continued at a leisurely pace during the second half of the 1980s. As it did, the Ministry of Finance lost control over the system. While its actions and inaction can be explained by the macro-economic and political pressures to which it was exposed, the consequences in the world of finance were like unleashing a pit bull terrier at Cruft's Dog Show. The lack of control over Japan's money contributed to a period of financial instability both at home and abroad: first the yen soared and the dollar collapsed; then world stockmarkets crashed; finally, Tokyo became the scene of manic speculation.

Endaka (or 'yendaka'), meaning the strong yen, is the name given to the period from 1985 to 1987. The yen hit a low of ¥260 to the US dollar in February 1985. It climbed rapidly to reach ¥160 two years later and more gently to a peak of ¥120 by the end of 1987. The soaring yen threatened to price Japanese exports out of world markets. By 1986 the domestic economy was heading for a recession. Industrial production fell and real GNP growth slowed to 2%. Industry's profits shrank, and investment plans were slashed. Japanese interest rates were progressively reduced. The Bank of Japan's official discount rate, at 5% in early 1986, was cut to a post-war low of 2.5% by early 1987. Rising capital outflows were expected to moderate the yen's fall, while lower interest rates would stimulate domestic demand.

Lower Japanese interest rates did not work as expected to weaken the yen. Although net long-term capital outflows from Japan doubled in 1986 and remained high in 1987, putting downward pressure on the yen, these were offset by short-term capital inflows and banking transactions. Confidence in the dollar was so weak that Japanese long-term investors were not prepared to run the exchange risk of holding more dollar assets. Japanese long-term investors continued to buy dollar assets, but they began borrowing the dollars with which to buy them. If they did use yen to buy dollar assets, they sold the dollars forwards to ensure they could

get back into yen safely even if the dollar fell further. A forward transaction is a contract to exchange, from three months to a year or more
later, a given sum in one currency for another, at an exchange rate fixed
when the contract takes place. The difference between this rate, the
forward rate, and the exchange rate at the time the contract is agreed,
roughly equals the difference in the cost of borrowing money in the two
countries whose currencies are being exchanged. Japanese banks, which
undertook to buy dollars from Japanese overseas investors, covered their
exchange risk by borrowing dollars immediately and exchanging them
for yen. When they had to meet their obligation to buy dollars, they used
the proceeds to repay their dollar loans.

The Japanese investor did not cause the October 1987 stockmarket
crash, but he contributed powerfully towards it. Trouble started with
nervousness in advance of the February 1987 US Treasury bond auction. It was widely feared that Japanese institutions would boycott them.
Fearing that the dollar would then go into free fall, finance ministers
from the Group of Seven leading industrial countries, meeting at the
Louvre in Paris, decided it was time for concerted action to save it. As it
happened, Nomura and Daiwa Securities had just been granted primary
dealers' licences, allowing them for the first time to enter the US
Treasury auction. They twisted every arm in sight to make it a success – it
was – but the damage was immense. When life funds finalised their
accounts for the year ending 31 March 1987, they found they had currency losses of ¥600 bn, or nearly $4 bn, on their US Treasury bond
holdings. Other investors, equally, had their fingers burnt. Even a 5%
differential between US and Japanese long bond yields could not compensate for a 40% fall in the dollar. And the loss would be enhanced if
US bond rates rose, causing their prices to fall. Japanese private capital
flows to the US started to fall. They were replaced by increased intervention by the Bank of Japan in support of the dollar. During 1987 it bought
almost $40 bn, borrowing yen at home with which to do so.

The Bank of Japan's borrowing at home began to mop up spare
Japanese cash. The cash shortage threatened to become acute when the
next tranche of government shares in Nippon Telephone & Telegraph
shares were due to be sold in November, which promised to realise ¥5.5
trn, or some $35 bn. As a matter of honour and in the hope of huge
profits, the entire NTT issue was bound to be bought by Japanese investors. Japanese institutions therefore began building up their war chests
in advance. Purchases of US Treasury bonds, which averaged $8 bn a
month in January to August, slumped to $1 bn in September. US bond
interest rates rose and bond prices slumped. Yields on bonds looked
attractive. Stockmarket prices looked seriously overvalued, prompting

investors to pull their money out of Wall Street. This is what triggered the October 1987 crash, which rapidly spread to most other world markets. None of these massive international capital movements could have happened before Japan embarked upon financial liberalisation. When they did, the Japanese authorities were powerless to control them.

Zaitech

Endaka frightened Japanese industry about business prospects, leading them to cut back severely on investment. It also frightened the Japanese government into making credit extremely cheap and plentiful, particularly following the October 1987 crash. Instead of borrowing the cheap money to boost their capital spending, Japanese companies began to play the financial and property markets. The name given to their financial operations was zaitech, meaning financial technology. The zaitech game began respectably, as a way of cutting costs when profits fell. Old high-cost debts were exchanged for cheaper new money. Wonderful new financial instruments had been invented by innovative stockbrokers – convertible bonds and warrant bonds – which companies had been set free to exploit. A convertible involves a company borrowing by issuing a bond with a life of four to five years. But the bond buyer is given the option, when the bond is repaid, of using the proceeds to buy the company's shares at a price set when the bond is issued. Warrant bonds are a variation on this theme. The conversion rights are in the form of a warrant, which is detachable from the bond and can be sold on its own. Depending on the terms of the issue, the right to purchase the company's shares may be exercised on a specified date or at any time within a given period. The purchase price is often as low as 5% over the price of the company's shares a day or two after the warrant bond is issued. The punter reckons on making a fat profit by exercising his conversion rights. He is betting that the stockmarket can go only up, and is therefore willing to receive only nominal interest on the bond during its life. The company obtains cheap funds immediately at the cost of the lost opportunity to acquire cheaper funds later. When conversion rights are exercised, the company regains the money needed to repay the bond. The snag is that, if the stockmarket falls, the conversion rights will not be exercised. The company then has to borrow expensively to repay its cheap bond loan. Warrants whose conversion price is above the market price of the company's shares are said to be 'out of the money'.

The issue of warrant and convertible bonds began slowly in the mid–1980s, but then built up speed. From a level of $20–30 bn in 1986, companies raised $66 bn in 1987, $80 bn in 1988 and $126 bn in 1989 –

money which cost next to nothing. Interest on bonds issued by top-notch borrowers in the late 1980s was reduced to 1% or lower. Securities houses themselves were into the warrant bond market in a big way with their own issues. Banks, forbidden to issue warrant bonds, went for convertibles instead. Japanese companies also issued bonds denominated in foreign currencies on the Euro-markets. The proceeds were then immediately converted into yen, which was even more risky. If the Japanese stockmarket, bond market and the yen fell, the cost of repaying foreign currency bonds would soar.

The tale of the tokkins

Tokkins sound like creatures out of Tolkien's *The Lord of the Rings*. They were certainly very imaginative inventions. Many companies wanted to boost profits by borrowing cheap zaitech money and using it for speculative property and share purchases. But first a snag had to be overcome. When company A holds shares in company B, these can be valued at cost for tax purposes, provided it does nothing with them. Unrealised gains do not count as profits and are not taxed. But if any new shares in B are bought, all of B's old shares must be revalued at the new price. This increases A's accounting profits on which taxes must then be paid. Since Japanese companies customarily hold a wide range of each other's shares, this limits the extent to which they are willing to speculate on the stockmarket.

The solution was to speculate indirectly, through what are called tokkin funds held by trust banks. A company can put its money into its own tokkin fund, to which nobody else subscribes. Better still, the trust bank need not be left to decide what investments the company's tokkin fund makes. Running the fund can be delegated to 'independent' advisers (usually the company's stockbroker), who do what the company asks them to do with the money. But since the brokers supposedly know which shares are going to be ramped, the company usually gives them the discretion to speculate on its behalf. When company A's tokkin fund buys and sells B's shares on its behalf, there is no need for A to revalue B's shares in its own portfolio. The tokkin pays it a dividend earned from its capital gains, on which A is taxed. But it escapes taxation on its unrealised gains on B's shares.

Tokkin funds were immensely popular in the later 1980s. The process was also short-circuited to cut out the trust banks. The securities houses ran illegal tokkin funds themselves, called eigyo tokkins, operated by the brokers' institutional sales departments where, owing to their different reporting requirements, they could easily be 'hidden'. The Ministry of

Finance Securities bureau knew about them, but turned a blind eye. Nomura even ran an illegal eigyo tokkin for the Ministry of Finance pension fund. Eigyo tokkins took as much in deposits as the regular tokkins. The trust banks complained to their regulators in the Bank of Japan, which in turn asked the Finance Ministry to investigate. In October 1986, it called in the heads of the big brokers' institutional sales departments one by one. Each denied that they ran such funds, but admitted that others might do so. None was found to be guilty and the Ministry of Finance happily reported that eigyo tokkins didn't exist. Nobody is sure how much money went into eigyo tokkins, but their size in 1986 was thought to have been ¥10–12 trn, around $70 bn. By 1989 it had risen to around ¥30–40 trn. Eigyo tokkins caused the 1991 Nomuragate scandal.

Zaitech operations were a wondrous money-making machine: the more money that companies borrowed to buy shares, the faster the stockmarket rose. The more the market rose, the larger the zaitech profits that companies made. The larger these profits, the more their own share prices rose. Rising share prices on the Tokyo stockmarket boosted company profits and earnings, higher earnings then boosted share prices. The market was able to pull itself up by its own bootstraps.

In the year to March 1987, when endaka made trading profits hard to come by, the top ten industrial zaitech earners made $5.3 bn pretax profits. Out of this, $3.4 bn came from zaitech operations. Toyota made $1.1 bn, Nissan $0.9 bn, which swamped a small trading loss, and Matsushita $0.8 bn. The five fund managers of these companies made more money that year than all their companies' other employees put together. The October 1987 crash should have come as a warning. Losses of a similar magnitude could be disastrous. But the Tokyo stockmarket climbed back above its 1987 peak by March 1988.

Non-bank banks

The property speculation story is almost as bizarre. The main source of finance for this was bank lending. But the main city banks have to be careful how much they lend against property development and speculation. Their operations are closely monitored by the Bank of Japan. Most finance for the most risky and speculative ventures therefore came from what were known as 'non-bank banks'. These are financial companies, which lend money as if they were banks, but cannot – as banks do – raise funds by taking deposits from the public. They therefore obtain their funds directly, if a subsidiary, from their parent banks or indirectly, when they are subsidiaries of large industrial and commercial companies (including the securities houses), from the banks. City banks' books then show as respectable loans to industrial and commercial companies, money which, in fact, is used to finance risky and dangerous property speculation.

Non-bank banks used mainly to be the city banks' consumer finance, hire purchase, leasing and credit card subsidiaries. As these traditionally played such a minor role in Japanese finance, and were under the control of the Ministry of Trade & Industry, they escaped the close scrutiny and control which the rest of the banking community suffered. The Ministry of Finance could not directly interfere on MITI's patch, so it left the banks to look after their own non-bank interests. This unregulated sector expanded massively in the cheap money days of the late 1980s. There are now reckoned to be up to 30,000 non-bank banks, but nobody knows their number for sure. Their traditional business – hire purchase finance – expanded, and by the end of the decade, HP debt owed by the average Japanese consumer exceeded that owed by Americans. But the non-bank banks' foray into the property sector was more dramatic. In 1990 the Ministry of Finance undertook the first-ever study of this murky area, concentrating on the top 200 non-bank banks, which are estimated to account for 70% of all non-bank lending. Their total lending amounted to ¥58 trn ($450 bn), of which over 40%, nearly $200 bn, was directly to property and construction companies. This was equivalent to a third of all bank lending to such companies. Moreover, during the previous year non-bank banks had lent more to property companies than banks. Their total loans doubled between March 1989 and March 1990. The latest loans were the most risky loans, since they were made when the property price bubble was closest to bursting. While the property price boom lasted, non-bank banks made substantial contributions to their parents' profits. So great was the land speculation that a National Land Agency survey reported in 1988 that major companies owned five times as much land as they used in their businesses.

The greatest money-making machine of all time

Financial deregulation severely squeezed banks' profit margins. In 1980 only 12% of city banks' deposits were obtained at market rates; by 1990 only 18% were not. The banks could not easily pass on their higher costs to their largest customers, who went directly to the markets themselves for their funds. So they increased their lending to smaller and medium-sized companies, which now account for two-thirds of their loan books. These loans were riskier than lending to large related companies, but they paid higher interest. The banks also borrowed short and lent long, making a profit out of the difference between long- and short-term interest rates. Long rates are usually higher than short rates; but above all, banks went for growth. The more they lent, the more they earned, even if margins were smaller.

In going for growth, Japanese banks had one immense advantage: they were not limited in their expansion by reserve asset requirements. Reserves to guard against losses were not considered important during the highly regulated days. How could banks make losses when they lent to the best borrowers at fat margins and with no fear of competition? In any case, the Bank of Japan would be forced to save any bank that got into difficulties. In the early 1980s, when opportunities for expansion at home were limited, going for growth meant going abroad. By 1986 Japanese banks had become the world's biggest lenders, accounting for a third of all international bank assets reported to the Bank for International Settlement (BIS).

British and American banks no more liked the Japanese invasion of their traditional markets than did car manufacturers. They complained of unfair competition; British and American banks were limited in their expansion by the reserves they were forced to hold. They pushed for the introduction of world standards for banks' reserve adequacy ratios and persuaded the Japanese government to play ball. Under an agreement negotiated with the BIS, Japanese banks were ordered to build up their reserves to assets ratios to 8% by March 1993. At the time, Japanese reserve ratios were about 4–5%.

That should fettle them, thought the Americans – but it didn't. Japanese banks held large portfolios of company securities, part of their cross-holding under the keiretsu system. It was argued that capital gains on these security holdings belonged to the banks and not to their depositors, and these should therefore count towards banks' reserve assets. It was agreed that Japanese banks could count 45% of their unrealised capital gains as part of their reserve assets. This ruling was dynamite; it was like letting a wild elephant free in a ferry boat. The growth of bank credit henceforth depended on the size of banks' reserves; the size of banks' reserves depended on their unrealised capital gains; which depended on the rise in share prices; while the rise in share prices depended on the growth of bank credit to finance speculation. The more Japanese banks expanded credit, the more they were able to expand credit; and vice versa: a perfect recipe for alternate explosions and implosions of bank credit.

First came the explosion, as endaka channelled easy money into financial markets. Japanese banks' reserve ratios automatically increased. But the banks also exploited the stockmarket boom to raise substantial extra capital, either by equity issues or convertibles. These issues were greedily taken up. The more the banks borrowed, the more they lent. They even lent keiretsu family members the money with which to buy the equity and convertibles that they themselves issued. Competition to expand was so intense, that bank behaviour became insane. They offered loans to their big corporate customers at lower rates of interest than they themselves paid borrowing the money on the money market. Company treasurers saw they were on to a good thing. They accepted bank loans that they did not need and lent the money back to the banks at a profit on the money markets. The more they borrowed from the banks, the more the banks had to borrow from them, increasing both the level of banks' assets and liabilities.

Crash of 1990

The fifth phase of Japan's post-war financial development ended in 1989. From May onwards the Bank of Japan moved to raise interest rates. At first little happened. The Tokyo bull market continued unheeding, peaking at the end of the year with the Nikkei index at 38,915. Average price-earnings ratios were 70, meaning that dividend yields on ordinary shares were less than 1%. The Bank of Japan's move to higher interest rates pushed bond prices down and yields up. The gap between ordinary share yields and bond yields widened, clear evidence that the stockmarket had become seriously overvalued. In 1990 the message finally got through: the days of cheap and plentiful credit were over.

The 1990 stockmarket crash began slowly. Prices slipped in January, slid faster in February and then plummeted in March. In the first three months of 1990 the Nikkei index fell to 28,000, down almost 30% from its December peak, wiping $1000 bn off the value of Japanese shares. Panic set in. The market was hit by the 'three weaknesses': weak bonds, which pushed up yields to 8%; a weak currency, the yen dropping from ¥147 to ¥157 between December and March; and the stockmarket weakness. The authorities were in a cleft stick. If the Bank of Japan pushed its interest rates higher in defence of the yen, the bond market collapse would intensify. But if it did not, the yen's slide would continue.

Nothing much could be done until the end of the financial year on 31 March. No investor would buy into a falling market, just before drawing the line under his year's results. But when the month ended a concerted effort was made by the major stockbrokers to manufacture a rally, and they were successful. Bargain-hunters returned and the market recovered weakly. The worst seemed to be over – but it wasn't. Iraq's invasion of Kuwait on 2 August and the threat of higher oil prices set Tokyo reeling once more. By the end of the half-year in September the Nikkei index was down to 20,222, a fall of almost 50%. Again, as the half-year ended the market steadied. But it still ended the year nearly 40% lower. These stockmarket movements were accompanied by a weakening in property prices. The fall was not severe – only some 10% – but this was more due to the collapse in transactions. The market in property died. Nobody bought or sold. Speculators who came unstuck included Itoman & Co, with outstanding debts of ¥1.3 trn, or almost $10 bn; Kyowa Co, a steel-processing company with about ¥200 bn debts ($1.6 bn); Nanatomi, a Japanese resort developer whose debts were put at ¥300 bn; Tobishima Corporation, a general contractor; and Yuho Chemicals.

The collapse of asset price inflation has put the magic money machine into reverse. Loan losses and falling share and property prices have eroded banks' capital adequacy ratios. They have been forced to contract, instead of expanding bank credit. This threatens to cause share and property prices to fall further, winding down the supply of credit in the process. So far Japan has avoided being caught in a debt-deflationary spiral. Credit and money supply growth has slowed dramatically: the Japanese money supply rose only 2% in the twelve months to December 1991, its lowest post-war rate. Banks are losing deposits to the postal savings system – teigaku accounts are now paying 8% on ten-year money, against the 6.3% which banks pay on deposits. The stockmarket recovered in early 1991, thanks to victory in the Gulf War, but moved sideways through the summer and autumn with the Nikkei index running at between 24,000 and 25,000. Below 23,000 the Japanese banks are in serious trouble with their capital adequacy ratios. But the issue of so many warrants and convertibles during the late-1980s roaring bull market, has left a horrendous hangover following Tokyo's 1990 collapse. By end–1990 over $100 bn of warrant bonds were 'out of the money' – many massively so.

Worst hit were property companies, banks and securities houses. Their shares lost up to two-thirds of their market value in 1990. Hopes are exceedingly slim that they can recover by the time that the outstanding bonds fall due for repayment. From 1992 onwards, money – which cost next to nothing to borrow in the late 1980s – will have to be replaced by money costing 6–8%. That's bad enough; but many companies used the proceeds from warrant and convertible bonds for stockmarket and property speculation. When the stockmarket crashed and property prices fell in 1990, they lost a fortune. They will have to repay the money they have lost, and many may be unable to do so. The big four stockbrokers – Nomura, Daiwa, Nikko and Yamaichi – are in this up to their necks. The 1991 Nomuragate scandal has lopped 85% off the value of their shares. Their domestic and international business operations are being crippled by the opprobrium which they have brought on themselves. The catch 22 is that only a major stockmarket recovery can save them. They need to go on behaving in a scandalous way, to push share prices back up; but they are now forbidden to do so.

Tomato banking

Two things remain to be done to complete the liberalisation of the Japanese financial system: the deregulation of interest rates on small amount savings; and the removal of the remaining restrictions over the kinds of business different types of financial institutions are allowed to do. Both are scheduled by 1993 – but they will take some doing.

So far, interest rate deregulation has mainly affected large banks. By 1990, city banks paid deregulated rates on some 82% of their deposits, regional banks on about 50% and shinkin banks only 30%. Credit co-operatives still obtained most of their funds at regulated rates – as did postal savings offices. The Ministry of Post & Telecommunications is in favour of scrapping all regulated interest rates as soon as possible. The postal savings system enjoys many unfair advantages over banks: it is under no obligation to make profits – if it does, it pays no corporations' tax, if it does not, its losses are met by the tax payer – it holds no reserve assets; its interest payments are guaranteed by the government. In a free-for-all for deposits, it would win hands down.

The Ministry of Finance Banking bureau wants the postal system to lose its borrowing advantages before it is willing to see unfettered competition for small deposits. But when it comes to lending, the postal system will be badly placed since it cannot invest its funds where it likes. It is allowed to put up to 10% overseas and to hand a part to private investment managers. But most of its deposits must be lent to the Trust Fund Bureau at below-market rates. The Post Office is ready to give up its borrowing privileges – provided it is given freedom to lend at market rates to whomever it likes. This brings the Ministry of Finance Trust Fund bureau into the argument. It needs postal savings to help finance off-budget the ¥430 trn public works programme, which the government has undertaken as a result of the SII talks. If postal savings funds go elsewhere, the public works programme will have to be financed on-budget, meaning a larger deficit. The government will then have to compete for funds in the market at higher interest rates. So far no solution to this problem has been found.

Even without full deregulation, small banks are already facing intense competition for deposits. Hardest hit so far are those in the middle – the regional banks, Sogo mutual savings and loan associations and the 450 medium-sized Shinkin, or credit associations. To compete for deregulated deposits at high market rates in the late–1980s, they plunged into speculative property lending. Many have already come unstuck. In March 1990 the Sanwa Shinkin Bank had to be taken over and bailed out by Japan's seventh largest bank, the Tokai Bank. Amongst other things, Sanwa had lent ¥10 bn ($70 m) to a private school owner to finance stockmarket speculation. The Ministry of Finance arranged the takeover – the first by a city bank of a shinkin since the Second World War. It hardly did Tokai a favour, which had gained more branches, but also the staff and debts that go with them. Getting rid of staff is not easy in Japan and the country is over-banked. It is reckoned that one-in-seven shinkin banks are in the red.

Owing to a regulatory loophole, the exact size of the banks' problem is unknown. The Bank of Japan closely monitors only those banks which borrow from it. Over 100 shinkin banks do not. Sogo banks, i.e., mutual savings and loans, have another problem. They were owned by their depositors, each of whom had a vote in how they were managed, and limited to lending most of their money to companies with no more than 300 employees. This put their managers under acute local pressure to make questionable local loans. But in 1990 they were allowed to change their status into second-tier regional banks and set free to lend how they liked.

Since medium-sized banks depend on regulated deposits for up to 70% of their funds, the pressures on them are bound to mount as deregulation proceeds. Competition for deposits has already produced some notable responses. In July 1990, the Kansai Shinkin Bank employed an astrologer to sit in its banking hall on Saturdays and read customers' horoscopes. Most were doubtless warned of the need to save. Another bank installed self-operated blood-pressure measuring machines for the benefit of their elderly customers. But the prize for originality must go to Kenji Yoshida, President of Okayama's Sanyo Sogo Bank. Over breakfast one morning, he hit on the idea of brightening up his bank's appeal by changing its name to the Tomato Bank. 'Tomatoes', he observed, 'are bright, delicious and popular, and that is what I want my bank to be. A Tomato Bank which loves human beings.' The name change hit the headlines. Articles on the Tomato Bank appeared everywhere in the international financial press, *The Economist, Financial Times, Wall Street Journal, Japan Economic Journal* and *Far Eastern Economic Review* all carried the story. It was a brilliant publicity coup, which led the Tomato Bank to collect telephone deposits from Tokyo, where it had no branches. It was also appointed Okayama Prefecture fiscal agency as a reward for its enterprise.

The Japanese banking system is in for its largest ever shake-up.

Doubtless the Ministry of Finance will do its best to encourage many more mergers, take-overs and bail-outs. This will not solve the problem. There are too many too small banks in Japan with too many too small branches. They are inefficient and must remain so. They exist only because of protection from competition they enjoyed and the large margin which existed between regulated deposit and loan rates. If, for example, Tokai succeeds in attracting deposits to the old Sanwa branch network, it will do so at the expense of other small banks which will risk going under. Individual small banks may be saved by mergers and take-overs – but the system cannot be.

Japan has never let a bank go bankrupt since the Second World War. But it is going to have great difficulty dealing with the consequences of interest rate deregulation. In 1991 the Shikoku-based Toho Sogo Bank was on the brink of insolvency as a result of hefty losses on shipbuilding and shipping loans. It did not actually collapse; instead the Japanese Deposit Insurance Corporation lent the regional Iyo Bank ¥600 bn to take it over. This was the first ever payment from the fund to cover bank losses. A further weakness in the system is that Japanese banks make negligible provisions for bad debts. The quality of their asset cover is far inferior to that of British and American banks. The National Tax Agency is to blame – it sanctions bad debt provisions and is always reluctant to do so, since tax relief has then to be given. When bank margins are squeezed by competition for deposits, all their bad property and stockmarket loans will come home to roost. Like the US savings and loans, it will be found that few have the money left to survive. The Deposit Insurance Corporation, financed 50% by the government and 50% by the banks, has nowhere near enough reserves to bail out the system and, like its US counterpart, faces bankruptcy. There will be numerous bank closures all over Japan during the next few years, and thousands of bank workers will lose their jobs. What has happened so far is only the beginning. As *The Economist* (2 June 1990) remarked: 'Japan could see its biggest banking crunch for decades.' Tomatoes are easily squashed.

Removing the barrier between banking and stockbroking is another thorny problem. Big banks desperately want to get into stockbroking at home. Small banks – eager to get into securities sales – have far more branches than the brokers and the extra activity could save a number from going under in the wake of deregulation. Brokers want to protect their monopoly position. The big brokers would do a deal, if they could keep the fixed commission system; but the Nomuragate scandal has ruled this out. The 200 small brokers, by contrast, are scared stiff of competing with banks and are dependent for their survival on fixed commissions; many will go under.

What angers the stockbrokers is that foreign banks have already been allowed into broking as members of the Tokyo stock exchange. Citicorp, Security Pacific and Chase Manhattan all have TSE membership, but through subsidiaries. The Ministry of Finance recognises home country rules. As there is no division between banking and broking in London, it has allowed Japanese banks and brokers there to transact each other's business. It has even allowed Japanese banks' London stockbroking subsidiaries to open branch offices in Tokyo. Its rules for foreign banks obtaining securities licences and stock exchange membership in Japan require that the operations should be done by a subsidiary in which the foreign bank holds only a 50% stake. The remaining 50% must be held by a 'sleeping partner', such as an unrelated industrial concern. British Petroleum and Ciba Geigy are sleepers.

The system proposed for Japan is similar. Big universal financial institutions would continue to be banned. But banks and brokers could set up separate and partly owned subsidiaries, which would be allowed to conduct each other's business. Since these subsidiaries would have to be large and well capitalised, this approach is similar to that taken with interest deregulation. Start big and gradually lower the limits. City and regional banks, however, fear that they will be the losers. Their capital has already been stretched meeting the BIS reserve ratios. It will be stretched further when they are forced to bail out smaller and weaker banks. The question must therefore be posed, why can't the Japanese leave things as they are?

Part of the answer to this has been given already. As long as Tokyo's financial markets remain more tightly regulated than London's and New York's, a large part of its domestic financial business will be transacted outside Japan and beyond the control of the Ministry of Finance – with consequent destabilising effects. In addition, pressure from the US for deregulation to continue remains intense. In October 1990 the US Congress passed the Fair Trade in Financial Services Act, which includes section 2028, modelled on the famous Clause 301 in the 1988 Omnibus Trade Act. This gives the President more power to retaliate against Japanese institutions in the USA.

During the past two years Japanese interest rates have gone up and US rates have come down. Japanese rates are now higher than US rates and capital outflows from Japan slowed to a trickle in 1990. The invasion of foreign markets seemed to have been checked and Japanese bankers and brokers have been in retreat – but this is only temporary. The US economy is now recovering and the Japanese economy is slowing down. While Japan's interest rates are set to fall, those of the US are close to their cyclical low and more likely to rise. Cyclically, the Japanese current account surplus has started to increase strongly again. Capital outflows from Japan are likely to be resumed shortly. All the old pressures will return when they do.

Scams and scandals

This story would not be complete without highlighting some of the scams and scandals which have recently come to light. The administrative guidance system allowed a great deal of wrong-doing to go undetected and unpunished. At times the regulators were parties to the crimes – either through negligence or by turning a blind eye to what was happening. Administrative guidance – instead of clear and detailed laws applicable to all – contributed, which is why there is now intense public pressure for this system to be reformed.

Easy money in the late 1980s obscured much skullduggery. Thieves and fraudsters made fortunes during the great bull market by speculating with stolen money, and were able to replace the funds they 'borrowed' with impunity. Maybe banks' and brokers' top managers were none the wiser; more likely they were much the richer. But then the bubble burst. Stolen money, lost when the stockmarket crashed, could not be repaid. Hence the recent rash of banking scandals. Recruit Cosmos, Nomuragate and the Fuji Bank fraud case, which deeply involved leading politicians, are described later. Other scandals – involving mainly businessmen, bankers and stockbrokers – show that crooks and swindlers are to be found at the top of major Japanese corporations and financial institutions.

Itoman, a family textile business founded in Osaka in 1883, failed in 1990 with debts of ¥1.3 trn, almost $10 bn. In the mid–1970s, Itoman was rescued from financial collapse by Sumitomo, Japan's third largest bank, and became a member of Sumitomo's keiretsu family. Sumitomo sent in one of its Vice-Presidents, Ichiro Isoda, to clear up the mess. He appointed one of his top Sumitomo aides, Yoshihiko Kawamura, to be Itoman's President. Isoda subsequently became Sumitomo Bank's Chairman. Sumitomo used Itoman in the late 1980s as a vehicle for property speculation. Isoda also encouraged other banks to lend to Itoman. Many small banks and credit co-operatives pitched in – they reckoned that if Sumitomo was behind the company, it was bound to be sound. From the mid-1980s, Itoman borrowed heavily to invest in property and land, and to finance its own offshoot, Itoman Finance, in its lending to property developers and speculators. Itoman regularly raised money internationally, selling Euro-dollar warrant bonds three years in a row. Its last issue was for $200 m in August 1990. The scandal broke a month later.

Kawamura plunged Itoman into some of the most risky ventures. As property markets started weakening, he played 'double or quits'. He got involved with a shady local Osaka property speculator, a young Korean businessman Ho Yung Chung. Ho used another such character, Suemitsu Ito, as his go-between. Ho's role was initially to suggest new ventures and secure development land for Itoman. But he also played a part, not fully clear, in an attempt by Kawamura to loosen Sumitomo's hold over the company. Both men were involved in buying Itoman shares. In 1989–90 Ho's holdings reached 19%. As a result, Ito was appointed to the Itoman board. The money for Kawamura's and Ho's Itoman share purchases appears to have come, by devious routes, from Itoman itself. One was an art scam. In 1990, Ito arranged for Itoman to buy 219 paintings and art objects from *Kansai Shimbun*, an Osaka news-paper owned by Ho. It paid ¥55.7 bn for the collection, which included works by the Italian painter Modigliani. The purchases were based on valuations issued by the Seibu department store, which were later found to be forged. The collection was worth only a quarter of what Itoman had paid for it.

Heads rolled: Sumitomo's President Isoda resigned; Kawamura was sacked by the Itoman board three months later. He and Ito were arrested in July 1991 on fraud charges. Sumitomo was Itoman's main creditor, putting up a third of the company's borrowing and it has taken responsi-bility for clearing up the mess. Properly handled, Itoman's losses should be manageable, but this depends upon how its assets are disposed of. In a fire sale, the losses would be huge – but Sumitomo should not allow it to come to that.

Wheels within wheels: Isoda's resignation was in connection with a different scandal – Sumitomo's links with Mitsuhiro Kotani, a share raider and ramper. Kotani was a self-made man, who got rich through owning hotels and golf courses. He turned his attention next to the stockmarket, where he specialised in greenmail. This involves acquiring a significant stake in a company, then forcing it to buy you out at a higher price. Kotani operated through the Kosin investment syndicate. In 1985 he turned his attentions on the sleepy Janome Sewing Machine com-pany. He surreptitiously built up a 20% holding in it, then demanded a seat on the board, which the management conceded. He then blackmailed Janome into giving and lending him ¥200 bn, by threat-ening to sell his stake to known gangsters. Janome paid up by raising the money from Sumitomo, Mitsui Trust & Banking, Sanwa Bank and Saitama Bank. The loans were obtained from branch managers, who knew they were for Kotani, in exchange for inside information. Four Mitsui Trust & Banking executives were subsequently arrested for tax evasion on undeclared capital gains, and three Sumitomo executives were arrested for making illegal loans.

Kotani used the money he obtained from Janome in 1987 for an attack on Kokusai Kogyo, an aerial survey company. It refused to be greenmailed and Kotani launched Japan's first successful hostile take-over bid. It took eighteen months to achieve but, in December 1988, he managed to have Kokusai Kogyo's board dismissed by the shareholders, when he and his cronies took over. Unfortunately, Katoni then faced the problem of re-paying some of his debts. He forced Kokusai Kogyo to lend him ¥25 bn. This was due for repayment in April 1991, but the stockmarket crash left him short of funds and he could repay only ¥6 bn.

This set Kotani off on his next escapade: his aim was to raise funds by ramping shares in Fujita Tourist Enterprises, a hotel and leisure group. Kosin already had a stake in this company, which Kotani arranged to sell to Tobishima Leasing in late April. With the help of Daiwa, two smaller Japanese stockbrokers and Citibank's subsidiary, Scrimgeour Vickers Securities, he generated considerable buying and selling activity in Fujita's shares, which sent them climbing 40% in a week. Whereupon Kotani then sold out as arranged to Tobishina.

Kotani was arrested in July 1990 for share rigging and charged in December with blackmail. Seven Kokusai Kogyo directors and executives were arrested for tax evasion or embezzlement. One politician was brought down by Kotani, Toshiyuki Inamura, an LDP minister in the late 1980s. Sumitomo's Isoda resigned in October 1990 to take responsibility for his bank's involvement with Kotani, although he personally had no hand in the affair. Reporting the scandal, The *Wall Street Journal* (13 March 1991) observed:

> Analysts say the rapid demise of the 53-year-old Mr Kotani as a force in Japan's financial world is no accident of fate. Rather there is a theory among bankers and stockmarket experts that Mr Kotani's troubles represent a concerted effort by the country's authorities to flush out some of the speculative and even extortionate practices that Mr Kotani and a crowd of other stockmarket speculators had been accused of depending on in the late 1980s to build their wealth. One weekly magazine even suggests a deal was struck between prosecutors and Japan's corporate establishment to rid the stockmarket of Mr Kotani.

In 1991 four similar bank frauds came to light, in which money was borrowed against the collateral of forged securities. The biggest, which broke in August, concerned the small Toyo Shinkin Bank. One of its branch managers forged deposit certificates worth ¥342 bn ($2.5 bn) and lent them to an Osaka restaurant owner, Ms Nui Onoue. She used them as collateral to borrow from some of the biggest and best banks in Japan – the Industrial Bank of Japan, the Fuji Bank, Nichiboshin – and financial companies affiliated to Sumitomo Life. They were only too willing to lend to Ms Onoue, as she was at one time the largest individual shareholder in IBJ and Dai-Ichi Kangyo, the world's largest bank. How the lenders could supply funds on such a scale against so obviously faked securities defies the imagination – the total deposits of the Toyo Shinkin Bank were only ¥360 bn – but they did. When the market crashed, so did Ms Onoue's fortune. The fraud came to light and she and her bank manager friend were arrested. The Bank of Japan moved promptly to prevent a run on the Toyo Shinkin Bank, although the banks which lent against its forged deposit certificates will probably have to stand the resulting losses.

Kyowa Co, a steel-processing company – which went under in November 1990 with about ¥200 bn debts ($1.6 bn) – may result in larger losses than Itoman. It is reckoned to be Japan's largest bankruptcy since the Sanko Steamship Co crashed in 1985. Kyowa recklessly invested in real estate. Some of its money came from the trading company Marubeni as a result of payments on fictitious orders. Former executives of both companies were arrested in July 1991 for fraud. Olympic, a condominium developer, filed for bankruptcy in November 1990, followed by Nanatomi, a Japanese resort developer, in January 1991. Nanatomi's debts were put at ¥300 bn, which further rocked Tobishima Corporation. When Yuho Chemicals collapsed in December 1990, it was revealed that its major creditor was Sanyo Finance, an arm of Sanyo Securities which, in its turn, is affiliated to Nomura Securities. Yuho Chemicals was small beer, but it still accounted for 10% of Sanyo Finance's total loans. Yoichi Tsuschiya, Sanyo's President, admitted that the firm had been lax in extending credit to Yuho. He explained that this was because 'the borrower is a subsidiary of a listed firm – Toyama Chemical Co, Japan's leading pharmaceutical firm – and other financiers had extended loans.' By pure chance, Tsuschiya's younger brother was President of Yuho.

12

Fearing Old Age

Reform has failed to increase the buoyancy or equity of the tax system. Financial liberalisation threatens to starve the 'off-budget' Fiscal Investment & Loans Program of the postal savings funds needed to finance Japan's expanded public works programme. While, as the population ages, the third source of public investment finance – pension fund surpluses – will dry up. Japan faces a budgetary crisis. The 'greying' of the Japanese nation is the subject of this chapter, which looks first at demographic trends, then considers the social causes of the declining Japanese birth rate, and finally assesses the economic consequences.

Middle-aged spread

The Japanese are growing older. So are we all, by one year every year. But what is true of the individual is not necessarily true of the population. The average age of the population goes down if more babies are born or older people die earlier. It goes up when fewer babies are born and if old people live longer, which is what has been happening in Japan.

Births have exceeded deaths in Japan every decade since the 1880s. The population has trebled. Its growth rate has varied. It was 1–1.5% a year before the Pacific War. In the decade following the war, it rocketed to 2.2% a year. At this rate, the population doubles every thirty-two years. This post-war baby-boom took the birth rate back to over 30 per 1000 of the population. There were 8 m Japanese born between 1947 and 1949; making children was the only activity to set all-time records in those years. At the same time, improved diet, better hygiene and modern medicine cut the death rate: infant and maternal mortality rates declined sharply; older Japanese lived longer. Population growth was thus boosted by more old Japanese as well as more young. The rising birth rate, coupled with war casualties amongst twenty- and thirty-year-olds, made Japan an exceptionally young nation. In 1950, 35% of the population was aged under fifteen, while only 5% was over sixty-five. The average age fell below twenty-seven, lower than it had been fifty years earlier.

The birth rate depends upon the number of women of child-bearing age and their fertility rate, i.e. the average number of babies each bears. To maintain the size of the population, a female must have at least two children during her child-bearing years. During the post-war baby-boom the fertility rate peaked at 4.5 in 1947. Ever since then, Japanese women have been having fewer babies. The fertility rate fell rapidly to 2.1 in the 1960s. By 1990 it was down to 1.5. In the 1960s this trend was offset partly by the large number of females of the baby-boom generation reaching child-bearing age. This produced an echo, though much smaller, baby-boom. There was a decline in the number of females reaching child-bearing age in the 1980s, which, combined with the continued drop in the fertility rate, caused the birth rate to collapse precipitately. By 1990 it was below 10 per 1000, one-third of its level a century earlier. Since the population has meanwhile trebled, no more Japanese babies are born today than a century ago. If the fertility rate now stops falling, there will be a second echo of the post-war baby-boom in about 2000, when the grandchildren of the baby-boomers are born. But it's a big 'if'.

Despite the declining birth rate, the Japanese population has continued to rise. Fewer births have been offset by fewer deaths. Life expectancy has risen from fifty for men and fifty-four for women in 1947 (levels reached in Britain and the US at the beginning of this century) to the highest in the world. Japanese life expectancy is now seventy-six for men and eighty-two for women. It is predicted to climb higher in the twenty-first century, but not by much, to seventy-eight and eighty-four by 2025. As the number of females of child-bearing age falls, the number of births per 1000 of the population will continue to decline. As the post-war baby-boomers reach old age, the number of deaths per 1000 of the population will rise, even though the Japanese live longer. Consequently, the Japanese population is forecast to peak at just below 130 m in 2010, and then fall to under 100 m by 2070.

The population is older as well as larger than it was just after the Second World War; the Japanese are now middle-aged. The average age has risen from twenty-seven to thirty-seven. By 2000 they will be the oldest nation in the world. By 2025 the average age is forecast to rise to forty-five. In the first half of the next century, more than half the population will be older than the life expectancy of Japanese born in the first half of this century. In 1950, one-in-twenty Japanese were over sixty-five and one-in-three under fifteen. By 2025, one-in-four will be over sixty-five, while fewer than one-in-ten will be under fifteen. The old and the young have to be supported by people of working age. The burden this represents can be measured by the 'dependency rate'. This is the ratio of the population of working age to those under fifteen and over sixty-five. A falling birth rate initially reduces this dependency rate; there are fewer young to be supported. But then the rising number of old people rapidly increases it. The figures for Japan are startling. In 1970 there were ten people of working age for every person over sixty-five. Now there are under seven. By 2020 there will be fewer than three. Taking account of the young as well, there will then be two dependents for every three people of working age.

Christmas cake kids

Why did the birth rate fall so steeply? Obviously, it was artificially high immediately after the Second World War. A decade of war, which towards its end left no time for anything but the war effort and survival, disrupted family life. When the men returned home, they made up for lost time. The high fertility rate of the late 1940s and early 1950s was, as elsewhere, a product of the war. Thereafter, a decline was to be expected.

The extent of the decline was not expected. In 1979 the OECD forecast Japanese births falling to 1.8 m in 1990; instead they fell to 1.2 m. Statistically, it occurred because girls married later, so missing a significant part of their child-bearing years in spinsterhood and, when they did have children, they had fewer. High birth rates are usually associated with youthful marriages. British Victorian child-brides frequently had an infant or two while still in their teens. Japanese women marry in their twenties; it used to be in their early twenties. Unmarried women aged over twenty-five were called 'Christmas cakes', meaning they were no longer wanted after the twenty-fifth. Now it is common for Japanese women to marry in their late twenties, with the average age for marriage moving up to twenty-five. Half of all women become 'Christmas cakes'. The average age at which a Japanese mother has her first child is twenty-seven, the second at thirty and the third, if there is one, at thirty-two. This two-to-three year spacing also reduces the number of children women have in their child-bearing years.

There are economic and social reasons for the steep fall in family size. Put simply, the idea of raising a big family in a home the size of a large holiday caravan, with a husband, chosen for you, who only comes home to sleep, has lost its appeal to a generation of educated, emancipated and affluent young Japanese women. For young men, too, the cost of marriage and supporting a young family has risen to the point at which early marriage is financially unattractive. Unlike their mothers and fathers, today's young Japanese expect to have a good time before, and increasingly after, settling down.

Immediately after the Second World War, children were a form of saving. When they grew up, they contributed to the family income and helped to keep their parents in their old age. Japanese newly-weds did not usually set up homes for themselves, but went to live with the bridegroom's parents. The bride was expected to serve and obey her mother-in-law. This was before there was adequate social security and when families had little money saved up for old age. These economic motives favouring large families have lost their force, particularly now that Japan has a generous social security system. Individuals have accumulated private wealth from years of hard savings. The young have left the countryside to live in the cities, where they set up their own homes. Not having children is now a form of saving. The wife can go on working longer earning more and education costs can be reduced or avoided.

Come back Malthus, all is forgiven

Malthus argued that population expands to the point at which food supplies are exhausted. Famine, plague and pestilence set the limits to population growth. This theory gave economics the reputation of being the dismal science. Evidence amongst advanced economies is the opposite, i.e., population growth slows with growing affluence. There is a precedent for this in Japan. In the 120 years after the establishment of the Tokogawa Shogunate in 1600, the Japanese population more than doubled. But from 1720 to 1850 it remained relatively static. It used to be thought that this was due to land and food shortages. There certainly were famines from time to time, but the reason was not a lack of food, but rapacious taxation. Japanese food production continued to expand throughout the later years of the Tokugawa Shogunate. Modern research has established that population growth was controlled by infanticide. This was not, as in other Asian countries, due to the despatch of unwanted baby girls. Boys were just as likely to be murdered at birth. The aim was to create small and balanced families; two boys and two girls was the norm. Where two girls were followed by a third, it would be murdered and the couple would have another go at producing a boy. A third boy suffered the same fate.

Malthus today might suggest that space, rather than food, sets a limit on population growth. Japanese homes are not large enough to house large families. Indeed one young man explained to me that, with his two-roomed apartment only 20 sq. m in size, he rented the cot for his first child; there was no point in buying one. He had no room to store it until his second offspring arrived. Cot-rental is commonplace in Japan. A bigger family, he explained, depended on moving to a bigger house. As this would take time, they might wait several years before having their second and probably last child. This problem has partly arisen because some Japanese have taken to Western beds and furniture. Traditionally the Japanese slept on futons on the floor, which were rolled up and put away during the day. It was easier then to fit in more children.

Both the need and the desire to earn more has reduced Japanese family size. Working wives became a rarity after the war. Historically, women worked in the rice paddies alongside their men. But as Japan became industrialised, married women were increasingly expected to stay at home and look after the children. Living away from their parents, the mother-in-law's main advantage – as baby-minder – was lost. Companies frowned upon working wives. Men were supposed to earn enough to support their families unaided. It was a matter of personal prestige that they should do so. This is changing. Following the 1973 oil price shock and the move to slower growth, incomes expanded less rapidly. Female participation rates in the labour force rose. Then, as the growth in the working population declined in the late 1980s and labour became scarce, the demand for women workers increased. The female participation rate in Japan, at 50% in 1988, while still lower than in Sweden (60%), Canada (56%) and the US (55%), was higher than in Britain (49%), France (44%) and Germany (42%).

Wanted: $20,000 to get wed

The high cost of marriage is another factor. It is a matter of family pride that a young couple should be wed in style and at great expense. Most weddings take place in hotels, which have their own chapels. About a third of all brides have 'Christian' church weddings. They are not believers, as most Japanese are atheists. But the church ceremony and garb have become popular. A white bridal gown with veil is preferred to the traditional kimono, which is a pity. Tokyo hotels do a roaring wedding trade. The New Otani did 1308 weddings in 1989 and the Imperial 1239. For its efforts the Imperial netted ¥7.6 bn, ($54 m). According to a Sanwa Bank report, the cost of a typical Japanese wedding in 1988 was ¥3 m (over $20,000). Engagement gifts cost another ¥1.4 m ($10,000). The honeymoon cost ¥1 m ($7000) and setting up house a further ¥3 m. The total came to over ¥8 m or $57,000. If lucky, the couple receive presents of ¥700,000 ($5000) to help defray these expenses. Families help out with the costs, but it still takes time for youngsters to save up to get married.

Social pressures are also working against early marriages. In 1988 a national survey on attitudes to marriage amongst single young Japanese showed that 95% wanted eventually to get married, but 80% of men and 90% of women preferred to remain single through their early twenties. All said that individual freedom was the main reason for delaying marriage. Men wanted to marry at twenty-seven and women at twenty-five. Their ideal family size averaged just over two. As yet, few women are attracted to a career rather than marriage, and married career women are almost unknown. So most do get married eventually. This could change.

Oyija Girls

The young Japanese woman does not want the life her mother leads. She is happy and affluent while single. Secretaries earn around ¥170,000 a month, or $20,000 a year, more than enough to keep them in comfort. They pay ¥400 ($3) for a canteen lunch and their commuting is subsidised. Many live at home, so that most of their income is pin-money. Single women are Japan's new rich. After paying tax and insurance contributions and other expenses, they have around ¥135,000 a month ($1,000) to spend on themselves. Their favourite pastime is shopping. They spend extravagantly on clothes, leisure and travel. One young woman, not exceptional, was reported to spend ¥1 m ($7000) a year on foreign travel and still managed to save ¥2 m in three years. Travelling abroad, Miss Japan leaves light and returns heavy. The average weight of her luggage on departure from Narita for Hong Kong is 15 kg; on her return it has increased to 35 kg.

The name 'oyija girl' comes from female golfers. A *Wall Street Journal* report in 1990 explained that oyija was the name applied to coarse, middle-aged, beer-swilling businessmen golfers, who monopolised many golf courses. Women usually confined their activities to golf lessons in big stores or at local driving ranges. But now they can afford to venture on to the fairways and greens. The cost is horrific, with the price of a single round up to $200. Nonetheless, the female of the Japanese species sallies forth with designer golf balls, $865 Mickey Mouse golf bags and $1000 worth of new clothes bought specially for the occasion. Slowly she slices and giggles her way round the course. Scores under 200, about three times par, are considered an achievement.

Love Hotels

Modern Miss Japan is emancipated, seeing no reason to rush into marriage to have sex. Traditionally, marriages were arranged between families and had little to do with love or sex. Men married for dynastic reasons and bought love in brothels or from mistresses. It was quite respectable to do so. Women were either housewives or kept women. Arranged marriages are still commonplace, but up to half of Japanese youngsters now insist on love-matches. Japan in the 1980s, like America in the 1950s, has discovered free sex. Few worry about AIDS. Prostitution and brothels were officially banned in 1956, but a ¥4 trn sex industry still prospers. The Japanese spend as much on sex as on defence. A quarter of the industry's income is earned by shinjuku or 'love hotels', which let rooms by the hour; short stays cost from ¥4000 ($30) upwards. Shinjuku are not sordid, backstreet dives, but magnificent, if gaudy and blatant, edifices. Some are like Disneyland castles, others sport replica Statues of Liberty on their roofs. They are sumptuously and erotically furnished. Rooms are booked by pressing buttons on back-lighted screens in the foyer. Love hotels – like most other things in Japan – are carefully regulated. Limits are imposed on number and size of mirrors allowed in each room. Beds must be stationary. Rocket-to-Mars devices are banned. All must have lounges and bars, to give the impression that they are normal hotels.

Love hotels serve a practical as well as an amorous purpose. Walls in Japanese homes are literally paper-thin. Married couples, who still live with their in-laws, frequent love hotels at week-ends. According to one owner, the patronage changes during each day. Senior citizens arrive in the morning, seeking inspiration. At lunchtime, it's office workers, usually in a hurry. Students and young couples take over in the evenings. The only couples turned away are pupils in school uniforms.

Where's Daddy?

Life after marriage offers Japanese women little. Bringing up children is hard work anywhere. In a tiny Japanese apartment, it is awful. Few women want to spend much of their time doing so, they would rather stay single and go on working a bit longer. The housewife's life is equal parts hard work and boredom. Male working lives have changed little so far. Although working hours are falling, they are still unendurably long by Western standards. The Japanese work on average 2044 hours a year, which is 10% more than the Americans and British work and 20% more than the French and Germans. At the end of his long working day, the

Japanese male drinks after hours with his buddies, before embarking on his long commute home. His wife must wait up late to feed him on his return home, then get up early to feed him again before he sets off for work the next day. Between times, she lives a lonely life. Alcoholism is a major Japanese problem: men drink together to relieve tension; their wives drink alone to relieve boredom. Another distraction, which helps the family budget, is prostitution. A 'date club' or escort agency in the Tokyo dormitory suburb of Shin-Matsudo was recently prosecuted; its forty-three women included thirty who were married to respectable salary-earners.

The Japanese employee is still expected to be a company man before anything else. He must put work and his career first, and family a long way second. An American baseball star, Randy Bass, playing for a Japanese club, Hansin Tigers, flew back to the US when his eight-year-old suffered a brain tumour. He was widely criticised for missing an important match and was sacked. A Japanese player would have put his team first. A bus driver stopped to help a woman who had collapsed with a heart attack in the street. He made a small diversion to rush her to hospital. He was reprimanded by his employers and would have been fired, but his exceptional action was reported in the papers and met with widespread approval. Companies habitually drive their employees into the ground. Nervous breakdowns are not unusual and the suicide rate is high. Shingo Furuya, Hansin Tigers' manager, was a former Hansin Electric Railway executive who knew nothing about running a baseball team. He was hounded by the company because of the club's poor performance and committed suicide in the New Otani Hotel's garden. Death from overwork, karoshi, is also commonplace in Japan. The National Defence Council for the relatives of its victims handles 2000 cases a year, adding that this is just the tip of the iceberg. More Japanese die of overwork, it believes, than are killed in road accidents.

Female emancipation is still only partial. Apart from a brief wave of interest in 1989, when Mrs Doi was leader of the Japanese Socialist party, most Japanese females are not interested in politics. They make no effort through the ballot box to change Japan's male-oriented society, nor are they much concerned by the discrimination (illegal) which they suffer at work. Japanese employers are notoriously wasteful of trained female labour. They employ large numbers of college graduates, but allow them to do only menial tasks. They are recruited to provide wives for their male employees, expecting them to be as loyal to their company as their husbands. Company men need company wives. Company wives are expected to socialise together in their company apartments, while their company husbands are socialising with each other at the company's expense and possibly in the company's bar. Female graduates from the prestigious Tokyo University wear neat little company uniforms and serve company tea to their male colleagues and visitors, even when working on equal terms in such jobs as bond traders. They do so as long as they remain company employees. They are never expected to make a career out of work and it is virtually unknown for any to move on to management positions. No man in Japan could be bossed around by a woman superior. A few women have management careers in companies they establish, notably in the fashion world or in the media. Elsewhere, their way ahead is firmly barred. But nor do they do much about it. Women's professional organisations, campaigning for equal opportunities, are poorly supported.

The generation of young Japanese women who are now marrying late, are all for delaying, but not much for changing, Japanese married life. But the revolution has begun – it will not stop here. When they marry, many women won't settle down. Having enjoyed single freedom, they won't accept married serfdom. Divorces are still rare in Japan, though the number is rising. The plight of the single-parent family is beginning to be recognised. The revolution will roll on. Women will increasingly demand a better deal at work and at home. With growing labour shortages, they will be well placed to have their demands met. The way in which Japanese men live and work will also be changed.

Few hands make hard work

Babies are cheap to keep; old people are expensive. Health care costs five times as much for the average over sixty-five than for the under sixty-five. This means that, when one-quarter of the population is over sixty-five, they will account for more of Japanese health care expenditure than all the younger Japanese put together. Moreover, in all advanced countries real expenditure on health is rising more rapidly than GDP. Modern medicines and surgical techniques perform miracles in prolonging life or improving its quality – but they are expensive.

Japan has universal health insurance, made up of various public schemes covering different categories of people. The self-employed on average contribute ¥10,400 a month per household. Private sector employees, seamen and private school employees contribute between 7.3% and 8.3% of their wages to their schemes. Government and local government employees and former employees contribute from 5.5% to 9.3%, according to the size of their families. Retired workers also pay a premium determined by income and family responsibilities. So when health costs go up, contribution must rise. But while the bulk of the additional spending will be on the old, the bulk of the increased contributions will fall upon the young.

The country has a generous and complex national pension system. Everyone gets a basic pension while employees also get a second pension attached to their job. The self-employed pay a flat ¥8400 a month into the basic national pension fund. Employee pension funds pay in the same amount on behalf of each of their members. These contributions cover two-thirds of the cost of the basic pension. The government chips in the remaining one-third from taxation. Employee funds collect contributions of 10–15% of wages. They pay out contribution-related benefits, which currently average ¥195,000 per month or $1400. Both basic and employee pensions are index-linked to inflation.

When the Ministry of Finance pushed the 1988 tax reform through the Diet, it made much of the growing burden social security contributions will impose as the population ages. It estimated that pension payments would rise fivefold to ¥220 trn by 2010. Their share of national income would almost double from 15% to 29%. The Ministry forecast that employees' contributions would have to rise from 11% of incomes to 17.5%. In addition, the government's contribution out of taxation would rise from ¥18 trn to ¥50 trn. These numbers were meant to scare, but they were probably realistic. By 2000, social security expenditure could account for a fifth of Japan's national income, and a quarter by 2010. The baby-boomers in the 1960s provided the young, active and hard-working labour force which produced miraculous economic growth. In their old age they expect to be generously rewarded by the smaller, middle-aged workforce they have sired.

Misspent contributions

The economics of providing for old age are the same no matter how pensions schemes operate. Funded schemes sound more prudent than pay-as-you-go systems. Under the former, the pension fund builds up assets during the contributor's working lifetime, which are run down when he retires; under the latter, the more contributors there are and the fewer beneficiaries, the less each contributor pays. As the number of beneficiaries increase while the number of contributors decline, the cost of pensions has to be met out of higher contributions. Pay-as-you-go schemes thus appear to place a greater burden on the young; they don't. Most of the assets acquired by funded schemes are government bonds. The young pay lower contributions into funded schemes as the population ages, but more in taxes to pay the interest and redemption costs on the larger amount of government bonds. The only difference is that funded schemes create financial obligations to pay more taxes, whereas pay-as-you-go schemes create legal obligations to pay higher contributions. Either way, the economic resources to look after the old come out of the pockets of the young.

Whether the ageing population imposes a burden on the young depends upon how the old spent their income while they were young. If they consumed too much and invested too little, the young inherit an inadequate industrial base and social capital stock. The amount of real assets which the baby-boomers leave behind when they retire will determine the burden they place on younger Japanese. Thanks to their high savings, they will leave a fine industrial base. The fewer workers in the coming generation will not need to devote 25% of national income to private investment. But they may inherit a woefully inadequate stock of social assets.

In the 1970s and 1980s, the government misappropriated pension fund contributions to finance current expenditure. By 1989, the value of outstanding deficit financing bonds totalled ¥65 trn, or 15% of GNP. The government has nothing to show for these bonds. Consequently, Japan's funded pension schemes' claims will impose a burden on tomorrow's taxpayers. The baby-boomers paid more than enough into their funded pension schemes to finance their retirement. But part of their payments was returned to them in low taxes. Taxes were low because part of public consumption was financed out of their pension fund contributions.

The story does not end there. The lightly taxed Japanese saved rather than spent. Their surplus savings were invested abroad, instead of at home. They will leave a large stock of foreign financial assets to the next generation of Japanese, instead of decent homes, roads, schools and hospitals. The foreign assets will produce income which can supply the real resources needed to pay for higher pensions. But there are three snags to this. Foreign income will only supply real resources if used to buy more imports. Japan will have to run a trade deficit. You can't import roads, sewers, homes and hospitals. So the Japanese will have to stop making so many exports and switch resources to construction. The industrial sector must be contracted, which won't be easy. Thirdly, most overseas investments are privately owned. The income from them will still have to be taken in higher taxes to pay for the roads, sewers, homes and hospitals which need to be built. An overvalued yen and higher taxes will be required to mobilise the resources created by the older generation.

A taxing time ahead

The Japanese government is not waiting until the twenty-first century before tackling the inadequate stock of social capital. As a result of the

SII talks with the Americans, it has agreed to raise public investment by 63% in the 1990s compared with the 1980s. This involves expenditure of ¥430 trn spread over the fiscal years 1991 to 2000. The cost can be met from either higher taxes or higher borrowing. But public sector gross debt already equals 70% of national income, and debt interest payments cost 4% of national income. Moreover the government still borrows cheaply at regulated interest rates. Financial liberalisation will increase the cost of servicing existing debt and future borrowing. The Japanese government, already alarmed at the size of government debts, has eliminated deficit financing bonds and now plans to cut the issue of construction bonds (which finance public investment) from 8.4% of general expenditure in fiscal 1989 to 5% in fiscal 1995. This is incompatible with financing the expanded public works programme out of borrowing.

During the 1990s, the Japanese will have to pay more tax. There are three ways they can do so: the system can be reformed to eliminate tax dodging; the sales tax rate can be raised; and bracket creep can be allowed to increase the income tax burden. All these options are unpalatable to the government. But one of them will have to be chosen if public investment is to rise as planned.

Even the old save too much

This brings us back to basics. The ageing population will lead to an income transfer from young to old. The more money taken from young Japanese to support old Japanese, the less income the young will have available to save. The old save less than the young, so the generational change in the distribution of income should reduce the average rate of saving. Unfortunately, the saving rate does not differ substantially between old and young Japanese. In 1985–8 the average personal savings rate was 24%. Youngsters in their twenties saved 20% of their incomes. In most years they saved much more, but they dissaved in the year they got married. In their thirties, the Japanese saved 25% of their income, dropping to 24% in their forties and 23% in their fifties. Over sixty, the savings rate dropped to 18%. The high savings rate of people in their thirties was partly offset by their lower income. In 1990, people in their thirties had an average annual income of ¥5m, against ¥7m for people in their fifties. Those aged seventy and over had slightly higher average incomes than those in their thirties.

If savings behaviour and relative incomes remain unchanged, ageing will do little to reduce average savings. If no Japanese died or were born between now and 2010 (so that the population aged faster than it can possibly do) the average savings rate would drop by only 1% to 23%. If

Japanese savings are to fall, ageing alone won't cause it. Changes in behaviour could have a much bigger effect. Tomorrow's old will receive better pensions. Their saving rate could fall. On the above assumptions, if the over-sixties save only 10% of their income after they retire, another 5% points is knocked off the average savings rate. But these assumptions are unrealistic. They would mean that half the population would be over sixty by 2010. On more reasonable assumptions, the drop in savings would be only 2–3%.

Two further factors suggest that savings will not fall significantly. Labour shortages are already causing Japanese employers to recruit workers who are beyond their retirement age; mostly they are former employees. Meister 60 company, an Osaka engineering firm, employed fifty-one new workers in 1991, with an average age of sixty-two. The oldest new boy was seventy. As the retirement age rises, so Japanese will go on saving more for longer. The rise in life expectancy is also increasing the number of years people will spend in retirement. Those at work may try to save more for their longer old age. The 'greying' argument for lower Japanese savings has been overstated.

Even if the Japanese do save less, they may still continue to save too much. Investment needs will also fall as Japanese age. In the extreme case above, where nobody dies and nobody is born, there would be no need to increase the housing stock other than to improve it. Personal investment would fall. A smaller and older population needs fewer dwellings. A smaller labour force needs fewer new machines. The OECD has looked into this, observing that 'With a gross capital output ratio of 3.3 (average of the 1980s, including government capital) and a decline in labour force growth from 1% (average 1980s) to 0%, the equilibrium gross investment/GDP ratio would be reduced by 3.3% points.' This alone would take care of a significant fall in gross savings.

13

Little Boxes

The Japanese live in little boxes. Although they are no longer the size of rabbit hutches, they remain small by Western standards. There are 42 m dwellings in Japan, 10% more than the 38 m households; some are empty, but a significant proportion of Japanese have two or more homes. The average dwelling has a floor space of 108 sq yds, up from 90 sq yds in 1970. It has five rooms and is shared, on average, by 3.2 people. Each person has 33 sq yds of living space. The average size of British houses is almost the same. But in Britain only 2.5 people occupy each dwelling. Each British citizen has a third more space to live in than the average Japanese. Kitchens, bathrooms and entrance halls are not much smaller in Japan, so normal living space in Britain is significantly greater. In the US houses are much bigger; Americans enjoy more than twice the living space of the average Japanese.

Averages conceal as well as reveal: dwellings are inevitably small and expensive in major cities, where land is at a premium; they are larger and cheaper in dormitory towns within commuting distance; and even bigger and cheaper in remote country areas. The Japanese, more than most, face a trade-off between space and time. The 3 m who commute daily into central Tokyo have bigger homes than the 8 m who live in the city's twenty-three wards, an area bigger than Luxembourg. But they spend on average three hours a day getting to and from work. The lucky ones commute 125 miles or more by shinkansen, the famous Japanese bullet trains, in which they enjoy reserved seats and can sleep, read or socialise with their neighbours in comfort. But the cost of commuting such distances can top $1000 a month.

The shortage of living room in Japan is not because too many people are crowded into too little space. There is plenty of land in Japan. It is just badly used; 124 m Japanese occupy islands with an area of 145,000 square miles. Population density is 848 per square mile. Belgium's is about the same. Holland crowds in 100 more inhabitants per square mile. Singapore has twelve and Hong Kong fourteen times the number. Bangladesh, South Korea and Taiwan are all more densely populated than Japan. Unfortunately, much of the land in Japan is mountainous. It is possible to build and live in hilly country – look at San Francisco – but the Japanese are flat-earthers. Consequently, over two-thirds of the country's area remains woodland; half what is left is farmland; a quarter is used by industry, commerce, administration, roads and railways; while dwellings occupy just 4% of the available land.

More people live in Paris

The Japanese are gregarious: more than 60% live in areas where the population density exceeds 2000 per square mile; half live in the three biggest conurbations, centred on Tokyo, Osaka and Nagoya; one-third live within 100 miles of their Emperor's palace. A quarter live in the Tokyo metropolitan area, that is the twenty-three wards of the Tokyo prefecture together with the neighbouring prefectures of Saitama, Chiba and Kanagawa. Even so, Tokyo is less densely populated than Paris. There are three reasons for this: low-rise buildings; urban farmland; and corporate land hoarding.

Central Tokyo excepted, most of the city is a sprawl of single- and double-storey detached houses, most are flimsy and many are wooden. They are packed tightly together in ugly little alleyways, so narrow that a large American car would get wedged trying to turn corners. Full-sized trucks, coaches or fire engines never stray from the highways. Dust carts look like Dinky toys. On-street parking is impossible or illegal, and often both. Only mini cars with pretty yellow number plates are allowed to park on Tokyo streets. Larger, white-plated cars must be privately parked. Commercial vehicles have blue number plates, something to watch out for when hiring a cab at Narita International Airport: a white plated cab is a cowboy's. Before buying a new car, a Tokyo resident must show that he has somewhere, off-street, to park it.

Low-rise Tokyo is partly the legacy of the great Kanto earthquake, which destroyed much of the city in 1923. Before the big Kanto 'quake, serious earthquake activity was common in the region. There were devastating tremors two or three times in every decade. But since 1923 there have been no really big ones. This means tension has been building up for nearly seventy years. Top Japanese seismologists fear another giant tremor is coming shortly. But modern buildings can stand up to big earthquakes; the 1990 San Francisco earthquake did surprisingly little serious damage and caused relatively few casualties. The Japanese need not stick with their small, low and flimsy homes. The reason they do so has more to do with the Japanese taxation and other regulations. Nonetheless, instead of being spread out vertically, as Parisians are, the Japanese prefer to be cramped together horizontally. If the average height of buildings were increased to eight storeys, twice as many Japanese could live in apartments twice as large in half the space. There would be room for wider roads and more parks. Perhaps the opportunity could be taken to place neatly underground all the ugly telephone lines and power cables which festoon the streets.

The world's most expensive cabbage patch

Urban farms are the second reason the Japanese live so tightly packed together in their cities. The 8 m inhabitants of Tokyo's twenty-three wards account for two-thirds of metropolitan Tokyo's 12 m population and occupy only 60,000 acres of housing land. Yet some 89,000 acres are farmland, about 10% of metropolitan Tokyo's total area. More than half the cabbages eaten in Tokyo are grown in the city's Nerima ward, the most expensive cabbage patches in the world. The Ministry of Construction claims that, if all this urban farmland were used for housing, a further 3 m condominiums could be built. The third reason is corporate land hoarding: Japanese companies own five times as much land as they need. The National Land Agency reported in April 1990 that companies had no specific plans to use 78% of the land that they owned. The top 210 company landholders own 2000 square miles of land. In Tokyo, 56,000 acres are left empty by factory owners.

There is no shortage of dwellings in Japan. Housing starts totalled 1.8 million in 1990, a 4% increase in the stock of dwellings in a single year; 145,000 apartments were built in Tokyo, but only 90,000 were sold. It is not difficult to find somewhere to live at a reasonable rent. Young Japanese men and women are initially housed in company dormitories, often free of charge. These used to provide only rudimentary accommodation, but thanks to labour shortages, company dormitories are being rapidly upgraded. Swimming pools, saunas, exercise and games rooms are now frequently provided. After the dormitories come subsidised company apartments, which may be small but are usually cheap. My young Tokyo friend's two-room apartment rents for ¥90,000 ($650) per month, but his company pays 80% of the rent, leaving him paying only ¥4500 ($30) a week. It also subsidises his rail commuting and gives him ¥5000 ($35) lunch vouchers a month. A standard three-bedroom condominium with an area of 85 sq yds in a suburb twenty miles from the centre of Tokyo rents for around ¥150,000 ($1070) a month. The

Japanese can live all their lives in relatively cheap rented accommodation. Many baby-boomers, now in their forties, will be forced to do so. They don't want to and that is the problem. Everybody wants to own; nobody wants to rent; while nobody who already owns wants to sell. Consequently although rents are cheap, purchasing is prohibitively expensive.

There are many dramatic ways of illustrating the absurd price of Japanese property. The extreme example is the cost of land in Tokyo's high-class Ginza shopping and nightclub district, which in 1990 reached ¥50 m per sq yd. To buy the area covered by a one dollar bill placed on the ground in the Ginza, 10,000 more had to be piled on top of it. The price is astronomic, because opportunities to buy land in the Ginza are about as frequent as snowstorms in the Sahara. When a plot does come on to the market, the competition for it is intense. The Ginza as a whole could not be sold for so high a price. If it were all put on the market, the price would collapse. A more realistic measure of Tokyo prices is the average price of a 70 sq m condominium, which reached ¥70 m at the market's 1990 peak. Prices elsewhere are lower. Osaka prices are about 80% of Tokyo prices. Even so, at 1990 property prices Japan was worth four times more than the US, which is twenty-five times bigger, meaning that at the current yen–dollar exchange rate, Japanese property prices are 100 times US prices. Put another way, the property price purchasing power parity for the yen–dollar exchange rate is ¥13,000=$1. At ¥130=$1, the current exchange rate, the land occupied by the Emperor's palace in Tokyo is worth more than the whole of California.

Idiotic economics of land ownership

Well might the mind boggle. The Japanese must be crazy about owning property. To buy a ¥70 m condominium with a 100% mortgage at 7% interest would cost at least ¥5 m a year, but the same condominium rents out at only ¥1.8 m. Better still, under a 1921 Law, the rent cannot be raised by more than 10% in any two-year period, and Japanese tenants have lifetime security of tenure. The same absurdity applies to the low-yielding Japanese stockmarket. Anyone in his right mind should have sold real estate and shares in 1990 and invested the proceeds in government bonds, safely yielding 7–8%.

The Japanese are not out of their minds; land is not held for income, but for capital gains. Over the thirty-five years from 1955 to 1990, residential land prices in the six largest Japanese cities rose two-hundred-fold. During the same period wages rose twenty-one times and consumer prices merely fivefold. The conclusion that the Japanese have drawn is that you become rich by what you own, not from what you earn. Japanese owners became more rapidly rich in the late 1980s than at any other time since the war. The pace of house price inflation varied from one area to another. Prices first rose sharply in Tokyo, doubling between 1986 and 1988 and then rising less rapidly in 1989 and early 1990, by about another one-fifth. Prices in the Osaka area were up less than 50% in 1986–8, then increased to three times their 1986 level by 1990. Nagoya area prices rose only 80% in 1986–90 and the average for other areas was up little more than 30%.

$2 m to play golf

Anyone owning property in the late 1980s made a killing. Speculation was not confined to development land and housing. Golf club members collectively own their golf courses. Club memberships are bought and sold; in 1988 the going rate for a single membership at the Koganei Country Club, the country's most expensive, reached ¥280 m ($2 m). Membership of more ordinary clubs cost $250,000–500,000. Between 1982 and 1985 the Nikkei index for the cost of club membership in the Kanto area doubled; between 1985 and 1987 it tripled; the index, based on January 1982=100, peaked in March 1990 at 948, following a last-gasp spurt in which it rose 50% in eight months. But there it stopped. The stockmarket began to crash in February 1990 and the price of golf club memberships followed two months later. By June 1991 the index was down by 300 points, a loss of a third of its peak value.

Wealth, illegally gained and inequitably shared

Gains from asset price inflation are inequitably shared. In a country where official statistics on almost everything abound, none is collected and published showing the distribution of wealth. This information is too dangerous for the government to reveal. At a guess, one-third of Japanese now own almost all the country's physical assets. The remaining two-thirds rely mainly on what they earn for their living. Statistics on home ownership are available but misleading. Some 60% of homes in Japan are occupied by their owners, while 40% are let to tenants. But this does not mean that 60% of Japanese own their own homes. Grown-up children, living with their parents, do not; although they may expect to inherit them. But then they will face hefty death duties, which they may not be able to afford. In many households, the property has to be sold to pay estate duties. There are 90 m adult

Japanese and 38 m households in Japan owning 42 m dwellings. Given 60% owner occupation, there is a maximum of 22 m home-owners. Assuming all home-owners were married couples, 46 m Japanese, just over half of all adults, would not own their homes. This is the minimum estimate. The true figure must be significantly higher. Even amongst the lucky home-owners, the majority cannot realise their property wealth as they must live somewhere. They cannot sell and rent without facing extortionate capital gains taxes. The best they can do is to move from cramped, high-priced city-centre plots to larger homes in the suburbs. A significant number have done so, causing the population of Tokyo's twenty-three wards to fall slightly in recent years.

The 100-year mortgage

The 1980s property price boom made Japan a nation of 'haves' and 'have-nots'. The 'have-nots' have little chance of ever becoming 'haves' no matter how hard they work and save. The average Tokyo house costs 10 times the average Tokyo salary. US and German homes cost about 4.5 times average earnings, British about 4 times (although these ratios vary considerably from year to year). To buy a home, young Japanese must first save a large proportion of its purchase price. They could then take out a 100-year mortgage for the balance of the purchase price, leaving their grandchildren to pay it off. Many Japanese do save hard out of their earnings. But while they are doing so, house prices rise. The *Far East Economic Review* (Sept. 1990) reported the case of a young Japanese journalist, who, in 1985, had been close to buying a 100 sq. m flat in southern Tokyo for ¥35 m, but decided not to do so; two years later its price had risen to ¥100 m and he no longer could do so. By 1992 the price had fallen to perhaps ¥70 m, but this was probably still beyond his reach.

HUDC the only hope

There is one way some dreams can come true. The government's Housing & Urban Development Corporation builds 25,000 dwellings a year and sells them at cut prices. It determines who gets them by running lotteries. The *Financial Times* reported that in June 1990, 4517 people applied to buy a single three-bedroom apartment on offer at ¥45.4 m ($325,000). The lucky winner, had he been allowed to, could have sold the next day at a 50% profit. Instead he must wait five years before selling. Even so, he won a small fortune. HUDC has a club for twenty-time lottery losers who get priority on certain vacant apartments.

The 'haves' are the lucky ones, who inherited a paddy field or bought their homes years ago. The fewer parents of the baby-boom generation are mostly sitting pretty. Many of their more numerous sons and daughters, now in the forties, are still struggling to get on to the first rung of the home-ownership ladder. When the Tokyo house boom reached its peak in early 1990, a survey showed that up to 85% of tenants had given up hope of ever owning a home. This helps to explain the fall in the personal savings rate in the late 1980s and the consumer boom which caused the economy to overheat. But it does not mean that savings have been permanently lowered.

Why are property prices so high?

Despite their decline during 1990–1, house prices in Japan remain much higher relative to income than in other advanced countries. The persistence of small and low detached houses is partly due to planning laws and building regulations, set under the Constitution by local authorities. The government can do little to change them, but can only advise and exhort. The rules local governments impose are of their own choosing. These often prevent tall buildings from being erected; in many areas, for example, there is a 10 m height limit, which restricts buildings to four storeys. The government wants this increased to 12 m, but it cannot force local authorities to comply. Wooden houses are not allowed to exceed two storeys, and wood is still regarded as a desirable building material because it withstands earthquakes rather well; unfortunately it also burns. Strict fire-proofing regulations are applied.

Local authorities impose plot ratios. These limit the area of floor space in a building to a given multiple of the area of the building plot. If the ratio is two, for example, a four-storey building can be constructed, but only if its base occupies half the site area. It is cheaper to build high than to build wide. Roofs are expensive. But most sites are extremely small, perhaps as little as 40 sq yds. All of a very small site must be used for the ground floor – which means that the building can be only two storeys high. The staircase would take up most of the room in a taller building on a smaller base. The smaller the building plot, the lower the building.

Large rewards for leaving land idle

The government can do something about the tax system, which discourages the sale of development sites. The owner may rebuild his own house and the Japanese do so about once every generation, but few families sell their small homes. It is difficult to acquire adjacent vacant sites in order to amass a larger building plot. Capital gains tax is punitive. The rise in house prices has been so rapid that many Japanese live in houses which they could no longer afford to buy. If they sell, the tax bill would break them. Death duty favours property versus cash or stock and shares. Duty is levied on the basis of property tax valuations, which can be as low as half the market value of real estate. Old people hang on to their homes to leave them to their children.

It is no easier putting rented property together into large development sites. Lots of little shops and businesses stand on small urban plots. Landlords may be willing to sell to developers. But their tenants legally cannot be forced to quit. They have to be bought out or forced out. Both methods are employed. During the boom, many respectable landlords cashed in on the high prices which jiageya, property sharks, were willing to pay. The jiageya first offered fat bribes to tenants to move out, then sent in the heavies. Yakuza gangsters obtained further profitable employment for their persuasive skills. Arson was not unusual. Even so, the process of collecting together large development sites is an expensive, protracted and generally an unpopular one. Old folks don't like to change their way of life. It's often easier to wait for them to die.

Many local authorities, representing people already living there, do not want the nature of their communities to be changed. Tough zoning laws are applied. An effort has been made to preserve green belts around cities. The individual's right to light, so many hours of sunshine a day at street level, and to his view of Mount Fuji must be respected. Many buildings in the suburbs of Tokyo have their tops shaped like right-angled triangles, so that the sunlight can reach the lower floors of buildings on the other side of the street. Developments require the provision of public services, which add to local governments' costs. So while everybody favours large development projects, nobody wants them in their own back yard.

Sweet potatoes

The government can sometimes have as much trouble getting hold of land as the private property developer. Tokyo's Narita International Airport is grossly congested. It has only one runway. The authorities hope to complete a second runway in 1992, eighteen years behind schedule. But to do so, it still needs to buy eight farms, occupying 21 ha of land, which is used to grow sweet potatoes and carrots. The owners have refused to sell for the past twenty years as they don't want to move. They are supported by violent left-wing radicals, who opposed the airport's original construction and still sometimes launch rocket attacks on it. The airport is consequently surrounded by barbed wire fences, moats and concrete stockades. It is guarded by 1500 riot police, who inspect every one of the 55,000 people who enter the airport each day. In theory, the government could be given the right by the local prefectural council to seize the land. But when it seemed it might do so, its chairman was beaten up with steel pipes and the council changed its mind.

Companies hoard land

Corporate land hoarding is partly speculative. It also reflects the steep taxes imposed on profits from land sales. Land can be valued at cost on Japanese companies' books. Regular revaluations, which Shoup proposed when setting up the Japanese tax system after the Second World War, were abandoned. Unrealised capital gains from increased prices do not therefore appear in profits and remain untaxed. Real estate companies that sell land within two years of purchase face a punitive 95% composite corporation tax rate on their profits. Land held for five to ten years before sale attracts 42% corporation tax on profits, plus a 20% premium and local taxes which bring up the total to 80%.

Urban farmers receive exceptional tax treatment. Local taxes are imposed annually at 1.4% on the value of residential property and farmland. The value of residential property for tax purposes is reviewed every three years. But the assessed value for tax purposes is kept artificially low and averages only some 35–50% of current market values. Even so, the rise in property prices has significantly increased the holding cost of residential property. Farmland, however, is valued at its original purchase price, which is only a fraction of its market worth. Holding costs of urban paddy fields are negligible. Property taxes on farmland work out at only about one-thirtieth to one-seventieth of residential property taxes. A typical 2000 sq yd 'farm' in central Tokyo, with a market value in 1988 of ¥790 m ($5.6 m), incurred only ¥22,300 ($160) in property tax, or 0.003% of its capital value. Moreover, farmland can be passed tax free at death to any heir who promises to continue to farm it for the next twenty years. If, during that time, the land ceases to be farmed, the original death duties plus interest must be paid. Since capital gains tax on the sale of such land is extortionate, nobody sells. Rural farmland could also be used to increase living space.

Feeble reforms

What action is being taken to deal with the property price problem? Not a lot, and most of it is misguided. Since August 1987 the prices of all property transactions involving sites over a specified size have had to be registered with the local authorities. They have the power to prohibit transactions in which the proposed sale prices are considered to be exorbitant. The limit was originally 500 sq. m, but was dropped to 100 sq m. Needless to say, larger plots were broken up and sold piecemeal to the same buyer. Some were caught doing this, but not many. Capital gains tax on sales within three months was pushed up to 96% in 1987 and in March 1988 the capital gains tax break on money ploughed back into property was withdrawn on land resold within two years of purchase. This was designed to stop speculative property churning, but the main effect was to reduce the number of land transactions thereby cutting the amount of development space coming on to the market, which pushed prices higher.

A feeble start has also been made to reform property taxes. A new Land Tax law was passed in April 1991 designed to increase the cost of holding land. An annual 0.3% tax was imposed on the value of all land owned by individuals and companies from 1 January 1992. It sounded tough, but it was not. The tax is payable only on the value of land in excess of ¥1.5 bn ($12 m) and a maximum valuation of $230 per sq. m is set for moderate-sized plots. Farmland in urban areas was exempted until 1997. Such timidity will solve nothing.

Falling prices can cause a financial crisis

Lowering property prices to reasonable levels by increasing the supply of development land presents the Japanese government with an impossible dilemma. To use market forces to lower prices, as it has been doing, will succeed only if it causes a financial crisis, widespread bankruptcies and an economic depression. Whatever the Governor of the Bank of Japan may want, the government will not allow this to happen. Japanese interest rates started to come down again in July 1991. The rising balance of payments surplus, combined with fears of trade protection, will force Japan to move back towards monetary expansion before the job of deflating property prices is half complete. Effective tax reform must include lower capital gains taxes on land and property sales. But these will be seen as rewarding landowners and property speculators at the expense of other tax payers, which is a foolish view. Landowners will lose far more from lower prices than they could possibly gain from lower taxes.

Japan's housing problem can be solved only by measures which substantially reduce land prices. This means a transfer of wealth back from owners to earners. There is no way in which a political consensus can be reached to produce this result as the losers will never agree. If any such measures were forced through the Diet without consensus support, there would be a political crisis of even greater severity than that which followed the introduction of the sales tax in 1988. Either the 'haves' or the 'have nots' must be alienated. The former if something is done to solve the problem; the latter if nothing. The question is merely which is it to be?

14

All for a Bowl of Rice

Urban farms in Japan reduce the land available for building and contribute to high house prices. City dwellers could enjoy a little more living space at more reasonable prices if urban farmland were developed. What about rural farmland? If the population were more evenly spread throughout the countryside, house prices would tumble and the Japanese could enjoy as spacious a way of living as most Europeans. Strict land-use regulations, locally applied, together with all the usual tax problems, inhibit the development of new towns in rural areas. As a result, too much land in Japan is inefficiently farmed by too many people. Japan's 3 m farmers live off 20,000 sq. miles, 14.4% of Japan's area, and nearly four times as much land as the remaining 121 m Japanese live on. Farm workers' productivity is one-tenth of manufacturing workers, but farming household incomes are 30% higher than the urban average. The 121 m Japanese pay through the nose, in taxation and exorbitant food prices, to give 3 m farmers high enough incomes to stay on the land. That, in a nutshell, is why the Japanese live cheek by jowl in the world's most expensive little boxes. The economy is grotesquely distorted.

The problem can be traced back to the Americans, who imposed far-reaching land reforms to break up the concentration of wealth and power in Japan. Land was confiscated from thousands of landlords and sold cheaply to millions of their former tenants. A country of serfs became a country of peasant farmers. More than half the population acquired a stake in farming and land ownership. In 1947 there were 6 m farm households; 18 m people, over half the labour force, worked in agriculture; less than one million were employees. The rest were landowners and their families. To prevent the re-emergence of large landlords, laws were passed restricting land transfers, controlling rents and making it almost impossible to evict tenants. These laws still inhibit the development of urban and rural land.

In 1947 the Americans also established a government-sponsored co-operative, the Nokyo, to look after farmers' interests. When the nation faced starvation following the war, it became the government's agent for buying and selling food. It has grown into one of Japan's largest bureaucracies and, by all accounts, one of its least efficient.

Naughty Nokyo

Nokyo has its fingers in many pies, agricultural, commercial, financial and political. At its top are national federations; at its base are 4200 local co-ops, divided into forty-eight regional federations. The system as a whole employs 380,000, one bureaucrat for every ten farm workers and four for every five full-time farmers. Nokyo has a trading arm, Zen-Noh, which has a near monopoly of fertiliser, seed and cattle-feed sales to farmers. It also sells cars, electronic goods and other consumer products. Zen-Noh markets mostly farm products, collecting 90% of the rice produced in Japan for sale to the government. Nokyo also handles insurance through its Zenkyoren organisation and is allowed to sell life and non-life policies, something that ordinary insurers are forbidden to do. It operates the country's sixth largest bank, the Norinchukin Bank, which acts as central banker to the Nokyo savings and loans system; the network as a whole has more deposits than Japan's largest commercial bank. Both financial arms enjoy the advantage that, as government-sponsored co-operatives, they pay no tax.

Nokyo's political and lobbying arm, Zenchu, in its heyday could control the destiny of two-thirds of LDP Diet members. It supplies cash and delivers votes to local politicians, or withholds them. It can make or break individual Diet members, and even the government if it chooses. The LDP defeat in the 1989 upper house election was partly engineered by Zenchu to punish the party for liberalising beef and citrus imports. According to a survey by *Mainichi*, a national newspaper, thirty-one farmers' organisations in seventeen prefectures withdrew their support from the LDP. That was fatal.

The post-war peasant farmer sold his soul to the Nikyo company store, which lends him money, looks after his savings, provides his insurance, sells him seed, markets his products, even keeps his accounts and, in every way it can, rips him off. In 1987 rice farmers were forced to accept their first price-cut in thirty-one years. The government argued that the strong yen had lowered imported feed and fertiliser costs. It had. But Nokyo had not passed on the savings to farmers. Nokyo has a life of its own, which spreads far beyond farming, with nearly 9 m members and associate members. In south Yokohama, for example, the local farm co-operative has 4500 farmer members, but 8087 associate members most of whom have never handled a rice plant or dug a hole in a field in their lives. As the number of farmer members has declined, the number of associate members has risen. But associate members cannot vote – control remains in the hands of the farmers. In return for all Nokyo does for them and nicks from them, farmers have its total dedication to the protection of their privileges.

Nokyo has been a bastion of conservatism, resisting change of any kind. Its 380,000 employees are a special-interest group in their own right. To protect their role they prefer to see Japan remain a land of small and inefficient peasant farmers. Were farming to become large-scale and efficient, Nokyo would lose members. Its commercial and financial leverage over those who remained in the business would be weakened. But even Nokyo cannot resist change for ever and is now having to rethink its own future. But it remains one of the most powerful political lobbies in Japan.

Mass migration

While Japan's industrial economy was reconstructed, there was continuous migration from the countryside to the towns. As each year's crop of pupils graduated from school and college, they departed *en masse* by the trainload to find their fortunes in the cities. The farming population collapsed. Its precise size today is uncertain; it depends on how one defines anyone with an interest in farming or in agriculture. The OECD put the total of those principally employed in agriculture, forestry and fishing in 1988 at 6,611,000, or at 10.4% of the Japanese labour force. But these numbers include related activities, such as the provision of seed and fertilisers, marketing of products and support services. The number of farm workers is around 3 m, or 5% of the labour force, but only 470,000 work full time. The remaining 2.5 m are part-time, mostly weekend farmers, who draw most of their income from other employment. Rice farming still predominates; there are 2.2 m households growing rice, mostly in small amounts and combined with other activities; there are 286,000 full-time rice farmers, who account for less than 1% of the labour force and less than 0.4% of the population. At the same time, however, many who left the countryside retained farming family connections and often an interest in the ownership of land. It is estimated that 20 m Japanese, many elderly, still receive some income from the land.

Most of Japanese farming is highly inefficient. The average farm is tiny: five-sixths of the country's commercial farmers till three-acre plots. (By contrast, the average British farm is 74 acres; the average American farm 340 acres.) Such minute farms are too small for mechanisation; they are labour intensive, with the result that labour productivity is low. Most full-time farmers are old, half being over sixty; even the part-timers are ageing. Less than 3% of farm families' children want to stay at home after finishing their schooling. Men who stay to help out their parents face a lonely life. Few girls remain and their prospects of marriage are slim, unless they buy and import Filipino brides.

Lopsided growth

The Japanese economy is lopsided. The one-in-ten Japanese who work in agriculture, forestry and fishing produce only one-fortieth of the country's GDP. The agricultural worker's average productivity is one-fifth of a manufacturing worker. But the Japanese is forced to pay double what he should for his food. If allowance is made for this, agricultural productivity drops to one-tenth of manufacturing productivity. When overall GDP per head is compared internationally, it takes 137 Japanese workers to produce the same output as 100 Americans; Germany requires 140 workers; and Britain 144. The US is still by far the most efficient and productive economy. Japanese workers are not much more productive than German or British.

The illusion of Japanese economic might stems from comparisons which concentrate on industry. Japan's manufacturing productivity is about 30% higher than Germany's and 35% higher than Britain's. Japanese agricultural productivity is abysmal; German productivity is almost as bad as it also has many small farms and part-time workers; by contrast, British and American farm productivity is far higher. The image of efficiency, which Japan presents as its cars and consumer electronics flood world markets, obscures the reality of a desperately inefficient nation in almost all the things it supplies its own people at home.

Subsidising the rich

Farmers everywhere are subsidised and protected; the Japanese more than most. There are government subsidies from taxation, which directly boost farming incomes. Sometimes these depend on how much the farmer produces; sometimes on how much he does not produce by leaving land idle. The consumer subsidises the farmer through needlessly high food prices, resulting from import controls, protective tariffs and direct price controls. Since the wartime 1942 Staple Food Control

Act, Japan's farmers have been forced to sell most of their rice to the government, which then sells it to licensed rice shopkeepers. When farm incomes lagged behind rising urban incomes in the 1950s, the government fixed both producer and consumer rice prices at inflated levels. Starting in 1956, the producer price (i.e., the amount paid to farmers) was raised every year so that, by 1986, it was ten times the world price. Consumer prices were increased accordingly. The government itself made no profit, but found itself landed buying more rice than it was able to sell. So in 1969, it imposed mandatory cuts in the area of land used to grow rice – but to no avail. The demand for rice fell faster than the supply. Today, half the taxpayers' bill for subsidising farm incomes is for the purchase and storage of unwanted rice. Japan's rice mountain stands at 1.5 m tons. Annual consumption is 10 m tons.

In 1990, the Japanese farmer's income from subsidies was more than double the value of the food he produced. For every ¥100 he was paid, ¥68 came from subsidies; ¥50 came from the artificially high prices consumers paid in the shops and ¥18 from the taxpayer's pocket. In 1988 the Japanese consumers paid $73 bn more for their food than they need have done. As taxpayers they shelled out a further $17 bn in farming subsidies. The total bill was $90 bn, or 3.2% of Japan's GDP – a mighty generous subsidy for a mere 3 m households to be given. But Japan's generosity to its farmers is not unique. The European Community also feather-beds its farmers, through the Common Agricultural Policy. The European subsidies, accounting for half of farmers' incomes, costs $121 bn or 2.6% of GDP. American subsidies provide a third of farm incomes at a cost of $76 bn or 1.6% of GDP. Nobody is blameless when it comes to buying farmers' voters.

The high cost of food is a feature of Japanese family budgets. They spend on average 30% of their disposable income on food. The average European spends only 20% and Americans spend 17%. In Tokyo the cost of beef is three times as much as in New York and twice what it is in London. A single melon in a department store can cost more than a whole truckload in Australia. Rice is sold, ironically, at six times world prices in Japan. But the greatest cost to the Japanese from their overly protective farm policy lies in the unnecessarily high price of housing. The ultimate absurdity is that for many years the Japanese government has been paying rice farmers to take land out of production. Almost a third of rice paddies now lie fallow. This is equivalent in area to half the land used for dwellings. But it is not being used for building. Instead of selecting whole areas and switching them from rice production to new towns, the government paid every farmer to use less land growing rice. In consequence, four-out-of-five Japanese rice farms have idle rice paddies. This reduced the size of small farms and increased their ineffi-ciency, without in any way easing the shortage of building land. Paying all farmers a little to produce less rice was politically more acceptable than paying a few ex-farmers a lot to produce no rice.

The political power of the agricultural lobby explains why the govern-ment has failed to introduce long-overdue land and agricultural re-forms. It has been under pressure for years to do so, not only from foreigners who want to see the Japanese market opened, but also from industry and urban voters. There has been some progress.

Opening the doors

American cattle and citrus farmers have long demanded that their government force Japan into opening its markets for imports of these products. In 1978 the US government tried, but without much success. A decade later it had better luck. The Prime Minister, Noboru Takeshita, was pressured into agreeing in June 1988 to lift import restrictions on beef, oranges and a number of other foods. The concession was not as great as it seemed: the end of restrictions was delayed until April 1991; and when quota controls were lifted, punitive tariffs were imposed. The duty on imported beef was increased from 25% to 70% in fiscal 1991, which will drop to 50% in fiscal 1993 and thereafter. The tariff on imported oranges remained at 20–40%. The government gave ground on these items because relatively few Japanese farmers were affected. Only one-in-ten farmers raise livestock or grow citrus fruit. Moreover, Japanese kobe beef is markedly different from American beef. It is marbled with fat, whereas American beef is lean with fat round the edges. Japanese beef is exceedingly tender, particularly when sliced very thin and quickly fried (sukiyaki) or boiled (shabu-shabu) in the tra-ditional manner. American beef is coarse and tough, better for barbecues and burgers. The Japanese are willing to pay more for their own beef. Moreover, Japan's farmers were given three years in which to prepare for the American invasion; they did so. Much of Japanese beef comes from the southern parts of Kyushu and Hokkaido, Japan's northern island, where farms are bigger. Herd sizes are being increased. The little pro-ducer, with an average herd of 9.7 head of cattle, is going out of business, but his place is being taken by bigger and more efficient farms.

Despite its protective agricultural policies, Japan is the world's largest food importer. In calorific terms, it grows less than half its own food and imports the remainder. Its self-sufficiency rate in cereals, including fod-der, is only 30%. Nonetheless, it is committed to self-sufficiency in rice, its staple food. The reasons are strategic, emotional, political and ironic.

The irony is that pre-war Japan was a large rice importer. But after the war, when it lost its Korean and Chinese empire, it was cut off from its traditional foreign supplies. The importance of self-sufficiency was rubbed in during the days of near starvation in the late 1940s. Nonetheless the ban on rice imports is of fairly recent origin; it was imposed in 1969 as an adjunct to measures to reduce over-production at home. Japan's emotional commitment to rice production goes back far further: rice has been grown in Japan for 2000 years. The requirements of rice farming, notably co-operation and groupism, permeate Japanese society. Even the housewife has, until recently, favoured paying high rice prices rather than see foreign rice freely imported. Politically, the power of the farm lobby and vote has prevented any politician from advocating reform. The farming backlash in the 1989 upper house election was so fierce and so damaging that not a single candidate supported rice import liberalisation during the 1990 lower house election campaign. Ministers insisted that Japan's traditional closed-door policy would remain sacrosanct, and all agreed that 'not a single grain' should be allowed in. The farmers' vote was recaptured and the LDP fared better than had been feared.

But the problem would not go away. When efforts to reduce surplus production by mandatory cuts in rice acreage failed, a new tactic was tried. In 1987, for the first time, the producer prices paid by the government were cut, going down by 5.9%. This was followed by a 4.6% cut the next year. Prices were frozen in 1989, because of the upper house election, but they were cut again in both 1990 and 1991. Rice producer prices have thus fallen from ten times world price levels to six times. Inefficient small farms producing less popular varieties of rice are being squeezed out and farmers are now being encouraged to amalgamate land holdings to produce larger and more efficient farms. The aim is to cut production costs by 40–60% by 1995 – not an impossible target. Part-time farmers are ageing and retiring, leaving the land in their droves. So average farm size could increase dramatically, allowing the use of modern mechanisation. The Californian rice farmer spends only two days a year working each acre of his paddies. Japan still does not intend to import rice if it can help it. It plans to exploit the demographic decline in the farm population to produce cheap rice instead, even though this will do nothing to alleviate the shortage of land.

External pressure for change has intensified. Agriculture is the key issue in the Uruguay GATT round. The Japanese powerful employers' organisation has come out strongly in favour of rice import liberalisation. Opinion polls now favour it by a majority of two-to-one. Politicians are promising to allow imports of up to 5% of consumption, provided Europe and America make concessions on agricultural trade as well. The Japanese negotiating posture seems smart. It will be almost as hard for the US and European Community to reduce the protection they give their farmers. With luck the Uruguay round will fail because of the intransigent European attitude towards the EC's Common Agricultural Policy. Even so, retaliation against Japanese industrial exports would follow. The pressure for rice liberalisation will not continue.

15

Return of the Black Ships

The original black ships were Commodore Perry's, who arrived in Edo in 1853 to prise Japan open to international trade. The return of the black ships refers to the Structural Impediments Initiative talks, forced on Japan by the Americans in 1989. These resulted from clause super 301 in the 1988 Omnibus Trade Act, under which the President can impose unilateral trade sanctions on countries which unfairly persist in running large bilateral trade surpluses with the US. In May 1989, Japan was branded a prime offender, along with India and Brazil. The Bush Administration favoured free trade, so it initiated the SII talks as a last-ditch attempt to prevent Congress from launching a trade war. President Bush would prefer Japan to become a reformed character; it is more likely to remain a recidivist. Congress takes this for granted, but was bought off for a time by the talks.

Japan reacted angrily to being branded; it did not like being bracketed with Third World countries. But at least the US Administration did not issue a general condemnation of the country; it concentrated instead on certain specific unfair trading policies. What President Bush really wanted was wide-ranging talks on all matters which affected bilateral trade and at the Paris summit in July 1989, the Prime Minister, Sousuke Uno, unwillingly capitulated to this demand – his only important act in a brief and inglorious premiership. Talks between trade officials from both countries began in September 1989.

By agreeing to such talks, Japan allowed the US to meddle in what are strictly its domestic concerns and condoned America's move towards managed trade. (The process was carried a step further in January 1992 when President Bush visited Japan, accompanied by a team of top US industrialists. They openly wanted to bully the Japanese into 'voluntarily' importing more US products, such as cars and car parts.) Yet the domestic reforms which the US demanded were mostly in Japan's best interests. They bore a striking resemblance to recommendations contained in the two Maekawa reports and many Japanese favoured them. The US took up cudgels on behalf of the public interest against narrow producer interests; were the 'Occupation' re-sumed, America would build a new and better Japan. Where SCAP sculptured a miraculous economy, today the Americans would design a Dallas paradise. Unfortunately, this requires that a not insignificant minority lose the concentration of wealth, power and privilege they have so painfully and dishonestly regained since the Second World War.

The SII talks

The SII talks started in September 1989, and by June 1990 the negotiators reached an initial agreement which was hailed as a great success; it wasn't, but it was the best that the Americans could get. Claiming great success was a way of humouring Congress. In the follow-ing year officials monitored progress: they said that things were going more or less according to plan, although Japan continued reforming at its usual snail's pace. But the deal coincided with a cyclical decline in Japan's global trade surplus; progress could be claimed for reducing payments imbalance, although awkwardly the bilateral imbalance between the two countries remained substantial. Unfortunately, with America's feeble recovery in 1991 and a slow-down in Japan, the Japanese current account surplus is rapidly rising. It could exceed $100 bn in 1992 and Congress is considering putting teeth into clause super 301 to force the President to retaliate.

Most of the areas in which the Americans are demanding greater progress, such as financial liberalisation and land reform, have already been discussed. The main subjects remaining to complete the picture are Japan's retail distribution system, its keiretsu system of cross-sharehold-ings and its construction industry.

Family-owned shops

Japan's retail distribution system makes it difficult for new producers to break into markets, whoever they are. Like farming and banking, the system is regulated to provide generous profit margins, so that the smal-lest and least efficient shop can survive. Existing retailers are protected from competition from new entrants in order that high profit margins can be preserved. In 1988 there were 1.6 m retail shops in Japan (875,000 with fewer than three employees), compared with 1.5 m in America, which has twice the population. These shops were served by 430,000 wholesalers, again more than in the US. More than half of Japanese retail stores are little family-owned shops, housed in small wooden buildings with limited shelfspace and living accommodation behind. They are mostly specialist shops, selling a limited range of related products. There are a few chain stores and supermarkets, selling a wide range of products, and big high-class city department stores.

Goods leaving the manufacturer pass through three layers of wholesalers before reaching the retailer, each taking a generous cut. Wholesale turnover is four times the value of retail turnover in Japan, compared with twice in Britain and America. Most wholesalers are owned or controlled by manufacturers, as are many of the shops – Matsushita, producing electrical goods, owns 27,000 stores; Toshiba owns 14,000. Most wholesalers and many retailers deal only in goods produced by a single manufacturer. The supplier fixes the final retail price and the margins the wholesaler and retailer receive. The final price is often bogus; the shopkeeper is expected to give the customer a discount, while still collecting a 20–25% cut on the sale. The real price is the one the customer pays; the price printed on the box is merely to mislead. All margins are kept secret. Favoured wholesalers and retailers get bigger margins. They still charge the customer the same price, but push these goods harder. Suppliers give generous trade credits, usually ninety days or more and most stock is supplied on a sale-or-return basis. Clearance sales are virtually unknown in Japan. Prices of goods sold at home can be 50% higher than the identical Japanese products on sale in New York; it is not only imported goods which suffer high mark-ups in Japanese shops.

The Japanese system is highly fragmented: in its extreme form, this would mean every single producer had his own distribution system carrying only his own goods. In the British and American systems, goods from different producers pass through the hands of general wholesalers and retailers market a range of rival products to give consumers a wide choice. The American and British systems are easier for importers and new producers to penetrate. To sell goods in Japan, one must either persuade a Japanese company to distribute them, or set up a whole distribution system of one's own. Companies which try the former find that their goods are the poor relations and are rarely promoted. Schick, the safety razor producer, is an exception: Hattori Seiko, the watch and calculator manufacturer, distributes its goods and it has secured a 70% share of the Japanese market. Coca-Cola went the other way and built its own distribution system and grabbed 60% of the soft drinks market. BMW's sales jumped when it dropped its local agent and set up its own dealers. But the cost of setting up a distribution system is astronomic and only the largest foreign companies can afford to do so.

Why has Japan retained so many small shops? Shortage of space is again part of the answer. The Japanese tend to shop locally and daily, at friendly family-owned stores, because stocking-up once a week at a supermarket would mean storing large quantities of food. They don't have room at home for that – an American-sized fridge and a deep freezer would occupy the whole kitchen! Equally, big delivery vans cannot penetrate the narrow alleyways of residential suburbs and where would one get the space for the large car parks which supermarkets require? What would be the cost?

These considerations have inhibited the development of American-style supermarkets and shopping malls. But another major constraint has been the Large Scale Retail Store Law, passed in 1956. It says that MITI must be informed of plans to open stores with a floor space of more than 500 sq m (1500 sq m in the eleven largest cities). Applications must then go before the local chamber of commerce and all existing retailers in the neighbourhood must be informed and consulted. The chambers of commerce cannot legally veto a planned store; but they can kick up such a fuss over details that negotiations to get their approval could be strung out for up to ten years. During this time, the hopeful new shop owner would doubtless have shown his civic pride by contributing to some worthy neighbourhood cause.

Under American pressure, the Japanese agreed to reduce the delay on approval for store opening to twelve months and to consult the consumer interest in their decisions. Existing stores have been given an immediate go-ahead to extend their floor space by up to 100 sq m if the new space is dedicated to selling imports. The Large Scale Retail Store Law is being reviewed and could be abolished. This won't do much for imports; the shortage and high price of land continues to inhibit supermarket development. The most rapid expansion is likely to be in food stores, where US products have already penetrated the Japanese market or are barred from it. Specialist shops will remain small. Nothing is being done to change manufacturers' pricing and discounting methods; but at least these are under attack from within. In textiles, some Japanese firms have cut out the middlemen to sell cut-price goods in 'roadside' stores in city suburbs (stores deliberately just below the Large Scale Retail Store Law size). They have grabbed a 10% share of the market. Cowboy operators are appearing in the electronics sector, getting discounted goods illicitly from official wholesalers struggling to meet excessively ambitious sales targets.

The retail system is another source of grass-roots support for the LDP. Small shops are concentrated in urban areas, where votes are most needed. The Japanese consumer shows few signs of protesting against being ripped off. He was taken to the cleaners during the period of endaka, when the yen soared and oil prices collapsed. *The Economist* calculated that between October 1985 and January 1988 these developments should have lopped ¥29 trn off prices in Japanese shops, but distributors and retailers grabbed ¥18 trn for themselves. Until the consumer starts complaining, the LDP will continue to step warily in reforming distribution, but when it does act, the main beneficiary will be the Japanese. The more efficiency in distribution and service industry increases, the easier it will be for manufacturers to hold down wages and costs. Better shops will help everyone, not just importers.

Kill the keiretsu

The Americans also object to Japan's corporate structure; they say Japanese companies conspire with each other, rather than compete. They are grouped together in families of firms, known as keiretsu, with large cross-shareholdings in each other. Members of the same keiretsu families buy from and sell to each other, even when cheaper products are available from other sources, which locks out competition from other Japanese companies as well as from foreigners. US companies do not belong to Japanese keiretsu families and they are left out in the cold, which inhibits imports and prevents foreign firms setting up in Japan. The Japanese, on the other hand, found it easy to set up car plants in America.

The keiretsu is not one system but several. One branch can be traced back to the zaibatsu which dominated and controlled Japanese industry until 1945. After the Second World War, the Americans dismantled the old zaibatsu. But as soon as they were gone, the Japanese put them back together again. Mitsui, Mitsubishi and Sumitomo are trading groups, which contain their own banks. Fuji, Sanwa and Dai-Ichi Kangyo are banking empires which include trading and manufacturing companies. Bank-centred keiretsu are horizontal conglomerates, with member companies in a range of different but complimentary types of business. The trading company-led keiretsu, sogso shosha, which also include C.Itoh and Marubeni, are more vertically integrated. Traditionally, the sogso shosha was the marketing and purchasing arm for its members, monopolising much of Japan's international trade. To this activity was added the provision of trade finance. The bank-based keiretsu sprang from the post-war shortage of capital in Japanese industry. New families have been added to these older families. Hitachi, a manufacturing firm, has collected together 688 subsidiaries; Matsushita, which has developed a

226

vertical chain stretching from suppliers to wholesalers and retailers, has 340 direct subsidiaries. Toyota and Nissan have linked up with suppliers and sub-contractors. Nissan's holdings include a 20.9% stake in Ichikoh Industries, a company producing car rear-view mirrors. When Ichikoh's boss and founder, Tetsuya Tsukatani, demanded more independence to trade with other companies, Nissan forced his removal. Tsukatani also claims that they prevented his son succeeding him as President. Uncharacteristically, Tsukatani decided to write to President Bush, spilling the beans about what goes on in keiretsu.

The keiretsu operate in restraint of trade; their activities would be illegal in America and probably are in Japan. But Japanese anti-monopoly laws have never been seriously enforced. In 1991 the Fair Trade Commission, which is responsible for this, brought its first criminal indictments for alleged price-fixing in seventeen years. The last occasion that any such action was taken was against petroleum companies at the time of the first oil shock. Cross-shareholdings are estimated to account for up to 70% of all Japanese company shares. They are held by other companies or financial institutions, who never trade them. This partly explains why Japanese companies are able to pay such small dividends, retaining a large share of their earnings cheaply to finance further growth. The majority of corporate shareholders don't mind; they are more interested in capital gains. It also explains why shareholders rarely force directors to resign, although they always step down if scandal taints their company's reputation. Hostile take-overs are almost unheard of in Japan; Kotani's success with Kokusai Kogyo was unique. When the American raider, T. Boone Pickens, bought a 26.4% stake in Koito Manufacturing, the country's second largest maker of car lights and a member of the Toyota group, he became its largest single shareholder, but he failed to obtain a seat on the board. Toyota, with a 6% stake has three board members. Pickens had to get a court order to see the companies' books and then could not find a Japanese accountant willing to explain them to him. He gave up and sold his stake.

The keiretsu system is not as damaging to competition as it seems; often it is the reverse – which is almost as bad. Rival keiretsu families compete viciously against each other for market share, so that when one sets up in a big new plant to produce anything, all the others rush to do the same. This results in over-capacity and cut-throat competition. But the Japanese prefer to cut each other's throats politely and abroad; over-capacity boosts exports and they are charged with dumping. The Japanese justify the keiretsu system as a superior form of corporate organisation. They point out that it leads to long-term relationships and shared technology. They can point to Japanese industrial success compared with American failure. American managers, they say, are always looking over their shoulders. They are forced to think short term and go for quick profits. They spend less on research and development, with its long pay-off period. The Japanese have a point.

But the keiretsu, like the old zaibatsu, have become the vehicle through which power and wealth are concentrated in relatively few hands. The route to the top in Japan is no longer through marrying into the zaibatsu owner's family but, instead, through selection to self-perpetuating oligarchies. Powerful families may no longer be the owners of Japanese industry, but they monopolise control of it.

It's fine to dango

Japanese construction companies do ten times more work on US public projects than Americans do on Japanese. Japanese dirty tricks get the blame. Ordinarily no Japanese public sector body would dream of handing a construction contract to a non-Japanese – that's not the way the system works. In Japan, construction companies form bid-rigging rings called 'dangos' which decide who shall 'win' which contract. The price has to be a high one, because the 'losers' receive pay-offs. The winner also sells sub-contracts to other contractors, who get their turn to win in due course. Funds are also generated for political contributions and bribes. The construction industry employs 10% of Japan's labour force and its activities account for up to 20% of GNP. It is infested with gangsters. Police reckon that the yakuza own or control over 1000 construction companies. Half of all bribery and corruption cases implicating local and national government officials involve construction companies. The standard political pay-off for a contract is 2% of its value; the venal Japanese politicians, local and national, love this system. They are smacking their lips over the 1990s ¥430 trn public works programme – at 2% a ¥8.6 trn pay-off is due. This makes the Ministry of Construction one of the most sought-after Cabinet posts. To allow an outsider to put in a genuine bid would spoil everything. Moreover, with the Lockheed scandal in mind, when the company was forced in America to spill the beans on the bribes it paid to the former Prime Minister, Kakuei Tanaka, nobody would feel safe about accepting American money.

The Japanese insist that they take an extremely dim view of dangos. But sucessful investigations by the Fair Trade Commission are rare. Amusingly, one that succeeded showed bid-rigging for work done on American military bases in Japan. The Japanese are willing to reform their bidding system a little; allowing longer notice when calling for bids and making the specifications clearer. But they are not going to seriously change anything. Instead, they have agreed to allow American participation on twenty-three projects, meaning that US contractors will get a modest share of this work.

16

Money Politics

The Japanese political system, in its present form, cannot possibly implement a radical reform programme. Japan is not a democracry and never has been but, on the contrary, is a country run by and for powerful vested interests, masquerading behind the formal trappings of democractic institutions. Democratic institutions alone do not create democracies. The Japanese do not vote for parties and policies. They either vote in the way that they are coerced to vote, or for the greatest scoundrels who offer the biggest bribes. Rival political dynasties, called factions, have emerged, controlled by a handful of robber barons. A civil war is raging within the ruling Liberal Democractic party, as these barons battle for power and the wealth it brings. Japan is not a society in which all men are equal under the law. This requires precise and detailed legislation, against which the actions of executives and bureaucrats can be tested in the law courts. Instead, laws are left deliberately vague. Bureaucrats invent their own rules and impose them through the system of 'administrative guidance', which cannot be challenged. Within their own spheres, they run Japan with largely unfettered dictatorial powers – used both to reward and to punish.

The lifetime employment system is modern-day serfdom. Japanese workers' lives are not their own, but the company's. Once they have joined it, sometimes forcibly recruited, they have little chance of escape. If they lose their job, their chances of getting another as good are nearly non-existant. Consequently, they are subject to the direction of labour little different from that in a former communist state. They are told what job to do and where to do it. They have no effective unions to protect them. Outside work, yakuza gangsters have replaced the old pre-war terrorist cliques; they prevent street crime, while their own organised crime goes largely unchecked, since often they operate in collusion with the police and politicians. Overt or covert intimidation are part and parcel of everyday life. If you have a car crash in Japan, do not expect insurance companies or courts to decide who was to blame and must pay for repairs; the yakuza settle such matters.

Money politics dominate Japan, a web of corruption which penetrates every corner of the land. Its roots lie in a crazy voting system, less-than-secret ballots, rural over-representation, bureaucratic power and social pressure to conform. Japan is notionally a parliamentary democracy. The Parliament, or 'Diet', has upper and lower chambers, the House of Councillors and the House of Representatives. The Prime Minister and government are supposedly appointed by and answerable to the lower house, the House of Representatives. But as one party has ruled continuously since 1955, ministers are appointed by and answerable to the junta that controls it.

A crazy voting system

Both houses are elected by universal franchise. Like the American Congress, there is a fixed period between upper house elections. These are held every three years; the next is due in July 1992. The upper house is never dissolved; only half its 252 seats come up for re-election at each election. Councillors individually serve six-year terms. The British system applies to lower house elections. The maximum period between them is four years, but the lower house can be dissolved at any time the government wishes. Only once since the war has a parliament run its full term (Dec. 1972 to Dec. 1976). The average life of a parliament is three years. There are currently 512 Representatives, who are elected from 130 constituencies. Apart from the small island of Amani Oshina, which sends only one member to the Diet, all other constituencies are repesented by between two and six members; most have three to five. Voters, however, are allowed to vote for only a single candidate. Upper house Councillors are elected in two ways. The lower house multi-member constituency, single ballot system is used to select 76 out of the 126 Councillors elected at each election. The remaining 50 seats are filled by proportional representation. The voter votes for a party list and not individual candidates. If the LDP wins 60% of the party vote, it gets 30 seats. These go to the 30 candidates it has put at the top of its list.

Money politics is blamed on this odd voting system, which works as follows. Suppose that 60% of voters in a five-member constituency support the LDP, 30% support the Socialists and 10% the Communists. Suppose also that the LDP puts up five candidates, the JSP two and the JCP only one. If each party's votes are shared almost equally between its candidates, the two Socialists will top the poll with about 15% of the votes each. Three of the five LDP candidates will win the remaining seats, each with about 12.5% of the votes. The two LDP candidates who poll the lowest votes will be defeated, as will the single Communist with 10%. But suppose that one LDP candidate is much stronger than the others and gets 32% of the vote. The other four will be left with an average of only 7% each. If they are all about equal, the Communist's 10% will win him the fourth seat. One of three LDP candidates will get the fifth, meaning that only two LDP candidates will be elected instead of three.

Wanted: mediocrities

This system has many consequences. Charismatic politicians are unpopular. The last thing a party wants is a candidate who will take more than his fair share of its vote. The aim is to have influential unprincipled mercenary mediocrities. In a five-member constituency, the LDP likes candidates with local followings in different parts. They can pull out their own voters, without attracting other LDP candidates' voters. A popular orator or superstar, capable of appealing to voters throughout the constituency, is dangerous. This is one reason why Diet members are so grey and uninspiring. The popularist candidate will often be forced to fight first as an independent. If he wins, he will probably be accepted into the LDP, but as an independent, unless he is exceedingly rich, his chances of winning are limited.

The fewer candidates the better

Since votes are divided between candidates from the same party, the fewer candidates from a party, the more likely each is to win. For example, the rural Ibaraki prefecture is represented by four Councillors, two of whom are elected every three years. In the upper house elections in July 1989, the LDP put up two candidates and won one seat and the Socialist's single candidate won the other. This left Ibaraki with its normal balance of two Socialists and two LDP Councillors. But shortly after the election, one of the Socialist Councillors died. A by-election was held in October 1989. As only one seat was contested, it became a first-past-the-post race. Only one LDP candidate was nominated and he won it. Ibaraki is now represented by three LDP Councillors and one Socialist, which more accurately reflects the votes normally cast for each party.

More money equals more votes

A voter is more likely to switch from one LDP candidate to another, than from voting Socialist or Communist to voting LDP. So it is easier for a candidate to win votes off another in his own party, than from an opposing party's candidate. Consequently, election battles are fiercest between rival candidates from the same party. Candidates from the same party in the same constituency usually support all the same policies. These are to promise whatever serves the narrow self-interests of voters in that constituency. Policies often differ more between candidates of the same party in different constituencies, than between candidates of different parties in the same constituency. All LDP candidates in a rural constituency will oppose lifting the ban on rice imports. Candidates in an urban constituency may support it. Consequently, elections are fought over personalities rather than policies. The candidates who have done or could do their constituents the most favours, usually win. But favours cost money; so candidates who spend most generally win.

More votes equals more money

Money is more easily raised collectively than individually. An aspiring young politician, following in his father's or father-in-law's footsteps, has it easy. He inherits a ready-made band of supporters. A politician without wealth or connections has little hope. But if he wins an election, he will have a Diet vote. Successful old politicians have the power, position and influence to get money. But they need Diet votes to win and hold the top jobs. This is why factions fragment Japanese political parties, especially the ruling LDP. They exist solely for the purpose of trading money for votes. They are held together by money, personal loyalty or family connections. Policies and principles are irrelevant. Each young politician needs an older patron to supply him with the money to get into and stay in the Diet. Each older politician needs protégés to supply him with votes. The higher the office he can obtain, the more money he can get by exploiting it, the more young protégés he can afford to launch into the Diet, enabling him to rise even higher.

One big unhappy party

There is only room for one big party, which is why the LDP has monopolised power since it was formed in 1955. The maximum number of seats a party can win is limited by the total number of candidates it puts forward in each election. Consider the first example above: if the Communists and Socialists had each put up five candidates, none of them would have been elected; all five seats would have been won by the LDP. Only a party with a large proportion of the votes can field enough candidates to win power. In the February 1990 general election, the LDP put up 325 official candidates. Between them they received

233

30,315,000 votes, a 46% share. So each LDP candidate obtained an average of 93,000 votes. The LDP won 275 seats, 54% of the total. Three out of twenty LDP candidates lost. (Eleven successful independents joined the LDP giving a total of 286 seats.) The Socialists put up only 148 candidates, less than the number of LDP candidates; between them they polled 16,025,000 votes, more than half the LDP total and won 136 seats. Only one in twelve Socialist candidates failed to get elected. This success rate reflected the fewer Socialist candidates. But had all of them won, the party could still not have obtained a lower house majority; while had it put up enough candidates to have a chance of wining a majority, its votes would have been shared out more thinly and it would have won fewer seats.

The LDP's monopoly of power is self-perpetuating. It provides a monopoly of top jobs which can be used, by fair means or foul, to obtain the massive amount of money needed to field many candidates and win elections. If the opposition parties were to unite, they could dislodge the LDP from government. A new left-wing party could then monopolise power. But the opposition parties have never been willing to ignore policy differences in the pursuit of power. They get their pay-off from the bribes they receive for allowing the Diet's business to run smoothly.

Politics is an extremely expensive business in Japan. Most of the cost comes from the battles within the LDP between rival factions. Each aims to get as many of its members into the Diet, by beating members of other LDP factions. It costs a large fortune to become an ordinary Dietman; and it costs a small fortune to be one. Faction leaders must find much of these fortunes on behalf of their younger followers. They must bribe other faction leaders to obtain top ministerial jobs for their faction members. More and bigger bribes are often needed to secure the top job, that of Prime Minister. Finally opposition politicians must be bribed to ensure legislation gets through the Diet.

Cost of becoming a Dietman: ¥1 bn

The first step up the political ladder is probably hardest. A young man with family connections in the constituency might win at a cost of only ¥500 m ($4 m). A man without connections could spend ¥1 bn ($8 m) and still lose in a marginal seat. During election campaigns, money is put into envelopes and through letter boxes with notes expressing the candidate's hope that he will get the recipient's support. ¥10,000 notes ($80) turn up at the bottom of gift boxes of chocolates, even in pork pies. But normally brown envelopes stuffed with money simply change hands. In a land where a favour received is a debt owed, local politicians, bigwigs, businessmen, bankers and anyone with influence to peddle, can rally supporters. In return for favours received, they vote the way they are asked to. Naturally they are asked to support the candidate who will do the most favours or gives the most money to their patron.

The LDP's 325 candidates each spent on average ¥650 m ($5 m) during the fifteen-day February 1990 campaign. This gives a total cost of over ¥200 bn, or some $1.5 bn. Cost per LDP vote works out at around ¥6500 or $50. Moreover this figure excludes most of the costs normal in an election campaign. Japanese candidates are not allowed to buy expensive radio or TV time or to advertise in newspapers. The posters they can show are strictly limited in size and in number, and can be displayed only in specified places. Door-to-door canvassing is forbidden, but widely practised. Even campaign meetings on behalf of a specific candidate are prohibited. Indeed all modern means by which a candidate addresses the electorate are off limits during the campaign. A low ceiling is set on campaign spending, calculated from the number of voters and seats in a constituency – about ¥20 m is the average – even if it is not observed. During the 1990 campaign, for example, 2.5 m people were caught breaking the electoral laws; so many that all were pardoned. On polling day 7000 were arrested on the streets handing out bribes; one was caught brazenly distributing socks full of ¥1000 notes to passers-by.

Favours are expected as well as cash. Members must help constituents find good jobs for their sons, or get them into the best schools and universities. In June 1991 two Meiji University staff members were arrested on the suspicion of forging examination documents as well as on suspicion of having arranged stand-ins at entrance examinations. They were reported to have done so for an LDP Dietman's secretary on behalf of parents in his constituency. Local businessmen wanting licences, to sell hard liquor for example, expect their Diet member to fix it for them with the bureaucrats. Public procurement contracts must come the way of local concerns; similarly, when the politician rises to ministerial status, public works projects and state subsidies are expected to be directed towards his constituency.

Unsecret ballots

Why shouldn't the voter, bribed or coerced to vote for say, Ishi, vote instead for Kawasaki? It is supposed to be a secret ballot, but it hardly is. The voter arrives at the polling station and, having established his identity, receives a completely blank ballot paper. He goes to a three-sided booth. Posted on the wall of the booth which faces him is a list of the candidates. He writes in the name of his chosen candidate on the ballot paper. All the time he is watched by 'election observers' there to see 'fair play'. If he writes the longer name, Kawasaki, instead of Ishi, it may be all too obvious. If he endeavours to hide what he is doing, the observers will suspect him of cheating. He must then return to place his paper in the ballot box, keenly observed the whole way. It requires guts and good acting to vote the wrong way. Suspicion alone will bring instant retribution. This is a major problem in small rural constituencies, where LDP support is concentrated. It is less so in big urban constituences, where more voters pass through the polling station and each is less well known.

Nepotism

The best way to become a Dietman is to be born into it or marry into it. Being the son of a Dietman means that you can inherit Dad's support organisation. This is the group of interests which your father has gathered about him. They supply money and votes, he supplies favours. Support groups are usually territorial. The politician tries to get all important interests and people in a part of the constituency on his side. He will try to expand his power base into his rivals' neighbouring territory. There are specialist interests when it comes to the larger constituencies for upper house elections. Yoshihisa Oshima, Councillor for Aichi, has the support of the dentists' association. But the territorial nature of support organisations means they represent local groups within which there are strong personal and business ties between the members. They don't disband when their sitting parliamentarian retires or dies, but adopt a new member, who is usually the son or son-in-law of their old one. Every LDP Dietman under forty, except one, is related to another present or past politician. Half of all LDP Dietmen are related to one another by ties of blood or marriage. For example, Shintaro Abe was the son-in-law of the Prime Minister, Nobosuke Kishi. Shin Kanemaru's son is married to Noboru Takeshita's daughter. Takeshita's sister-in-law is Ichiro Ozawa's wife's sister.

A half of all LDP Dietmen are nisei or second-generation members. The second-generation has a better than 50% chance of getting elected at his first try. The candidate without connections has about a 15% chance. Once in the Diet, the advantages of being an incumbent are substantial. Sitting candidates rarely get beaten unless they really blot their copy books. Since promotion goes with seniority, and the nisei are usually younger when elected for their first term, their monopoly of top jobs is assured. In 1989, *The Economist* profiled nine possible young contenders to succeed Takeshita as Prime Minister. The list included five sons of former Dietmen. It did not include Sousuke Uno, who got the job. But it did include Toshiki Kaifu, of whom *The Economist* remarked: 'Lightning would have to strike for him to make it to the prime ministership.'

Become a bureaucrat

There are other routes into the Diet: becoming a bureaucrat is one. After the Second World War, the Americans purged most of Japan's older politicians, but bureaucrats were spared. The obvious way to fill gaps in parties was to recruit civil servants. They were better at pulling the wool over the Americans' eyes than young inexperienced local politicians. A practice was thereby begun of recruiting senior bureaucrats into politics. In the 1950s as many as a third of LDP Dietmen had begun their careers as bureaucrats. Moreover they progressed somewhat faster to ministerial office than non-bureaucrats. More recently the promotion of former civil servants has been the same as that of other new members. Consequently the age at which they enter politics has fallen from around fifty to between thirty and forty. The other two routes are to make your own fortune, as Tanaka did, or graduate from local to national politics.

Cost of being a Dietman: ¥200 m a year

Once elected, it costs a great deal of money to be an LDP Dietman. The Diet member gets a small office free with his job, the cost of two secretaries and free rail travel. But he has to have another office in Tokyo and a further one in his constituency. He employs at least twenty people full-time to look after his support operations and collect money. The member or prospective member must attend weddings and funerals in his constituency, where he must give a small cash present to the happy couple or grieving relatives. On average a member attends eighty weddings a year and 318 funerals. He will usually give ¥25,000 ($200) to the newly-weds and ¥10,000 ($75) to the bereaved. It takes two to wed, but only one to die. So weddings, though dearer, are fewer. They cost the Dietman ¥2 m ($15,000) a year. Funerals are cheaper but more plentiful. They cost over ¥3 m yearly. During three weeks in December, the Dietman or his representative must attend thirty parties a day, giving the hosts a present of ¥10,000 at each. This costs another ¥6 m. There is also the summer gift-giving season, called chugen, at which time further small gifts are appreciated. But this is the small change of politicking. Some supporters have to be bought at a much higher price. The total ordinary cost of being in the Diet is reckoned to be approaching ¥200 m a year or around $1.5 m. All this supposedly comes out of a Dietman's after-tax pay of ¥11 m ($85,000).

Rice cakes from your leader

The young politician starts by receiving help from his seniors. As he progresses up the political ladder, he is expected to raise more money himself. In time, it becomes his turn to help his juniors. Once he has been in the Cabinet, he is expected to make a significant personal contribution to his faction's funds. The faction leaders themselves must raise billions of yen each a year, part of which are distributed to their younger followers. At oseibo, New Year, before elections and at other gift-giving times such as chugen in July, faction leaders hand out money to their followers, several million yen to each, nominally for 'rice cakes'. Kakuei Tanaka, on the eve of his downfall as Prime Minister in 1974, went even further, giving ¥3–5 m to every member of the Diet and to some bureau chiefs as well; it availed him little. Shintaro Abe, who died in 1991, is reported personally to have raised ¥2.6 bn ($20 m) for his faction in 1986. The fight for the leadership of the Abe faction after his death was won by Hiroshi Mitsuzuka, because, as the *Japan Economic Journal* explained: 'He has more money than fellow faction member, LDP Policy Research Council Chairman, Mutsuki Kato.'

Bribery is not confined to elections or electors. The elected bribe one another. Votes in the Diet are frequently bought and sold. The ubiquitous brown envelopes are not always large enough to contain all the loot and plastic shopping bags full of notes frequently change hands. In 1988 ordinary Socialist members of the Diet Budget Committee were persuaded to give Takeshita's tax reform plans an easy ride with ¥100,000 ($750) for their votes or abstention. The top JSP member was reputed to have received ¥1 m. The man doing the dirty work for the LDP was the Committee Chairman, Koichi Hamada, a Takeshita faction member. Hamada was rather more clumsy than most in his operations. An aged Communist committee member, kept in the dark about the deals the LDP was doing with the Socialists, brought accusations against Hamada, who replied by called him a 'murderer'. Possibly he was. The assassination to which Hamada referred happened in 1933, when a police infiltrator into the illegal Communist party was uncovered. He unhappily passed away while being asked a few questions.

Hamada was unwise to bring up the past; he had been a yakuza gangster and had a criminal record. It was suspected that he was using his knowledge of other member's private lives to threaten exposure where bribery failed. Hamada had to step down following this incident, but

who knows, he could turn up again as a minister. Hamada had been put
into the job by Shin Kanemaru, a Tanaka henchman. Kanemaru himself
has only one known blemish on his reputation: he was caught in 1980 on
the minor offence of failing to report ¥32 m of income to the tax
authorities.

The carpet baggers

From the time a budding young politician enters the Diet, his sights are
set on one of the 'honey-pot jobs': the Ministries of Construction,
Transport, Posts & Telecommunications, International Trade & Industry and Agriculture. The route to ministerial office does not depend on
ability, but on seniority, and follows the path of legislation. The first
stage of this is through LDP policy committees, which are twinned with
ministries. These are normally the forum within which legislation is first
considered. Moreover ministry bureaucrats habitually attend LDP
policy committee meetings, helping to advise on policy formulation.
Once a measure has been agreed by a policy committee, it goes to a
committee of the Diet, where it is negotiated with opposition parties.
Communists have seats on Diet committees, but they are usually excluded from inter-party deliberations, which often take place informally
between the other members. The JCP members had the habit of publishing their version of what goes on in committees in their party newspaper *Akahata*. It is not normally until the main opposition parties have
been squared, that a bill ends up in the Diet, hopefully for a swift and
easy passage.

A young politician chooses the area in which he plans to specialise and
usually stays on that track all his career. In his second or third term in the
Diet, he becomes a vice-minister on one of the policy committees. Next
he moves up to a divisional chief on a Policy Affairs Research Council. In
his fifth or sixth term, he becomes chief of the relevant Diet standing
committee, and by his seventh term, he should become a minister. There
have been eighteen lower house elections since 1946, giving an average
term of less than three years between each. This means that a politician
should reach Cabinet level twenty years or less after entering the Diet. A
few get there faster. But to get a honey-pot ministry, the member needs to
belong to a powerful mainstream faction. Nor will he keep it for long.
Cabinets change at least once a year and the average time a member
remains a minister is only eleven months; pedestrian plodders get only
one short stay at the top.

On his way up, the politician will expand his network of contacts with
bureaucrats, companies and other policitians, thus placing him in the

position both to ask and do favours. A favour given is a debt owed. So the higher he rises, the more valuable he becomes to his constituents. The more strings he can pull, the safer his seat. The former Prime Minister, Kakuei Tanaka, even after he had been convicted of bribery in the Lockheed case and resigned from the LDP, continued to be elected for his home constituency, topping the poll every time. Not a single major politician tainted by the Recruit Cosmos scandal lost his seat in the 1990 election.

Where does all the money come from?

LDP politicians are financed from many sources and in many ways, legal and illegal. They get donations from big industry, banks, credit co-operatives, and from stockbrokers through shady share deals. Even hospitals and dentists join support groups. The farmers' co-operative, the Nokyo, is a major political paymaster. The construction industry chips in with part of the profits from dangos. Gangster-run, tax-cheating pachinko hall operators need friends in high places and yakuza/political links are well established. Businessmen reward politicians who put contracts their way. Almost all Japanese organisations exist and prosper as a consequence of their role in pouring money into politics.

The original fund-raising system was called the 'iron-triangle'; its three corners were big business, bureaucrats and politicians. Bureaucrats are consulted at length on all policy and legislation, often by ministers who will be in their jobs less than a year. They can do a great deal to advance the interests of the industries they regulate through their powerful influence on legislation. But directly bribing bureaucrats is not considered fair play, as they are not supposed to be corrupt. When they are it is taken seriously.

Bribing politicians is a different matter. Big business contributes huge sums to political parties. Politicians obtained favours for big businesses; which make large profits as a result of those favours. In the early 1950s, before the LDP was formed by a merger of the various conservative parties, big industry was the dominant paymaster. Funds were channelled from companies through their employers' organisation to party leaders. The Keidanren, the Federation of Economic Organisations, represented the old basic industries such as steel, chemicals and electric power. It set quotas for donations from its member industries and for individual companies, collected the money and handed it over to the parties in return for favours. The companies themselves made donations out of their profits. They also 'encouraged' their employees to contribute to party support associations. The farmers' organisation, Nokyo, was the other powerful source of funds.

When the LDP was formed in 1955, the merging parties continued as factions within it. Their leaders, rather than the LDP, remained the main recipients of political donations from the Keidanren and the Nokyo. But the bitter battles for power within the LDP, first between the factions formed by Shigeru Yoshida and Ichero Hatoyama and later between Kakuei Tanaka and Takeo Fukuda, demanded much more money than could be supplied through these regular and legitimate channels. It came from the growing corruption of business and politics.

The man from Niigata

Kakuei Tanaka was the man who did most to develop money politics in Japan. Born near Niigata on the Sea of Japan side on Honshu, he was the son of a dealer in cattle and horses who went bankrupt. Tanaka left school at twelve and is the only post-war Prime Minister who never had a university education. Starting with neither money nor education, he nonetheless became the most powerful man in Japan and dominated Japanese politics for the best part of two decades. He made his first fortune by not building an armaments factory in Korea, while failing to repay the government the money he had received for doing so. He was too young and too unimportant to be purged by the Americans and was first elected to the Diet in 1947 aged twenty-nine – its youngest member.

From the start, Tanaka exploited the bureaucracy for the benefit of the construction industry. He set up ghost companies, without employees or offices, to buy and sell land designated for development. When he became Minister of Finance he ordered the sale of government-owned land, making sure that he, or his supporters, bought it at knockdown prices for resale. He promoted public works projects on a grand scale – indeed his plan for 'Rebuilding the Japanese Archipelago' would have been better described as the 'Plan for financing Tanaka'.

The world's largest pork-barrel

Tanaka was the master pork-barrel-roller. His Niigata prefecture, for example, had a bullet train branch line blasted through the mountains to it; mile for mile, it was the most expensive railway ever made. He was also responsible for a local road tunnel, 500 yds long, leading to the village of Shiodani with a population of seventy. It cost over $4 m to build and is used by twenty cars a day. Izumi Sano, by contrast, a coastal city of 91,000, has a single and inadequate road linking it to nearby

Osaka. The island of Shikoku, with a population of 4 m, is underdeveloped, but it was the home of two former Prime Ministers, Takeo Miki (called 'Mr Clean') and Masayoshi Ohira. Their dynasties still serve it well. It is being joined to the mainland by three bridge systems including the construction of sixteen separate bridges, one of which is the longest suspension bridge in the world. (There is still no bridge across Tokyo Bay.)

Tanaka was forced out of office in 1974 after a magazine revealed details of his shady dealings. The Lockheed scandal did not surface until 1976. Following the Tanaka scandal, an effort was made to clean up political finances. The Political Fund Control Law was passed in 1976 limiting the amount that a politician could receive from any one source and setting a maximum on the amount any company could give in political donations. This, however, did more to reduce the Keidanren's influence than to reduce the politicians' income. A large variety of methods was evolved to evade the restrictions. Although the amount that a politician could receive from a support organisation was limited, the number of support organisations was not. There was exponential growth in their number. There was no ceiling placed on companies' donations to research organisations and advisory bodies. Soon every leading politician was setting these up. They 'laundered' donations. Takeshita fell out with the ageing and stricken Tanaka in 1983 when he set up his own research group made up of Tanaka faction members. This group could obtain its own money instead of being beholden to Tanaka for funds.

The ¥2 bn free dinner

A legal method of raising money was to sell tickets for dinners in support of individual politicians, i.e. 40,000 tickets were sold at ¥30,000 ($230) each for the Abe faction dinner in July 1988, although only 8000 people turned up. The dinner netted a profit of more than ¥1 bn ($8 m). Takeshita holds the record with a ¥2 bn profit from a single dinner. He sold 70,000 tickets in June 1987 for a party in the Phoenix Room of the Tokyo Prince Hotel. Fortunately only 13,000 turned up and most stayed for less than ten minutes. The sale of tickets for such occasions is anything but legal. Companies received visits from ex-ministers and top politicians, often accompanied by bureaucrats. The advantages to the company of buying a block of tickets are gently explained, together with the undoubted disadvantages of refusing to do so. Takeshita's party launched him on his way to the Premiership in succession to Nakasone.

The way in which stockbrokers ramp political shares and allocate new issues has already been explained. This method of fund raising was exposed by the Recruit Cosmos scandal. It led to a clamp-down on some of the more obvious abuses. In early 1989, LDP politicians stopped giving dinners as they attracted too much media criticism. Companies became wary of making contributions and the flow of funds to individual politicians and faction leaders dried up. When the LDP lost its upper house majority in the July 1989 election, the outlook was bleak. A lower house election was due to be held in July 1990 at the latest, and the LDP needed even more money to fight it. The possibility that it would lose was taken seriously.

The task of filling the LDP's war chest was given to its Secretary General, Ichiro Ozawa, who set out to raise ¥30 bn for the party. He went first to the Keidanren and told them he would set the quotas for target donations from industries and large companies. In this way he squeezed an extra ¥3 bn out of industry, which paid ¥12 bn into the LDP kitty. He next threatened the banks, construction companies, electric machinery producers, securities and auto industries with what would happen if the LDP lost its majority. But these industries were already contributing the maximum that they were allowed, yet this was easily solved. The twelve city banks and three long-term trust banks were persuaded to give the LDP a ¥15 bn loan on easy terms. The industries were persuaded to underwrite this loan by the promise of contributions of ¥16 bn over the following three years. The LDP got its money and won the election.

Plans are afoot to reform the Japanese electoral system in order to curb the worst abuses of money politics. Although first mooted following the Recruit Cosmos scandal, to date they have not got far. The former Prime Minister, Toshiki Kaifu, introduced legislation in the Diet special session in October 1991, only to see it scuppered by members of his own party. This incident cost him his job. His successor, Kiichi Miyazawa, has been forced to put reform again on the back-burner.

PART III

Harvest of Failure

17

Warring Factions

There has been an unending civil war between rival factions within the LDP since its formation in 1955. The original post-war battle-lines were drawn even earlier, between former bureaucrats and professional politicians. The Liberal party, led by a pre-war politician, Ichiro Hatoyama, won most seats at the April 1946 General Election, but not a majority. Hatoyama was set to become Prime Minister, but immediately after the election he was purged by the Americans. A former diplomat, Shigeru Yoshida, took over instead. Except for a break of one year, Yoshida remained Premier until December 1954. He recruited former high government officials turned politicians to his side, many of whom were swiftly promoted to Cabinet posts. They had shared expertise in administration and wide-ranging contacts with industry and the bureaucracy. His two main protégés were Hayato Ikeda and Eisuku Sato; both entered the Diet in 1949. Ikeda had been a vice-minister in the Ministry of Finance and Sato vice-minister in the Ministry of Transport. They were given Cabinet jobs during their first terms – unthinkable these days.

The purge on Hatoyama was lifted in June 1951 and he returned to the Diet at the October 1952 General Election. His strength lay in his grass roots support in rural Japan. He gathered around him other older politicians such as Nobusuke Kishi, who was Sato's elder brother. (Kishi had been adopted by an uncle who had only daughters.) Like Hatoyama, Kishi had been purged, but with more reason; he had been Minister for Commerce & Industry in General Tojo's wartime cabinet. He was locked up for three years in Sugamo Prison as a suspected Class A war criminal, although in the end no charges were brought against him.

On his return to the Diet, Hatoyama wanted the Premiership. He said Yoshida had promised him it; Yoshida denied this and refused to go, thereby starting the political civil war. Hatoyama conducted a guerilla campaign against Yoshida, by splitting the Liberals and regrouping his supporters into the Democrat party. Yoshida held on grimly for two more years until Hatoyama finally ousted him and became Prime Minister in December 1954. He called a General Election in February 1955, hoping to consolidate his position, but unfortunately the Socialists made significant gains. The two wings into which they were split won 156 seats between them, against 185 for the Democrats and 112 for the Liberals. The Socialists smelt power and, in October 1955, re-united. Industrialists became alarmed; they feared that if the conservative parties continued to fight each other, the Socialists might succeed in returning to government. The Keidanren urged party leaders to settle their differences – it was their paymaster – but it was a gangster, Yoshio Kodama, who did the match-making by bribing the rivals into forming the Liberal Democratic party.

Before and after the war, all major political developments in Japan were accompanied by bribes and scandals – politics and corruption were heads and tails of the same coin. This produced a vicious circle: politicians were held in such low esteem that few decent Japanese would embark on a political career; most politicians therefore continued to deserve and preserve their corrupt reputation. The brief centre-left coalition government, led by the Prime Minister, Hitoshi Ashida, collapsed in 1948, because of bribes from the Showa Denko chemical company, which was seeking government loans. Ashida, his vice-Premier, and Takeo Fukuda were indicted, but not found guilty. Yoshida lost power because of another scandal: both of his top aides, Ikeda and Sato, were up to their ears in a shipbuilding scam which broke in 1954. Yoshida, who was milking the coal industry for money, shielded them. He ordered the Justice Minister to forbid Sato's arrest on the excuse of parliamentary privilege. It is hardly surprising that the LDP itself was born of corruption and weaned on it, became addicted to it. Stamp out corruption in Japan and you stamp out the LDP.

The 1955 set-up

The 1955 set-up was a watershed in Japan's post-war political history. It led to unbroken LDP rule, making Japan effectively a one-party state. The formation of the LDP internalised the political divisions on the right; the parties which merged preserved their identity by becoming parties within the party, called factions. Instead of fighting in public to obtain power, henceforth they fought in private to share it. As long as the left was not a credible alternative, LDP politicians had little incentive to explain or consult the voters on what policies to pursue. Policy remained the prerogative of the bureaucracy, while politicians pursued power and wealth. All they were interested in was to protect the special interests they represented.

There were originally eight factions in the LDP in 1955, named after their leaders. They were all relatively small, since many Dietmen chose to remain independent. Politics was not so expensive in those days, because most first-generation Diet members had constructed their own local support groups without outside help. Three of the original eight factions never produced a Prime Minister, lost the money politics game and were dissolved; one other produced a Prime Minister but died with him; the remaining four fathered the factions which still fight for power.

The first LDP leadership battle followed Hatoyama's resignation in December 1956, owing to old age and ill-health. Henceforth, whoever became LDP President automatically became Premier. It was a three-cornered fight between Nobusuke Kishi, Hatoyama's protégé; Tanzan Ishibashi, another faction leader; and Mitsujiro Ishii, one of Yoshida's stars, a former economics journalist who had been Finance Minister. Helped by considerable bribery and promises of office, Ishibashi won; it is said that his chief-of-staff promised the same Cabinet job to ten different men. His Premiership got off to a bad start and came to a quick end; less than two months after becoming Prime Minister, Ishibashi had a stroke and resigned; after he died his faction dissolved.

Kishi followed Ishibashi as Premier after being elected party President by an overwhelming majority. In 1960 he used the LDP majority to ram the revised Japan–US Security Treaty through the Diet, high-handed action which led to riots and demonstrations throughout Japan. Kishi was forced to resign. Today's factions are directly descended from four of those involved in these early battles.

Faction family trees

Yoshida		*Hatoyama*	*Kishi*	*Miki*	*Ishibashi*
Ikeda	Sato	*Kono*	Fukuda	*Komoto*	
Maeo	Tanaka	Nakasone	*Abe*	(Kaifu)	
Ohira	Takeshita	(Uno)	*Mitsuzuka*		
Suzuki	*Kanemaru*	*Watanabe*			
Miyazawa					

The names in brackets are Prime Ministers who did not lead their factions. Names in italics are faction leaders who did not become (or have not yet become) Prime Minister. All the other faction leaders became Prime Minister.

Japan's post-war Prime Ministers

	From	To
Kijuro Shidehara	9 Oct. 1945	22 May 1946
Shigeru Yoshida	22 May 1946	24 May 1947
Tetsu Katayama	24 May 1947	10 March 1948
Hitoshi Ashida	10 March 1948	15 Oct. 1948
Shigeru Yoshida	15 Oct. 1948	10 Dec. 1954
Ichiro Hatoyama	10 Dec. 1954	23 Dec. 1956
Tanzan Ishibashi	23 Dec. 1956	25 Feb. 1957
Nobusuke Kishi	25 Feb. 1957	19 July 1960
Hayato Ikeda	19 July 1960	9 Nov. 1964
Eisaku Sato	9 Nov. 1964	7 July 1972
Kakuei Tanaka	7 July 1964	9 Dec. 1974
Takeo Miki	9 Dec. 1974	24 Dec. 1976
Takeo Fukuda	24 Dec. 1976	7 Dec. 1978
Masayoshi Ohira	7 Dec. 1978	12 June 1980
(Masayoshi Ito)	*12 June 1980*	*17 July 1980*
Zenko Suzuki	17 July 1980	27 Nov. 1982
Yasuhiro Nakasone	27 Nov. 1982	6 Nov. 1987
Noboru Takeshita	6 Nov. 1987	2 June 1989
Sousuke Uno	2 June 1989	9 Aug. 1989
Toshiki Kaifu	9 Aug. 1989	5 Nov. 1991
Kiichi Miyazawa	5 Nov. 1991	

Post-war elections to the House of Representatives

date	total seats	largest party	% of vote	seats
10 April 1946	466	Liberals	24.4	141
25 April 1947	466	Socialists	26.2	143
23 Jan. 1949	466	Dem-Liberals	43.9	264
1 Oct. 1952	466	Liberals	47.9	240
19 April 1953	466	Yoshida Libs	38.9	199
2 Feb. 1955	467	Democrats	36.6	185
22 May 1958	467	LDP	57.8	287
20 Nov. 1960	467	LDP	57.6	296
21 Nov. 1963	467	LDP	54.7	283
19 Jan. 1967	486	LDP	48.8	277
12 Dec. 1969	486	LDP	47.6	288
10 Dec. 1972	491	LDP	46.9	271
5 Dec. 1976	511	LDP	41.8	257
7 Oct. 1979	511	LDP	44.6	248
22 June 1980	511	LDP	47.9	286
18 Dec. 1983	511	LDP	45.8	250
6 July 1976	512	LDP	49.4	300
18 Feb. 1990	512	LDP	46.4	286

Bureaucrats in the ascendancy

Following Kishi's resignation in 1960, the in-fighting for the LDP leadership was more intense that it had been in 1956. It was a battle between the Yoshida bureaucrats and Hatoyama politicians which the politicians should have won. But Kishi – smarting over his forced resignation – joined his brother Sato to support Ikeda for the job and by his defection switched the balance of power back to the Yoshida bureaucrats. Ikeda became LDP leader and Prime Minister. He took note of how Kishi had come to grief and settled to lower the political temperature, initiating consensus politics by seeking conciliation rather than confrontation. Kishi kept a low profile on foreign affairs and concentrated on economic prosperity, seizing the initiative with his 'National Income Doubling Plan'. These were the golden days, when the 'iron triangle' worked to perfection to give the Japanese the tranquillity and prosperity they desired. Nobody worried much about money politics while the system worked so well to satisfy everyone.

Ikeda won three successive two-year terms as LDP leader, before ill-health forced him to resign early in the third. Sato followed him and was the longest-serving Japanese post-war Prime Minister, holding office from November 1964 to July 1972. For more than a quarter of a century after the Second World War, the bureaucrats had the best of the political civil war. Between them, Yoshida, Ikeda and Sato held the Premiership for eighteen years, while Hatoyama, Ishibashi and Kishi held power for less than six. But Ikeda and Sato's long twelve years in power had been possible only by means of compromise with the opposition factions, whose leaders were promised that they would get their turn at the top. The partial truce between the warring factions during the 1960s would probably have continued, following Sato's resignation, if the heir-apparent, Fukuda, had become Premier. But Kakuei Tanaka – who had infiltrated the mainstream factions – staged a *coup d'état*. By interrupting the smooth transfer of power back to the opposition factions, Tanaka broke the truce. A violent battle for power began between Tanaka's supporters and Fukuda's and their confrontation dominated LDP factional politics for the following thirteen years. The cost of the battle soared and the means of waging it became increasingly dirty, leading directly to the Recruit Cosmos scandal in the late 1980s.

Root of all evil

When Eisaku Sato stepped down from the Premiership in 1972, Tanaka challenged Fukuda for the party Presidency. In doing so he split the Sato faction and took eighty-one of its members to form his own faction. The rump of the faction went over to Fukuda and a splinter group from the Kono faction joined them, which made the Fukuda faction the largest. Two other men joined in the Presidential battle: Takeo Miki, leader of one of the smaller of the original eight factions; and Masayoshi Ohira, the Yoshida-Ikeda faction boss. One faction was not in the race, the old Hatoyama faction led by Yasuhiro Nakasone. It was easy for Tanaka to recruit Nakasone to his side; Nakasone and Fukuda were bitter electoral rivals; representing the same local constituency, Gunma–3. The party was split into warring camps: Tanaka and Nakasone versus Fukuda and Miki. The enmity and rivalry between these men was such that for once faction leaders could not strike a deal behind closed doors, and there was then no machinery for a wider election involving all party members. The order of business was reversed and the battle was taken first into the lower house where Tanaka obtained the majority he needed to become Prime Minister. He was then elected to the LDP Presidency.

This battle for the leadership was one of the most vitriolic and the most expensive since the Second World War. Tanaka paid Dietmen of all parties vast bribes to get the job; bought off the Ohira faction, which shared his Yoshida ancestry; and used his links with the construction industry to raise vastly more money than Fukuda could amass. The cost of this battle broke all records; so blatant was the bribery that the contest was dubbed the 'root of all evil' election. In July 1972, Tanaka became Japan's youngest post-war Prime Minister, aged only fifty-four.

Faction strength in 1972 and 1973

	mainstream		opposition		
	Tanaka	Ohira	Nakasone	Fukuda	Miki
1972	81	62	33	93	50
1973	86	63	39	81	50
Change	+5	+1	+6	−12	0

Tanaka's methods have already been described: he rewarded his faction members and friends in other factions with honey-pot jobs. His own faction took control of the Secretary General's, which paid off handsomely in the election held in December 1972. Although the LDP lost seventeen seats in an enlarged House of Representatives and its overall majority dropped from forty-five to twenty-five, the Tanaka, Ohira and Nakasone factions gained strength at Fukuda's expense. In his second

Cabinet Tanaka had a freer hand and his faction members got the Ministries of Finance, Agriculture, Transport, Posts & Telecommunications, Construction and the LDP Secretary Generalship. Tanaka's ally, Nakasone, was given the Ministry of International Trade & Industry.

Money politics probably would not have mattered, if the golden age of miraculous growth had continued, but inflation and the 1973–4 oil shock brought it to an abrupt end. Tanaka's popularity collapsed with the economy, while the bust which followed the early 1970s stockmarket and property price boom, produced the usual crop of scandals and bankruptcies. The period 1970–5 was a precursor to that between 1985–90; most of what happened then was repeated in a similar fashion.

Tanaka fell from office in 1974 when scandals sparked an irresistible storm of popular anger. But although the public outcry forced Tanaka to resign in disgrace, he did not lose his Diet seat or control over his faction. It was eighty-one strong when he beat Fukuda and reached 141 ten years later. Tanaka was on his way to becoming the kingmaker – but not immediately.

The first Mr Clean

Three candidates were ready to step into Tanaka's shoes: Fukuda, Nakasone and Ohira. But with LDP popularity at a low ebb and a lower house election due within two years, the LDP rank-and-file opposed another dirty leadership battle. It was therefore decided that the party elders should select the next leader. They ignored all three rivals and selected an outsider, Takeo Miki, who led his own little faction and was regarded as 'clean'. Miki had neither wanted nor been able to raise the money needed to run a large faction, so he was an ideal choice. Tanaka wanted Miki because he was the weakest candidate and thought he would be a puppet on a string. Miki could take the blame if the LDP did badly at the next General Election, and then be easily pushed aside, to allow Tanaka to make a comeback. (Miki's faction remained small and subsequently became the Komoto faction, a member of which and Miki's protégé, Toshiki Kaifu, was chosen as 'Mr Clean' in 1989.)

Miki turned out to be no puppet and too clean for Tanaka's liking. The first thing he did was to tighten the rules controlling money politics. But Tanaka's hopes of a comeback were dashed when the Lockheed scandal broke in 1976, which revealed that Tanaka as Prime Minister had accepted ¥500 m in American bribes to persuade All Nippon Airways to buy Tristars rather than Boeing 747s. Tanaka expected Miki to protect him from prosecution as prior approval is required from the

Justice Ministry before a member of the Diet can be arrested. There were precedents for corrupt politicians being shielded – Yoshida saved Sato – but Miki would have none of it; public outrage was so great that he allowed the prosecution to go ahead. Tanaka was arrested and charged with corruption, by Yusuke Yoshinaga of the Tokyo District Public Prosecutor's Office. Yoshinaga is a name to be remembered.

Tanaka probably could have got off, if he had admitted to accepting the money and claimed it was for his party not himself. A blind eye was traditionally turned on shady money received by politicians, as long as it was not used to accumulate personal wealth. Tanaka's problem was that he operated more independently than other politicians; he did not take kick-backs from construction companies who received public contracts, he owned the companies himself. He was personally rich and not at the beck and call of big industry. Tanaka had benefited from the new rules on political donations; now he lost out – without powerful benefactors, he lacked protectors to take up his cause with other money politicians. Tanaka was not pilloried because he was corrupt, but because he was independently powerful; three years after his arrest, it emerged that McDonnel Douglas had paid ¥500 m to the LDP Director General of the Self-Defence Agency, but this scandal was hushed up and that politician got off scot-free.

The Tanaka/Nakasone axis was furious with Miki for not saving Tanaka. Miki, however, could not be ditched until after the next lower house election. As the Lockheed scandal had hammered popular support for the party, the election was delayed to the last possible moment in the hope that the storm would blow over. When it was finally held, in December 1976, the LDP suffered its worst setback since its formation; its popular vote dropped to 42% and it lost its overall majority. It survived in government, much weakened, only by dint of attracting independents to its ranks, which gave it a majority of one. But it lost control of half the important Diet committees. Obviously politics would become even more expensive with opposition members having to be bought off more frequently. Once the election was over, Fukuda and Ohira ditched Miki.

The Tanaka machine

Tanaka's disgrace and the unpopularity of the money-grubbing mainstream faction leaders meant that men such as Ohira and Nakasone (both of whom were suspected of being involved with Lockheed) had to bide their time before bidding once more for the party leadership. Fukuda was the only man who stood a chance of commanding a Diet majority and was nominated unopposed for the job. Tanaka and his henchmen reckoned they could still control the government. Like Miki, Fukuda was destined to survive only a single two-year stint. Tanaka had been forced to resign from the LDP, but was returned as an independent to the Diet by his grateful and loyal home constituents in Niigata. He continued to build up his power base in the party. The 1976 election defeat even helped him; fewer of his faction lost their seats, making it the largest in the party. Nobody could be elected leader without his support, and he had no intention of allowing another member of his faction to become Prime Minister. That person might grow powerful enough in the job to challenge his leadership. Nor could he allow any other faction leader to have the job for too long, as his faction might grow at Tanaka's expense. The answer was to bargain the leadership in exchange for honey-pot jobs for Tanaka faction members, keeping his supporters happy and the money rolling in. The key political job was the LDP's Secretary General, who controls party money, dishing it out to candidates; the sponsorship list by which the factions limit the number of official candidates at elections; and the party list for Councillors elected by proportional representation. This job gives the holder the ability to favour one faction over another, enhancing its size; it regularly went to Tanaka faction members.

In 1978 Fukuda wanted a second term, but the other tarnished leaders – as happened in 1991 – felt it was again safe to seek the Premiership. Fukuda was challenged by Nakasone, Ohira and Komoto. The rules governing the leadership contest had been changed: instead of LDP Diet members and hence faction leaders deciding the issue, there now had to be a primary election in which all party members could vote. The primary was to be followed by a run-off in the Diet between the top two candidates. As the incumbent, Fukuda thought he could win; instead Ohira topped the polls, thanks to solid support from the Tanaka machine. Money politics had simply been extended from the Diet to the constituencies, making life even more expensive for faction leaders. Fukuda withdrew from the run-off.

Ohira soon ran into trouble as support in urban areas was evaporating. In an effort to retrieve the situation before the next election, he announced plans to introduce a value added tax. Whatever this did to please urban salary-earners and big business, it caused a howl of rage from all the LDP's other supporters. VAT, in itself, was not bad. What mattered was that, in collecting it, the tax authorities were bound to find out most shopkeepers' and businessmen's true incomes. Ohira also planned to introduce a green card identity system to curb anonymous postal savings accounts. This annoyed all tax dodgers. The party was for once split over a policy issue and the factional fighting which followed led the LDP to field too many candidates in the election, held six months early in December 1979. In consequence it fared worse than it had in 1976; its vote increased, but its seats fell from 257 to 248, an all-time low.

Ohira soldiered on, but under open attack from other LDP factions. He was finally defeated, when the Fukuda and Miki factions failed to support him in a Diet censure vote in May 1980. But instead of resigning as expected, he dissolved the lower house and called another election. The LDP was on the verge of disintegration; for the first time, factions would fight each other in the constituencies on issues of policy. The LDP was saved when, ten days before the election, Ohira died. It fought the election under a provisional leader, Masayoshi Ito, and dropped all Ohira's unpopular policies. It had put up twelve fewer candidates than a year earlier and the election was held on the same day as the regular upper house poll which produced a higher turn-out. The LDP's vote rose several points, the party won 286 seats and obtained a thirty-seat overall majority.

The mainstream Tanaka/Ohira/Nakasone factions still commanded a majority. Zenko Suzuki, who took over the Ohira faction, was appointed party leader and served the next two years as Prime Minister, under constant pressure from potential successors. He decided not to seek a second term and the fight for the leadership came out into the open again. The opposition factions knew that they could not win in the Diet, but hoped they could win in the party as a whole. So they put up Toshio Komoto as their prime candidate and two others to force the primary: Shintaro Abe from the Fukuda faction and Ichiro Nakagawa from the Suzuki faction. But the Tanaka and Nakasone forces were as strong outside the Diet as in it, Nakasone won comfortably and became Prime Minister in November 1982. He appointed six Tanaka faction members to top jobs in his first Cabinet, in what was jeeringly nicknamed the 'Tanakasone' government.

Tanakasone rules OK?

Tanaka, wielding money and influence, was now at the height of his power. But his trial for corruption in the Tokyo District Court was almost over and he was duly found guilty in October 1983, fined ¥500 m and sentenced to four years in jail. There was uproar in the Diet – the opposition parties wanted him to be expelled from it – and business was brought to a standstill with the Budget debate stalled. An election – the only way to defuse the crisis – was called for December 1983. The 1983 election was fought at the wrong time and over the wrong issue: political morality. It was almost as disastrous for the LDP as in 1979: its popular vote fell by 2% to 46% and was shared between 339 LDP candidates, up twenty-nine from the 1980 field; it lost thirty-six seats and its Diet majority. To form a government, Nakasone had to persuade independents to join the LDP and form a coalition with the break-away New Liberal Club. Even so, the LDP had barely enough seats to control the major Diet committees.

1983 General Election:
House of Representatives: distribution of seats

	before	after	change
LDP	286	250	−36
Socialists	101	112	+11
Komeito	33	58	+25
Democratic Socialists	30	38	+8
Communists	29	26	−3
New Liberal Club	10	8	−2
Social Democrats	3	3	0
Independents	6	16	+6
Vacancies	13	0	−13
Total	511	511	0

Faction strength at Dec. 1983 General Election

	mainstream			opposition		
	Tanaka	Suzuki	Nakasone	Fukuda	Komoto	Others
Before	116	87	70	74	32	34
After	115	78	65	67	32	20
Change	−1	−9	−5	−7	0	−14

The line-up of factions in the lower house improved slightly from Tanaka's point of view. He lost only one member, Nakasone lost five while Suzuki, leading Ohira's old faction, lost nine. These losses were less than the damage done to opposing factions, which between them lost twenty-one. But if the mainstream factions were now relatively larger within the LDP, but with the LDP weaker in the Diet the only way to get business through Parliament was another truce in the civil war. This meant that Nakasone had to share the top jobs more fairly. The balancing job which Nakasone did when creating his new Cabinet left only two former ministers with their same jobs, Abe as Foreign Minister and Takeshita as Finance Minister. The plum job of LDP Secretary General was given to the Suzuki faction, to compensate for its losses. Komoto was given back his old job as Director of the Economic Planning Agency. Not only had the spoils of power to be shared more widely, but the graft and corruption necessary to buy off other factions and opposition parties increased still further. Tanaka himself was returned by his Niigata constituency by his biggest ever majority and the largest majority any candidate had ever received. His faction managed, at considerable expense, to defeat renewed moves to have him expelled from the Diet. But it was to be his last success.

The following year, Nakasone's first two-year term was due to expire and the leadership question was back on the agenda. The LDP's disastrous performance in the December 1983 election had weakened Nakasone and he looked like following the single-term precedent set by his four predecessors. But Nakasone was the last of the old guard faction leaders to be Prime Minister; only Toshio Komoto had missed having his turn and his faction was too small to matter. A younger generation of leaders were waiting for their turns at the top and, as the last round of musical chairs with five successive two-year Premiers had taken a decade, they were themselves getting older. They feared the succession might leap-frog to even younger men before their round was over.

Members of the younger generation had two battles on their hands: first to obtain leadership of their factions when their old leaders bowed out, because until the Recruit Cosmos scandal upset the succession, only faction leaders ever became Prime Minister; and secondly, to get the Premiership. Raising vast sums of money was the only way to become faction leader and further vast sums were then required to win the LDP Presidential race. It was therefore inevitable that, as the generational shift in the leadership approached, all the contenders would be deeply involved in the money-grubbing which marked the mid-1980s.

The younger hopefuls were Kiichi Miyazawa, who belonged to the Suzuki faction; Michio Watanabe, waiting to take over the Nakasone faction; Shintaro Abe, next in line in the Fukuda faction; and Noboru Takeshita in Tanaka's faction who also had his sights on the job. Takeshita was out of the running as long as Tanaka controlled his faction and he did not feel strong enough to form a break-away group. Throughout the summer of 1984 the rivals jockeyed for position, while Tanaka continued to support Nakasone. Suzuki, another old faction leader with a young hopeful, Miyazawa, in his ranks, was not particularly keen to press his protégé's claims. Suzuki preferred to sell his support to another faction's candidate rather than give it away to one of his own. His faction had already received the bribe of the party Secretary General's job. So when Suzuki lined up again with Tanaka to support Nakasone for a second term, the game was over for the other younger hopefuls. Nakasone was re-elected unopposed for a second term in October 1984.

Despite being an older generation leader, Tanaka at sixty-six was still a relatively young politician by Japanese standards. The succession problem therefore seemed relatively settled. After Nakasone's second term, Miyazawa would follow and then Abe. Takeshita would have to wait until last. But in early 1985 Tanaka suffered two massive strokes in quick succession which paralysed the right side of his body, leaving him unable to walk or talk. It is said that anger at Takeshita brought on the stroke, who had formed his own study groups within the faction – a way of garnering support. Henceforth, it would be only a matter of time before Tanaka lost control over his faction, leaving it ready for Takeshita to seize.

When Nakasone succeeded Suzuki in 1982, tax reform was once again on the agenda. But under Nakasone, the LDP approached the question with great caution. He set up his own special policy groups, by-passing the normal LDP horse-trading advisory system. The Maekawa Reports resulted from this process and a new set of tax plans were prepared. Nakasone set out to sell reform by appealing to the voter over the heads of the party. His popularity had been rising as Japan's economy prospered and he was having some success in getting legislation through the Diet. He decided therefore to go for an early election, timed to coincide with the next regular upper house poll due in July 1986. But he did not repeat Ohira's mistake, offering tax cuts to win votes while promising not to introduce any new sales tax.

The party leaders managed things much better in the 1986 election. They agreed to reduce the number of LDP candidates from 339 to 311 and the result was a massive victory. The party won almost 50% of the popular vote, its highest since 1963 and 300 out of the 512 seats up for grabs. Best of all for Nakasone, his faction strength increased by more than any other.

Faction strength at July 1986 General Election

	mainstream		*opposition*		
	Tanaka	Miyazawa	Nakasone	Abe	Komoto
Before	120	80	57	71	34
After	141	88	83	83	34
Change	+21	+8	+26	+12	0

Tanaka's faction reached its peak size at the same time as his control over it was slipping. The three other big factions were now of almost equal size. The factional strengths following the July 1986 election meant that any one of the three, combined with the Tanaka faction, could gain a majority; while all three would have to combine to out-vote it. The leadership issue was coming up again rapidly and a rule had been passed saying nobody could have the job for more than two terms. Nakasone wanted to stay on for a third term in order to push tax reform through the Diet and Takeshita still had not made his move to grab control of the Tanaka faction. He was possibly waiting for Tanaka to bow out gracefully, but the old man showed no signs of doing so, which meant Takeshita also needed more time. He therefore helped Nakasone to persuade the other factions to change party rules to give Nakasone a further year in office.

As soon as Nakasone's extension was secured, he broke his election promise. In late October 1986, he unveiled a new tax reform package, including plans for a 5% VAT. The package included substantial corporate and income tax cuts, but was revenue neutral, meaning that there had to be losers. Nakasone wanted to crown his last year as Prime Minister by getting tax reforms through the Diet and had the majority to do it. Unfortunately, he included his tax proposals in the 1987 budget legislation and the opposition parties promptly boycotted budget debates while mounting a vigorous anti-VAT campaign in the country. In March 1987, there were massive demonstrations throughout Japan, which drew 230,000 onto the streets; around 70,000 attended a rally in Tokyo.

Nakasone's position was weak; a lame-duck Prime Minister with less than a year left to serve, whose proposals had not passed through the normal LDP deliberations channels, but came from his own advisory groups. Civil war broke out within the LDP and intensified in early March, when a Socialist won an upper house by-election in the Iwate prefecture, which the LDP had held for the last twenty-five years. The Socialist obtained a two-to-one majority over his LDP opponent. Local elections followed in April in which the LDP fared moderately, but only because most LDP candidates stood on an anti-sales-tax platform. Nobody wanted Nakasone to visit his constituency during the contest. The 1987 Budget legislation remained stalled into April, after the financial year had already begun. The opposition threatened to continue their Diet boycott, until the LDP's tax reform plans were scrapped. The LDP was in uproar and finally Nakasone had to back down. All that remained of his tax reforms was the abolition of the Maruyu system, which went ahead in April 1988.

The power-brokers

In July 1987 Takeshita made his move, leaving Tanaka's faction and taking with him 80% of its members. His faction immediately became the largest with 113 supporters. The rump that remained continued to support Tanaka, who bowed out of politics in 1989 and died thereafter. The stage was now set for the leadership battle amongst the younger, but no longer so young, next generation. The LDP Presidential Election was to be held in October 1987, but the split in the Tanaka faction had changed the arithmetic. Takeshita's faction was not big enough to combine with any one of the other big factions to obtain a majority; whoever was to win would need both Nakasone's support and another faction's. The candidates got together and tried to strike a deal and failed, so that a bitter leadership battle between Takeshita, Abe and Miyazawa seemed inevitable – but it never came off. At the last moment, all three withdrew as candidates and Nakasone was allowed to choose between them. The rivals had agreed that whoever went first would be followed, at two-yearly intervals, by each of the others.

Nakasone chose Takeshita. It might have been gratitude for the support Nakasone had received from the Tanaka faction when he became Premier in 1982. But more likely, it was because Takeshita was also determined to get tax reform through the Diet. Takeshita himself made this abundantly clear. He told the Diet: 'The issue of liberalising imports of beef and citrus is something that was caused by pressure from abroad. Tax reform I personally picked for my administration.' He became Prime Minister in November 1987. Yet again the succession had been fixed by backroom power-brokers, rather than by open elections. *The Economist* described Takeshita as 'a product of the worst of Japan's money-politics', while the *Far Eastern Economic Review* referred to his 'legendary skills as a fund-raiser'. It was one of money politics' finest hours.

18

Recruit Cosmos

With Takeshita ensconced in the Premiership for only two years, the struggle to be next to follow him was bound to heat up. Each of the other main factions were of about the same size, and the winner would be the one which could amass the biggest war chest in the interim. The honeypot ministries were not as lucrative as they had been under Tanaka; public spending was being restrained, while the attempt to push controversial tax legislation through the Diet meant further big pay-offs were needed.

Faction strength

After 1986 Election		*1989 upper house Election*			*1991, after 1990*	
			Before	*After*	*lower house Election*	
Tanaka	141	Takeshita	114	106	Kanemaru	104
Suzuki	88	Miyazawa	89	82	Miyazawa	83
Nakasone	83	Watanabe	87	77	Watanabe	64
Abe	83	Abe	86	86	Mitsuzuka	79
Komoto	34	Komoto	31	31	Komoto	33

Takeshita, leading the strongest faction, was better placed than Nakasone to get tax reforms through and he was a much smoother political operator. He spent most of his first year as Premier organising full LDP backing for his tax plans. He was a pastmaster at behind-the-scenes deal making and did not make the mistake of tacking the tax reform measures onto the ordinary budget legislation. He got his first budget, for fiscal 1988, safely through the Diet before embarking on tax reform. In June 1988, the LDP adopted his measures. They differed from those which Nakasone had proposed because they included large net tax cuts of ¥2.9 bn, made possible by buoyant revenues due to the economic boom;

the proposed sales tax rate was cut from 5% to 3%; but most important, its method of collection was changed so that the small shopkeeper could keep his true income hidden from the taxman.

Takeshita needed a special session of the Diet to get his tax reform legislation through, which involved a deal with opposition parties to avoid a boycott of the Diet proceedings. Ever since Kishi lost office in 1960, using the LDP majority to ram legislation through against a united opposition had been regarded as taboo. The Communists didn't do deals; and the Socialists could be secretly bought off, so the main thing was to get Social Democrat and Komeito support. Both agreed to a special Diet session to consider tax reform on three conditions.

- The session had to be limited to seventy days, starting on 19 July 1988 and ending on 26 September.
- Tax cuts had to be considered separately from the proposed sales tax.
- Tax cuts had to be considered first.

The opposition hoped that time would run out after the tax cuts had been agreed, but before the sales tax had been considered. Takeshita accepted because he thought that if the special session ended with unfinished business, his chances of getting a second two-year term would be enhanced. But events took an unexpected turn when the Recruit Cosmos scandal exploded.

The scandal

The affair surfaced in mid-June 1988 as a minor local incident: a city official in Kawasaki, south of Tokyo, had been forced to resign in disgrace after confessing to buying Recruit Cosmos shares on inside information about the city's development plans. At first, this was dismissed as run-of-the-mill local government corruption. But a newspaper, the *Asahi Shimbun*, digging into the details, discovered a bigger scam involving a veritable 'Who's Who' of Japan's top businessmen, politicians and officials. Its exposure of those involved, published in a series of articles over the next two weeks, turned Japanese politics upside down.

The Recruit Cosmos scandal exposed many aspects of corruption in Japan. The Recruit Company was formed in 1963 by a young graduate from Tokyo University, Hiromasa Ezoe. As an undergraduate, Ezoe helped to produce a student's magazine. In doing so, he discovered the difficulty potential employers had in selecting which graduates to recruit and the difficulty students had in discovering what jobs were on offer. Since employment was for life, both students and their potential employers were eager to make the right choice. Students wanted to shop around, while potential employers each wanted to grab the pick of the bunch before their rivals could get a look in. As in all matters Japanese, there were regulations: employers were not supposed to approach individual students before 1 September, six months ahead of graduation. Consequently, when the hunting season opened, there was a mad scramble by employers to fill their quotas in which the less glamorous companies used dirty tricks to obtain recruits. One trick was to invite potential candidates to company presentations and kidnap them: students would arrive for a meeting, expecting to be there only an hour or two, and be whisked off in coaches to remote resort centres for several days. When they returned, jobs with the best employers were all gone and they had little option but to sign up with their kidnappers.

Ezoe saw a way to profit from this system and set out to plug the information gap caused by the ban on recruitment before the hunting season opened. He published an 'Exchange & Mart' type of magazine, in which employers paid to advertise. Their advertisements were often misleading or downright dishonest, a means of getting students to the vital first meeting at which they could be kidnapped. Ezoe's publishing company prospered and, over the next quarter of a century, he built an empire of twenty-eight companies with interests in information services, real estate and magazine publishing. In the process he became one of Japan's wealthiest individuals.

Like Tanaka, Ezoe was an ambitious outsider, a self-made man. He saw that for his companies to prosper, he must establish close contacts with politicians and bureaucrats. His aim was to gain political respectability and be admitted to the Zaikai, a closely-knit league of top business leaders who worked hand-in-glove with senior politicians and bureaucrats to formulate and implement policy. After that, his sights were set on a political career, which could lead him to the very top. To smooth his way upwards, he lavished gifts on all who could help him. The expansion of his enterprises in the 1980s was exponential; Recruit group turnover climbed by ¥80bn in 1982 to ¥270bn by 1988. Ezoe himself climbed the first rung of the Zaikai ladder with his appointments in 1985 to the government's tax and education advisory councils and in 1987 to its administrative reform and lands policy councils. Not only did these appointments bring respectability, they also gave Ezoe influence in matters directly affecting his own business interests.

Watergate had inspired in Japan a new style of investigative journalism. The *Asahi Shimbun* diggers discovered that the Kawasaki city official had been one of a large group of people who, between 1984 and 1986, had been allocated shares in an unlisted real estate subsidiary,

Recruit Cosmos, owned by the Recruit Group. Many also received loans from the group's financial subsidiary, First Finance, to pay for the purchase of their Recruit Cosmos shares. When the company was listed in 1960 and its shares came to market, their privileged holders were able to sell them at four or five times the shares' original cost. The journalists eventually uncovered the names of 159 people who had received Recruit Cosmos shares, including the secretaries or relatives of almost all Japan's leading politicians – former Prime Ministers Suzuki, Tanaka and Nakasone; the Prime Minister, Takeshita; other LDP faction leaders, Abe, Miyazawa, Watanabe; and the President of the Komeito or 'clean' party, Katsuya Ikeda; top bureaucrats in the Ministries of Education and Labour were found to have received Recruit favours; top businessmen were on the list, notably the chairman of Nippon Telephone & Telegraph, Hisashi Shinto; the President of Sumito Bank & Trust, Osamu Sakurai; and the President, Ko Morita, of a rival newspaper, the leading financial daily, *Nihon Keizai Shimbun*.

The Recruit Cosmos scandal became a long-running saga because there were several lists of names. The first distribution of 1.24 m shares took place in December 1984 to seventy-six people, intended to curry favour with politicians, bureaucrats and businessmen. This was the list which the *Asahi Shimbun* originally discovered and formed the basis of its exposures in early June. But two more issues, of 1.5 m shares in 1985, went to financial institutions and companies run by Ezoe's friends and were to raise capital. Finally, in the summer of 1986, Ezoe was in the middle of a complex deal with NTT and needed a little help from his political friends, while they were short of money after the 1986 General Election. Recruit Cosmos was due to be launched as a listed company in the autumn, but almost all its shares had already been handed out. Ezoe therefore bought 800,000 shares back from his friends and used them to oil the wheels of his NTT deal. With all these complicated manoeuvres, discovering at one fell swoop who had got what from Ezoe was impossible. Consequently, the deeper the investigators dug, the more names emerged.

Gifts of Recruit Cosmos pre-listing shares was only one of the ways that Ezoe distributed largesse. He bought blocks of party tickets, contributed to support organisations and even 'employed' Abe's wife as a 'consultant'. By the time the dust settled it had been revealed that one way and another Takeshita received over ¥200 m ($1.5 m) from Ezoe, Nakasone at least ¥140 m, and Abe and Miyazawa over ¥100 m each. There was nothing illegal in any of these gifts, provided no favours had been supplied in return. This was a matter for the Tokyo District Public Prosecutor's Office to discover, where the chief prosecutor's job was again given to Yusuke Yoshinaga. Remember him? He was the man who had nailed Tanaka over the Lockheed bribes. This time he was out to get Nakasone, who had been named in connection with five previous scandals, including the Lockheed affair.

Yoshinaga concentrated upon three issues: whether Nakasone had arranged for NTT to do Recruit favours; whether he had personally appointed Ezoe to the government's consultancy councils; and, unrelated to Nakasone, whether Ministry of Labour and of Education bureaucrats had done Recruit favours. The NTT affair was the most promising. In 1986 the company bought three American super-computers from Cray Research, two of which it had resold secretly to Recruit, helping it to grab a large share of the market in leasing high-speed digital communication lines. There had been something in this for everybody: Nakasone was under pressue from the Americans to increase public sector purchases of US products and NTT was still in the public sector, so that its computer purchases won Nakasone brownie points; NTT's superior bargaining power obtained the computers at a ¥170 m discount, which it passed on to Recruit; NTT's Chairman, Hisashi Shinto, pocketed a ¥22 m profit from his Recruit Cosmos shares.

Yoshinaga's investigative method was to start with the small fish and work up to the big ones. He had little chance of netting any of the big fish under the Japanese system, unless the smaller ones incriminated them. Diet members cannot be held for questioning while the Diet is sitting and while lesser mortals could be persuaded voluntarily to give evidence, top politicians could not. Faction leaders always operate through their secretaries and claim ignorance of what is done in their name. The secretaries carry the can for their masters, even committing suicide where necessary; Takeshita's top aide, Ihei Aoki, killed himself the day after his master announced his resignation from the Premiership.

During the Lockheed investigation, Yoshinaga had been criticised for conducting his inquiries in private; this time he went to the other extreme. Throughout his work, newspapers were supplied with a steady flow of leaked information to ensure that the case received maximum publicity. If he could not nail Nakasone directly, he might get him indirectly. If Nakasone were expelled from the Diet, his privileged status would be blown. If he was forced to testify before it under oath and lied, he could be charged with perjury.

Yoshinaga had some success at the lower levels. Ezoe and NTT's Shinto were both arrested and indicted. The 78-year-old Shinto was in hospital when he was dragged off to jail, done with full media coverage, indicative of the way Yoshinaga now worked. The two bureaucrats in the Labour and Education Ministries were also brought to trial, who had blocked moves to crack down on misleading job advertisements and changes in the closed season rules for graduate recruitment. Yoshinaga also got two minor politicians: Nakasone's former Cabinet Secretary, Takao Fujinami, took the rap for Ezoe's commission appointments; while Ikeda, the Komeito party boss, was indicted for lesser offences. But the main action was going on elsewhere, in the Diet.

Political blackmail

For months following the Recruit Cosmos exposé, Takeshita struggled to get his tax reforms through the Diet and to survive. Every time the scandal seemed to be subsiding, new developments brought it back to life and in the end it cost Takeshita his job. When the Diet assembled in July for its special session, the opposition demanded that the Recruit Cosmos scandal be discussed before the tax measures were examined. Takeshita refused and all the opposition parties boycotted the Diet's proceedings, bringing them to a halt.

Meanwhile, a repeat performance of the Iwate disaster threatened. (This was the 1987 by-election defeat which helped force Nakasone to drop his sales tax plans). Two rival LDP candidates presented themselves for the gubernatorial election in Fukushima, to be held on 4 September; Toshio Hirose, who stood on an anti-sales tax platform and was endorsed by the Socialists, who withdrew their own candidate; and Eisaku Sato, who supported the party line. When efforts to get both to stand down in favour of a compromise LDP candidate failed, everyone waited with baited breath to see who would win. If Hirose did brilliantly, Takeshita's sales tax might have to be abandoned; if he did badly, the opposition would cave in and attend the Diet proceedings. In the event, Sato won a landslide victory and the following day, Takeshita was able to persuade the opposition to allow the tax reforms to be considered by a special Diet committee, which got them off the floor of the House where they were stalled. But that evening, a secretly filmed interview was shown on TV, in which a Recruit executive attempted to bribe a Social Democrat Diet member, Yanosuke Narazaki, to withdraw demands that the affair be investigated by the House. The bribe attempt, in which ¥5m ($40,000) had been handed over to Narazaki, had been filmed some time before the Fukushima election, but was deliberately held back to torpedo Takeshita's plans. After it was shown, the Social Democrats dared not allow tax reform debate to proceed and Takeshita had to concede defeat. In return for being allowed a Diet inquiry, the opposition let the tax debate start, knowing it could not be completed before the special session ended on 26 September. Takeshita sought one month's extension, to which the opposition agreed on condition that leading LDP politicians gave evidence to the Diet inquiry. This was lethal: those who escaped the Tokyo Prosecutor's bribery charges, because of their privileged parliamentary position, now risked perjury charges.

By 10 November, despite the extension, the tax legislation was again running out of time. In exasperation, Takeshita did the unthinkable – he used his majority to railroad the proposals through a Diet committee although no opposition members were present. There was uproar and the police had to be called into the Diet to quell opposition anger. Once out of the committee, however, the bill still had to pass the lower house and further concessions were required for that; Takeshita agreed to publish the full list of all those who were implicated by the Recruit Cosmos scandal. Finally, it needed upper house approval to become law and this too had to be bought.

The Recruit Cosmos list included the top aides to Nakasone, Takeshita, Abe and Watanabe but the Finance Minister, Kiichi Miyazawa's, own name was on it. He was alleged to have obtained 30,000 shares, which he subsequently sold for a ¥20 m ($150,000) profit. Miyazawa was asked to explain and told the Diet the shares had been bought in his name and without his knowledge, by a business friend of Tsuneo Hattori, his top assistant; but it was soon discovered that this was untrue. Miyazawa next told the Diet that although his aide had bought the shares without his knowledge, Hattori had used his own money. This too was untrue: Recruit's chief, Hiromasa Ezoe, told the Diet that First Finance, a Recruit subsidiary, had lent Hattori the money. Miyazawa escaped prosecution for perjury because he did not give his evidence under oath; but, as its final condition for allowing the tax bill to pass into law, the opposition demanded and got his head. Miyazawa resigned from the Cabinet on 9 December 1988; the tax measures were passed on 24 December and the 3% sales tax came into effect on 1 April 1989. Once more Takeshita breathed a sigh of relief.

Takeshita's downfall

Takeshita believed that the Recruit Cosmos scandal was nothing out of the ordinary and had proved troublesome only because it broke during the tax reform battle. He and most leading politicians never realised its seriousness and, instead of dying down after Miyazawa's sacrificial departure, it blew up in their own faces. Takeshita immediately reshuffled his Cabinet to give it a new, clean image by appointing Takashi Hasegawa to head the Ministry of Justice. Hasegawa promised that he would do nothing to limit the Tokyo Public Prosecutor's inquiry, but when two days later his own name appeared on the growing Recruit list, he promptly resigned; to be following the next day by Ken Harada, the Deputy Prime Minister, who was chairman of the Diet committee investigating the scandal. The *Asahi Shimbun* revealed Harada had received ¥1m from Recruit in August 1988, two months after the scandal first broke.

Having tasted blood, the opposition parties wanted more. The first item on the Diet agenda in the New Year was the fiscal 1989 budget, which had to be passed by 31 March. The opposition continued boycotting Diet proceedings and stalling debates: they were after the bigger fish – in particular, Nakasone, who was refusing to appear before the committee investigating the scandal. Instead, he used a press conference to publicly deny any Recruit Cosmos connections, saying he would not testify until after the Tokyo Public Prosecutor had finished his investigation. Takeshita, whose political life depended on Nakasone's support, could not force him to appear: business in the Diet remained at a standstill throughout the first three months of the year; the regular budget failed to pass; and an emergency fifty-day extension of the previous year's Budget was needed to allow public business to continue into the new fiscal year. Takeshita started to crack under the strain: if he could not force Nakasone to appear before the Diet, perhaps he could shame him into it. On 11 April he himself gave evidence, admitting having received ¥151m from the Recruit Group over the years; but he claimed it had all been done by his secretary and he personally had known nothing about it. Moreover, he had done nothing illegal as no favours had been supplied in return.

Yet again Takeshita hoped that was the end of the matter, but within a week it was revealed that he had not told all. He failed to mention a ¥50m loan to his aide from Recruit in 1987, which had been secretly repaid. Takeshita's position was now undermined. In the Diet, the Budget legislation remained stalled; outside it, his popularity in the opinion polls had slumped to 3.7% – not much higher people said than his hated sales tax. He had been shown to have misled the Diet. A regular upper house election was due in July, which the LDP looked like losing. So finally, on 25 April, Takeshita announced he would resign as soon as the Budget was passed.

The big fish swim free

The stage was now set for the final act in the drama, which involved a complex three-way deal; the selection of a clean new LDP leader; Nakasone's resignation from the LDP; and the termination of the

Public Prosecutor's inquiries. Recruit Cosmos thus interrupted the orderly succession of the Premiership to the other faction leaders, who were all too badly tainted by the scandal. Finding 'Mr Clean' was not easy; everybody who was anybody was tainted. The choice lay between some young politician, who had been too unimportant to receive Recruit money, or some old politician, who had not needed it. The most popular candidate was 75-year-old Masayoshi Ito, the man who had stood in as acting Prime Minister after Ohira's death during the 1970 election campaign. Ito was not a well man and probably would not last long. Who better to entrust the Premiership to while all the fuss died down?

Ito was seen as a fall-guy, but he was not willing to be cast in this role. He would only accept the job on his own terms: demanding to be elected LDP leader for a full two years, not simply the remainder of Takeshita's term; and that all thirteen LDP politicians directly involved with Recruit Cosmos should resign from the Diet – which meant most of them would get locked up. This clean sweep of the discredited existing faction leaders was to be followed by the abolition of factions: the rules governing political contributions were to be severely tightened; and the electoral system was to be reformed to eliminate multi-member constituencies. This was not quite what the old LDP leaders had in mind; they wanted plenty of talk of reform, but no action; and to stay and pull the strings, not to go and serve time. Ito's terms were rejected.

The choice of the next leader was in Takeshita's and Nakasone's hands. They came up with the little known but experienced Foreign Minister, Sousuke Uno; independently wealthy; as clean as a whistle; and a member of the Nakasone faction without a large following of his own. He was the perfect fall-guy, who would do what he was told and lead the LDP into the next lower house elections. The Recruit-tainted old leaders would then stand for re-election and all be returned to the Diet by their grateful constituencies, thereby being purged of their sins. The LDP would probably do badly; Uno would be blamed and easily ditched; the old guard succession could then be resumed.

The second problem was to get Nakasone off the hook. Recruit money had been channelled to him via his former Cabinet Secretary, Takao Fujinami, who would naturally shield his boss. Fujinami voluntarily presented himself to the Public Prosecutor for questioning and was indicted on the charge of doing Ezoe favours in return, i.e. getting him appointed to the government's advisory bodies. That was as close to the top as Yoshinaga was allowed to get. Nakasone agreed to testify, but he simply stonewalled in the Diet, protesting his personal innocence and denying all knowledge of everything. He would take the blame for Recruit Cosmos, but only because it happened while he was Prime

Minister. His performance was unconvincing, but nothing could be proved against him. There was uproar and, on 28 May 1989, he atoned for his sins by resigning from the LDP. He handed over the formal leadership of his faction to Watanabe, but effectively remained its boss. Like Tanaka, he continued as an independent member of the Diet. Finally, on 29 May, it was unexpectedly announced that the Tokyo Department Public Prosecutor's investigation into Recruit Cosmos was complete.

In all forty-three politicians, civil servants, businessmen and journalists were forced to resign over the Recruit Cosmos scandal. Twelve people were prosecuted, a total which included only two of the thirteen politicians taking Recruit bribes. The Public Prosecutor's Office maintained publicly that the other eleven were not in a position to supply favours; privately, it said that it had not been able to get sufficient evidence on them to bring charges. The cut-out between a faction leader and his staff operated perfectly to protect top politicians. The big fish swam free.

19

Taisho versus Showa

On 2 June 1989, the 66–year-old Sousuke Uno was confirmed as leader of the LDP. He was not, however, given unanimous support: two former Prime Ministers, Fukuda and Suzuki, and thirty-eight other Dietmen boycotted the meeting. A dissident candidate was sponsored and received forty-eight votes to Uno's 392. Nonetheless, the party leaders breathed a sigh of relief. The Budget had been steam-rollered through the Diet and became law on 27 May; the Recruit inquiry was over; and the stream of new revelations, which had disrupted Diet business for nearly a year, was finally ended. A month remained in which to placate the electorate before the July upper house elections and a year before the next lower house elction had to be called. Peace at last – how wrong they were.

Within two days of Uno's appointment, a Japanese weekly magazine, the *Sunday Mainichi*, carried the story of his association with a second-rate geisha under the headline, 'You Bought my Body for ¥300,000 a Month'. Just as the LDP leaders never realised the seriousness of the Recruit Cosmos revelations until too late, so now they were astounded when news of Uno's past affair caused a scandal. Seamy stories often appeared in Japanese weekly magazines, but seldom made it to the pages of national dailies. Tokyo journalists did not pry into politicians' private lives; to do so risked being excluded from the flow of managed information. But the story, although written in Japanese, was picked up and reported by the world's press. The age of modern communications meant dirty washing could no longer be done secretly at home. But why the fuss? It was common practice for top politicians to keep mistresses – Tanaka had taken his with him to diplomatic functions. If, in addition to corruption, bought-sex outside marriage was to bar a politician from high office, the party would have difficulty in mustering enough members to fill a Cabinet. In the LDP leaders' eyes, the only crime that Uno had committed was to dally with a cheap prostitute and then not pay her enough to keep her mouth shut.

Thereafter things went from bad to worse: the press attempted to dig up fresh dirt almost daily. It ran stories saying Uno had a penchant for under-aged girls, which were retracted when no proof could be found. In late June the party was heavily defeated in a by-election in the rural rice-growing prefecture of Niigata. A 44-year-old Socialist housewife, new to politics, thrashed her LDP opponent. In early July, the party lost heavily to the Socialists in Tokyo's local elections. Female voters deserted the LDP because of the new sales tax and Uno's womanising. They were further offended during the upper house election campaign, when the Agriculture Minister, Hisao Horinouchi, denounced women as 'useless in the world of politics' – he was attacking the Socialist party's charismatic leader, Mrs Takako Doi. Finally the upper house elections took place on 23 July 1989. Farmers fed up by the liberalisation of beef and citrus imports, salary-earners mad about the Recruit Cosmos scandal, and housewives all deserted the party. The LDP received a thrashing.

Before the election the LDP held a comfortable majority in the 252 House of Councillors. As always, only half the seats in the chamber came up for re-election. The LDP defended sixty-nine seats and won only thirty-six and its strength dropped to 109, or seventeen short of a majority. The Socialists, defending twenty-two seats won forty-six and their strength increased to seventy-six. Komeito won ten seats to give it a strength of twenty-one – henceforth the LDP needed its support to get legislation through the upper house. Both houses of the Diet can initiate legislation, but in any contest between them the House of Representatives can usually prevail. If Councillors reject budget legislation or treaties, and the differences between the two houses cannot be resolved within a month, the Representatives' legislation automatically becomes law. On all other matters – including changes in tax rates – a two-thirds majority in the House of Representatives is needed to overcome an upper house veto. The LDP held only 293 seats of the 512 in the lower house, forty-eight short of a two-thirds majority. As in the upper house, it would henceforth need Komeito support if things came to a crunch.

The Prime Minister, Sousuke Uno, accepted responsibility for the LDP's election disaster and resigned the day after.

The second Mr Clean

Finding a replacement for Uno posed all the old problems: Abe and Miyazawa, still hoping for their turns at the top, did not want to see the succession pass irrevocably to the younger generation. They refused to support younger men in their own factions. Watanabe, the Nakasone faction candidate, was an older generation member tainted by the Recruit Cosmos scandal. This left either a candidate from Takeshita's faction or from the small Komoto faction. Takeshita's control over his faction was seriously threatened by its chairman, Shin Kanemaru, who was angry with his boss, who had failed to consult him over Uno's selection. Uno's disgrace undermined Takeshita and elevated Kanemaru to kingmaker. He was tipped to go for the job himself, but claimed not to want it. Although he was not directly implicated in the Recruit Cosmos scandal, he was well known for his involvement in shady construction deals. He thus seemed better placed to pull strings behind the scenes, as his old mentor Tanaka had done, and therefore supported younger men, but again from other factions. Kanemaru would not allow any other Takeshita faction candidate to replace Uno, which ruled out three of the party's most promising young men, Ryutaro Hashimoto, Ichiro Ozawa and Tsutomu Hata. Komoto, although old, would still have liked a go at the job. But he was ruled out because of his connection with the Sanko Steamship Company, whose collapse in 1985 (partly engineered by Tanaka) had been Japan's biggest post-war bankruptcy. Thus, in private and by default, the party elders' choice settled on a Komoto faction member, Toshiki Kaifu.

Kaifu turned out to be a popular choice. Having served out the remainder of the Takeshita/Uno term, he was reconfirmed in the leadership in autumn 1989 for his own two-year term. The LDP's popularity recovered as memories of the Recruit Cosmos scandal faded. The lower house election was held in February 1990 and the LDP performed far better than expected. It obtained a smaller, but still comfortable, working majority, winning 270 out of 512 seats with its official candidates and collecting the support of sixteen who won as independents. All the old generation leaders involved in the Recruit Cosmos scandal were re-elected, purged of their sins. Kaifu's popularity exceeded his party's and it was impossible to ditch him after he had done so well. The only way he could have been forced out was by a defeat in a Diet censure vote, which would have led to another election, in which those responsible for his defeat would have been savaged. So Kaifu was able to continue to October 1991.

Older versus younger

The battle-lines were immediately redrawn for the long run up to the 1991 leadership struggle – between old and young leaders. Abe, Miyazawa, Watanabe and Komoto still wanted their turns at the top, and Takeshita hoped to make a come-back. All had been born during the reign of the Emperor Taisho (1912–26). Nakasone's power had waned, putting him out of the running for another turn. His disgrace had reduced his ability to raise political contributions. He spent the General Election campaign in his own constituency fighting for himself, not outside it helping other faction members with theirs. Many did not want his help. He won his seat with ease, but immediately after the election handed effective control of his faction to Watanabe.

The young generation hopefuls were all born during the Showa era (1926–89): Hata, Hashimoto, Keizo Obuchi and Ozawa from the Takeshita faction; Mitsuzuka and Yoshi Mori from the Abe faction; Koichi Kato from the Miyazawa faction; and Taku Yamasaki from Watanabe's faction. If any of them got the job, or if Kaifu, also a Showa era man, obtained a second turn, that would be the end of the Taisho era politicians. Japanese factional politics therefore became a battle between generations, in addition one between rivals in the same generation. Kanemaru, although a Taisho politician, sided with the Showa generation; his battle to control the Takeshita faction was to be an important element in the in-fighting which followed. Kanemaru favoured one of the young contenders in his faction, Ozawa; whereas Takeshita was closer to another, Hashimoto. Rival alliances developed, with Kanemaru/Ozawa/Kaifu the most powerful. Takeshita was allied with Abe, who had been promised the next turn as Prime Minister.

The attack on Kaifu

The Taisho generation's hopes of making a comeback lay in discrediting Kaifu for his handling of the government. Their hopes of regaining the Premiership rested on resisting change and reform as their power came from money politics and the electoral system as it was. They were no longer government ministers. After the February 1990 election, Kaifu had insisted that nobody tainted by either Recruit Cosmos or Lockheed be given a government job. All the top jobs used to go to faction leaders, who also controlled the party; in Kaifu's Cabinets none of them did. He thus faced problems getting measures agreed in the party, in addition to the usual problems of getting them passed by the Diet. The old were champions of the status quo and hampered the preparation and implementation of policy: the younger men with governmental responsibility were forced, by economic circumstances and pressure from abroad, to campaign for change. The Showa generation, particularly Ozawa, are internationally oriented and outward looking; while many older Taisho politicians are totally insular. These old conservatives are widely supported by farmers and small businessmen, whom the younger men were bound to alienate. The Taisho leaders thus believed that they could still pull all the strings. On the young men's side was Kaifu's patronage in appointing ministers and constant reminders of past scandals and corruption – plenty emerged from the rubble of the 1990 stockmarket collapse.

This was the political background in August 1990, when Iraq invaded Kuwait; it explains Japan's sorry role in the Gulf crisis. Domestic political pressure created few problems for the government: when a majority of Japanese supported something, it could be got through the Diet without exposing Kaifu's flank to the Taisho generation. But foreign pressure for action placed the government in a cleft stick: it could be blamed for either capitulating to it; or take the consequences of resisting it. Japan's role in the Gulf crisis was regarded by Americans as pusillanimous and stingy; but at home there was strong opposition to the little that Japan was able and willing to do.

Kaifu was in an embarrassing position. The Japanese Constitution forbids the use of Japan's defence forces abroad. Nonetheless, President Bush called for both men and money to back the United Nations' intervention. The Taisho leadership saw its chance to embarrass the government. Japan was slow in condemning Saddam Hussein's aggression, as it had substantial Middle East interests and tried to get on well with all Arab countries. Opinion polls showed that a majority opposed Japanese involvement in the effort to evict Saddam Hussein from Kuwait. Nonetheless, Ozawa, the LDP Secretary General, persuaded Kaifu to try to change Japanese law to allow the Self-Defence Force to be used in a supporting role in the Gulf. Between August and October a controversial UN Peace Co-operation bill was cobbled together within the party. It was introduced into the Diet special session which started on 12 October 1990. All the opposition parties were against the bill and there was an outcry from the public and neighbouring Asian countries. The government failed to muster a Diet majority; in November the bill was defeated; and Kaifu lost face both at home and abroad.

If Japan could not supply men, it had to supply yen. Its initial aid offer, however, was a miserable $1 bn – not much more than a Japanese company had just paid for the Pebble Beach golf course. The offer was soon increased to $4 bn and, when the UN Peace Co-operation bill was thrown out, a further $9 bn aid package was proposed. Party elders favoured aid: they feared that if none was forthcoming the US would retaliate against Japanese trade, which would hurt their industrialist pals. Getting LDP support for the measure was no problem; getting it through the Diet was another matter. After his November failure, Kaifu's political life depended on success: if the aid package did not go through, retaliation from America would be swift and painful and he would be blamed.

Komeito party support was required in the upper house of the Diet and it was Ozawa's job to obtain it. Komeito demanded in return the LDP's help in ousting the eighty-year-old LDP Governor of Tokyo, Shunichi Suzuki, in the April 1991 local elections. His place was to be taken by Hisanori Isomura, a 61-year-old Tokyo television news anchorman. Ozawa dumped Suzuki as the LDP's official candidate and in early march the Komeito party repaid him by helping the $9 bn aid package through the upper house. The older generation saw another chance to stir up trouble and took it; the Tokyo election became a 'get Ozawa' battle. Local LDP chapters backed Suzuki and so did the Socialists, enabling him to win a resounding victory, which forced Ozawa to resign from the powerful LDP Secretary General's job.

Kaifu counter-attacks

Although Kaifu's main supporters, Kanemaru and Ozawa, lost ground as a result of local elections, the LDP as a whole did remarkably well. The 1988 disaster, which had forced Nakasone to abandon his proposed VAT, was reversed. The Socialists were routed. The tide which carried them to successes in the 1989 upper house election was on the ebb. After Socialist failures in the 1990 lower house and 1991 local elections, the LDP's monopoly of power had been re-established; Mrs Doi was blamed and in June she resigned the Socialist leadership. Gleefully the old Taisho generation claimed that the party had been forgiven by the voters for the Recruit Cosmos scandal, and that the way was clear for their return to government office. Takeshita promptly orchestrated Nakasone's re-admission to LDP membership; so skilfully was this accomplished, that when journalists asked Kaifu how he reacted, they discovered he did not know about it. While Nakasone could not run for the LDP leadership when Kaifu's term expired in October, Takeshita's actions gave a clear warning that he was preparing to do so.

Securities scandals

The old gang underestimated Kaifu, who knew that the big securities houses were hand-in-glove with the Taisho generation of corrupt politicians. By May 1991 rumours were even reaching visiting foreign journalists that Kaifu would be kicked out of the LDP leadership and Takeshita would reclaim it. The links between the securities industry and the Takeshita faction were extremely close and Setsuya Tabuchi,

Nomura's Chairman, was one of the country's most powerful men. Not only was he chairman of the world's largest stockbroker, but he was the boss of the securities houses organisation and executive vice-chairman of the Keidanren – tipped to become its next chairman.

Kaifu realised that if he could bring the securities houses' nefarious activities into the open, hopefully he could discredit them and brush aside Nakasone, Takeshita, and Miyazawa with a single swipe. The Justice Ministry had evidence that Nomura and Nikko had been paying off gangsters, and tax officials knew that Japan's largest stockbrokers, Nomura, Daiwa, Nikko and Yamaichi Securities, had compensated big corporate investors for losses sustained in the Tokyo bear market. The brokers had treated these payments as business expenses in their 1990 accounts, thereby avoiding tax payments on them. The tax men enforced payment, but in the typical Japanese manner. There had long been a system in Japan of 'voluntary' tax payments, by which anyone could come along and say, 'Sorry, I made a mistake in my last year's accounts and owe you more than I thought'. When this happened, it was customary for no further questions to be asked. During fiscal 1991 Nomura made a ¥16 bn voluntary tax payment, but this time questions were asked.

The yakuza connection

Apart from compensation payments, Nomura and Nikko had two further strikes against them: they had lent money to a prominent yakuza gangster and ramped share prices. Crime, like everything else in Japan is carefully regulated. The yakuza gangs are legal and their members' names are registered with the police. In 1988 there were 3197 yakuza gangs with a membership of 86,552. The three biggest gangs – Yamaguchi-Gumi, Inagawa-Kai and Sumiyoshi-Rengo – are amongst the largest privately controlled organisations in the country; Yamaguchi-Gumi, for instance, has over 20,000 members. A government report in May 1991 estimated that 41% of Japanese companies were under the influence or control of the yakuza. The police and the gangs often work together: the gangs help to prevent street and petty crime; collect debts; and sort out responsibility for road accidents. In return they are allowed a relatively free hand to run protection rackets, control the drug trade, prostitution and gambling, particularly the pachinko parlours. A special branch of the yakuza, the sokaiya, specialises in extorting money from large publicly quoted companies. One of the sokaiya's favourite tricks is to break up companies' annual meetings, unless they have been paid to keep them peaceful. An attempt was made in 1982 to stamp out sokaiya by making payments to them illegal. It failed: a recent report showed that 40% of companies holding their annual meetings in June 1991 were approached by sokaiya and most paid some protection money.

The securities houses' relationship with gangsters went back a long way. They used to pay off the sokaiya; but in the late 1980s refused to do so. As with over 90% of Japanese companies, they changed their accounting years so that all of them ended on 31 March, and arranged to hold all annual meetings on the same day. The sokaiya did not have enough members to handle them all at once. A 'war' broke out between the powerful securities houses and the yakuza. Over the last three months of 1988, when the old Emperor lay dying, right-wing extremist organisations employed the yakuza to ensure nobody was seen having a good time and enjoying themselves. The yakuza terrorised securities houses' executives, following them to bars and clubs, tracing their cars to find where they lived and generally made life uncomfortable. So strong was their power that they even forced a clampdown on entertaining by Japanese subsidiaries overseas. The securities houses were forced to buy them off.

The gangster connection involved loans of ¥36 bn from Nomura and Nikko to Susumu Ishii, leader of the Inagawa-Kai yakuza gang. Both companies made the loans through their finance company subsidiaries after Ishii had been introduced to the parent companies by a sokaiya extortionist. It was protection money. Ishii used the money to buy shares in Tokyu Corporation, a leading railway company. Tokyu was then targeted by securities salesmen in October 1989 and its share price rose 50% in four weeks. Some of the securities' branches did more than half their total business during that month in Toyku shares.

Favoured clients

The compensation story went back to the zaitech days of the 1985–9 great bull market, when companies raised billions of yen in financial markets to finance speculation. For tax reasons much of the money was handed to the major brokers to manage in discretionary eigyo tokkin accounts. These were illegal, stockbrokers were not supposed to manage money. In 1986 the Ministry of Finance securities bureau had turned a blind eye to eigyo tokkins, pretending that they did not exist. But in December 1989 the bureau changed its tune. It was worried by the speculation – which had lifted the Nikkei index by 120% in two years – and ordered the stockbrokers to wind up by December 1990 their 22,485 (officially non-existent) eigyo tokkins; it also outlawed compensation payments for losses.

The administrative ban on compensation did not have the force of law.

Provided no promises had been made to do so in advance, compensating clients for stockmarket losses was not illegal. The order was also vague as the brokers were not told when it was to come into effect. The securities bureau was simply covering its back. While in December 1989 the Tokyo market was booming, so in closing eigyo tokkins no compensation payments would be needed. Early in 1990 the market crashed and everything changed. Closing tokkins, as ordered, would force companies to realise large losses. The major securities houses' top management met and decided, with tacit securities bureau approval, that they could only obey the closure order, by disobeying the compensation order. In fact little progress was made in closing eigyo tokkins; 18,122 remained open in March 1991.

The securities scandal broke on Wednesday 19 June 1991, when the Tokyo Regional Tax Bureau leaked to the press a 'possible ¥16 bn compensation payment' had been made. This forced an ill-prepared Nomura to hold a press conference on Thursday, at which Vice President Yasuhiro Mizuuchi denied 'promises of compensation' had been made. Friday saw a flurry of further press conferences. Mizuuchi was forced to admit that 'promises of compensation may have been given'. He was clearly shaken. Nikko admitted similar compensation payments. But Nobuhiko Matsuno, Director General of the Securities Bureau, said neither broker had contravened any securities exchange laws. They had simply disobeyed administrative guidance, which had been imposed in December 1989 after Daiwa had admitted to making such payments. The securities exchange law would, however, have to be revised so that compensation payments were clearly and explicitly banned.

This was supposed to end the scandal, but it did not. Immediately after the weekend, Presidents Yoshihisa Tabuchi of Nomura and Takuya Iwasashi of Nikko publicly apologised and resigned. Nomura's Chairman, Setsuya Tabuchi, tried to bluff it out. But one month later he also resigned and was discharged from his Keidanren post – an almost unheard of thing.

The open secret of regulatory approval meant that the Ministry of Finance, as well as the brokers, had to be punished: the brokers were fined ¥9 bn and forced to stop trading for four working days; seventy-four securities company executives were dismissed, demoted or had their pay cut; the Minister of Finance, Ryutaro Hashimoto, publicly apologised and together with four top Ministry officials, took a pay cut – one of those punished had not been in his job when the payments were made.

The public demand for names – supported by Kaifu – was so great that there was no way of avoiding publishing a list. It included 231 favoured clients, who shared a total of ¥128 bn in compensation payments. It was a blue-chip who's-who: Toyota, Nissan, Hitachi, Matsushita, Marubeni, C. Itoh, Kawasaki Steel, Showa Shell Sekiyu were all on it, as well as several public sector pension funds, including the Ministry of Finance Pension Fund – but no politicians were named. Hot on the heels of the big brokers' lists came those of thirteen second-tier brokers, which increased the names released to 608 and upped the total compensation to ¥172 bn. Only a little political blood was spilt: a company run by Shin Kanemaru's wife was on the second list and so was the Buddhist lay organisation, the Soka Gakkai, which finances the Komeito 'clean' party.

That should have been the end of the securities scandal but, like the Recruit Cosmos scandal, it rumbled on. The lists published covered payments only to March 1990, and although the brokers at first denied it, payments had continued through to March 1991. Further details were dragged out following Diet hearings: the big four admitted to ¥44 bn compensation to seventy-eight clients during 1990–1. Again no political connections were revealed, but the details contained one surprise; Nomura, the largest broker, paid out only ¥435 m to six clients, compared with Nikko's ¥23.5 bn to twenty-three. Why were the Nomura pay-outs so low? It seems unlikely that it had stopped making payments during 1990. The Tokyo market had crashed a second time following Iraq's invasion of Kuwait in August and further large losses had been incurred. It is rumoured that Nomura's second list was sanitised.

The affair was wound up in typical Japanese fashion. Stockbrokers were forced to suspend most operations for four to six weeks and the ban on their government bond business was extended. But the securities bureau also announced that it could find no evidence that Nomura or Nikko had broken any laws by promising compensation or ramping Tokyu shares. Thus brokers received administrative punishment for disobeying administrative guidance. They were not indicted, tried, convicted and punished by court of law. The brokers' bosses were forced to testify in the Diet, but it was no inquisition. It was theatre in which the accused were publicly humiliated by being forced to apologise and show contrition. Gangster Ishii conveniently died and Finance Minister, Ryutaro Hashimoto, announced his resignation to take responsibility for the scandal. But first he saw reforms to the Securities and Exchange law through the Diet. These were half-baked: eigyo tokkins and compensation payments were made illegal, but the maximum punishment for illegal payments – ¥1 m fines for brokers and ¥500,000 for clients, plus minimal jail sentences – is ridiculously lenient; the definition of 'compensation' was left to the self-regulatory Japanese Security Dealers' Association; a watch-dog securities regulatory agency was established, but as part of the Ministry of Finance – the Japanese bureaucracy will not give up its arbitrary powers without further battles.

Unlike Recruit Cosmos, no top politicians were nailed in the securities scandal. Moreover, despite concurrent Fuji and IBJ bank scandals, there was no public outcry against political corruption. To this extent Kaifu failed; but he almost achieved one objective: Takeshita did abandon his leadership bid and supported Kaifu for a further two-year term. This possibly explains why the matter was closed without Nomura's second compensation list being questioned.

Electoral reform

The Takeshita faction, although the most powerful, could not outvote all the other main factions if they combined, and Kaifu's bid to remain Premier was defeated. The issue which settled his fate was electoral reform. A special session of the Diet opened on 5 August to consider four measures which Kaifu hoped to enact before his first term was over: a new bill to allow Japanese forces to serve overseas as part of UN peacekeeping operations; new securities laws; a Political Funds Control bill; and a Public Office Election bill, which proposed scrapping the multi-member, single-vote system. In its place 300 Dietmen would be elected to represent single-member constituencies and a further 171 would be chosen by proportional representation from party lists. Each voter would get two votes, one for his local Representative and one for a party. The total number of Dietmen would fall from 512 to 471.

With Takeshita's support, Kaifu had obtained party approval in June 1991 for this electoral reform bill. But Miyazawa, Mitsuzuka and Watanabe opposed it and combined to throw the legislation out of the Diet. They demanded further consideration within the LDP and between it and other parties, before any new legislation was tabled, which could delay legislation for months, if not kill it.

Following his Diet defeat, Kaifu considered one last gamble: if he could get Cabinet agreement, he could follow Ohira's example by dissolving the Diet and appealing to the public in a General Election. He was Japan's most popular post-war Prime Minister with the highest opinion poll support and this way the Showa generation, which controlled the government, could still possibly beat the Taisho party bosses. Kanemaru and Takeshita were horrified: Kanemaru prevented the Cabinet from meeting, and he and Takeshita withdrew their support for Kaifu's second term. Kaifu could not possibly win re-election without them and was forced to withdraw from the leadership battle.

Miyazawa makes it

Kaifu's withdrawal left three candidates: Watanabe, Mitsuzuka and Miyazawa. The Takeshita faction could have nominated a fourth from its own ranks, either Ryutaro Hashimoto or Ichiro Ozawa. But Hashimoto had been disgraced too recently by the securities and banking scandals; and although Ozawa was pressed to enter, he declined on grounds of both health and youth – he had suffered a mild heart attack in the summer. The Takeshita faction had then to throw its weight behind the leader of another faction. But which? The decision was made by competitive tender: each of the three contenders was interviewed by Ozawa to see what they would offer for Takeshita support. Miyazawa promised the most; aged seventy-two and in a hurry, he would be only a one-term Premier. In the LDP party election, held on 27 October, he won the Presidency, but by a moderate margin; Watanabe did surprisingly well; and Mitsuzuka did badly. The price Miyazawa paid became clear when his twenty-one-member cabinet was announced: only one of his own faction members was included in a minor job; the Takeshita faction obtained six places, all senior; Watanabe was chosen as Deputy-Prime Minister and his faction got three; Kanemaru wanted the Mitsuzuka faction frozen out altogether, but eventually it received a few minor posts.

Miyazawa's Premiership returned control of the government to faction leaders. It was expected that he would therefore be better able to control the party and the Diet – instead civil war within the party intensified; while the opposition parties turned the heat back on the corrupt LDP old guard.

A new UN peace-keeping bill was submitted to the Diet and in November was forced through a lower house committee – leading to brawls between Diet members. But Miyazawa failed to get it through the upper house and it lapsed when the session ended. It is unlikely to be reintroduced before the upper house elections in July 1992, as no opposition party will assist the LDP with legislation until that is over. The alternative, an international contributions tax of ¥1.3 trn, which was supported by the Ministry of Finance, was then killed by the chairman, Kabun Muto, of the LDP's tax-research commission – Miyazawa thus failed both to get legislation through the Diet and to get policy through the party, looking inept in the process. He fared little better in international relations where he was expected to score. He lost face when President Bush called off a visit to Japan scheduled for just before the fiftieth anniversary of Pearl Harbor, which was supposed to re-affirm the friendly co-operation and mutual dependence between the two countries. When Bush did arrive in January 1992, it was not for a meeting of world leaders to discuss global strategy, but as the head of a trade mission with twenty-five leading American industrialists in tow. Japan was pressed further along the road to managed trade; but what Miyazawa could offer both fell short of US demands and exceeded what Japan hoped to give – Miyazawa's popularity slumped.

All action to reform money politics was suspended in advance of the upper house elections and, as was expected, the return of the Taisho politicians to government led immediately to further scandals. The opposition reopened the Recruit Cosmos scandal, forcing Miyazawa to supply documents related to the affair to the Diet. These showed that his own personal secretary had authorised payment for Recruit Cosmos shares and not, as he had earlier maintained, his faction's top aide. The claim that Miyazawa had no personal knowledge of the pay-off is wearing thin.

While raking the embers of the Recruit Cosmos scandal may yield little, two new scandals could rock the LDP to its foundations. On 13 January 1992, Fumio Abe, formerly the Miyazawa faction's Secretary General, was arrested for taking ¥80 m ($640,000) in bribes from Kyowa, a steel frame maker. Two LDP members are under suspicion of receiving Kyowa money – the former Prime Minister, Zenko Suzuki and a former top official, Jun Shiozaki. The opposition parties, as usual, have boycotted the Diet's budget debate bringing government business to a halt. They are demanding that both men appear before the Diet to be questioned on oath. While, according to *The Economist* (8 February 1992), a new scandal is brewing involving a parcel delivery company, Sagawa, which 'in its size and political reach dwarf all earlier ones'.

Middle-aged militants

As the struggle within the LDP and between it and the opposition parties intensifies, two further skirmishes will play their part. The first is between men who owe their careers to connections and nepotism and those who have worked their own way up unaided. Under the seniority system, the latter stand less chance of reaching the top, because they first entered the Diet at an older age. They therefore have an incentive to discredit, whenever possible, their more privileged colleagues.

The second is a generational battle of a different kind. Consider the career of a bureaucrat; he reaches a position of power and influence aged around forty-five and retires from the civil service aged fifty-five, so that top bureaucrats are a generation younger than the top politicians. This generation gap used to be bridged by former bureaucrats becoming top politicians – it no longer is. The bureaucrat might still hope to 'descend from heaven' into a top job in industry or finance, but this is becoming harder: the Lockheed, Recruit Cosmos and securities scandals have made it less easy for bureaucrats to look after their friends; and deregulation is transforming the system of administrative guidance under which favours were done. The long years of hard work on low pay, spent getting to the top of the bureaucracy, do not promise the rewards that once followed. After the securities scandal, it will be much harder for a financial institution to appoint former top officials from the Ministry of Finance to plush jobs – this smells too much.

Men aged forty-five to fifty-five in 1990 were aged fifteen to twenty-five in 1960. They are the product of the student generation of the 1960s, when radical movements could mobilise 80% of all students to their protests. Those 1960s students who gained entry into the Civil Service were the pick of the bunch – the very brightest – and the brightest students are often the most radical and idealistic. They grew up opposed to the system and there is little reason to think that they are much less opposed to it now. The analogy is with the generation of left-wing Cambridge undergraduates of the 1930s, who infiltrated the British civil service and security services. They were the moles and the spies who, in the 1940s to 1960s, tried to destroy the system from within. In the story related above, every time the old politicians thought the Recruit Cosmos scandal was dead, something happened to revive it. The bureaucrat still has enormous independence from his political masters; the tax bureau official and the Public Prosecutor's office, once they have their teeth into a scandal, cannot easily be dragged off. Similarly journalists of the same generation have become more investigative, more willing to throw dirt. I doubt whether there is a conspiracy to bring down the present Japanese system of government and money politicians with it; I have no evidence of it. Nor need there be any; the generational gap simply means that the Japanese Establishment is now riven between those fighting to maintain the corrupt old ways and those wanting and able to change them. The independent actions of officials are attacking corrupt politics from within.

20

The Hara-Kiri Economy

The reader who supposed Japan to be like any other advanced economy will by now have been disabused. We have considered its grotesque tax system, in which the majority cheats, and seen how little is being done to reform it. We have looked at how the government spends tax-payers' money and found neglect and corruption. We have examined the financial system, designed to fleece the saver and reformed to finance the speculator. We have looked at a nation growing old, because young women are in no hurry to become housewives and mothers. We have noticed how the tax man encourages cabbage cultivation in city centres, while penalising the provision of decent housing. When the average worker on the average income cannot buy the average home in a hundred years, something is sadly awry. We have seen 3 m farmers, receiving subsidised incomes equalling thrice the value of the food they produce, as a reward for misusing four times the land the remaining 121 m Japanese live on, while double the needed number of shopkeepers go on charging extortionate prices to earn miserable incomes from providing wasteful services to complacent consumers, because they can veto new competition. We have looked at industry, riddled with cartels, price-fixing and collusion; at bid-rigging construction dangos in league with gangsters, greasing the palms of greedy politicians.

The reader who supposed Japan was a democracy should by now know better. Politicians fairly elected, laws precisely drafted, impartially applied and widely obeyed, could never have produced such a monstrosity. Bribes and threats determine how unequal votes are cast in unsecret ballots to elect politicians without policies or principles to pursue the interests of their corrupt and criminal paymasters. All are not equal under the law; robber barons of politics, business, finance and organised crime are above it. This is no economic superpower bent on world domination. It is a hara-kiri economy, set to self-destruct.

Trade war or civil war?

Can power, dishonestly obtained, be honestly used? The old generation of politicians has been at the forefront of pressure for economic reform. Masayoshi Ohira died while trying to sell fairer taxation to the nation. Yasuhiro Nakasone and Noboru Takeshita struggled to impose tax reforms until each lost their jobs. Toshiki Kaifu went down fighting for electoral reform. Even Kiichi Miyazawa, who became Prime Minister in November 1991, favours reform. Why? All have followed in the footsteps of their forebears. Twice in modern history Japan has had to choose between foreign war or civil war. The Tokugawa Shogunate bowed to pressure from abroad and was forcibly overthrown at home. General Tojo bowed to domestic pressures and launched an unwinnable foreign war. Today's LDP leaders face a similar choice, between trade war and political civil war. A gulf has emerged between the interests of Japan's advanced industrial and financial sectors, exposed to foreign sanctions, and of its sheltered and backward services and agricultural sectors. Urban workers bear the burden of inefficient farmers, shopkeepers and small businessmen. Foreigners no longer demand change at Japan's frontiers, they urge reform within Japan. Industry, urban workers and foreigners are on the same side. If reform is not forthcoming, industry suffers from foreign reprisals. With political power drifting from rural to urban Japan, the LDP will be driven from office unless it heeds industry's needs. For the past decade, the Japanese government has tried to steer a middle course, pushing reform as far and as fast as it dared at home, while hoping it would not be considered too little too late abroad. But time is running out.

The bubble that burst

The problem of excess savings remains to be solved; until it is, Japanese growth will depend upon how long foreigners remain willing to allow its exports free access to their markets. Optimists see some reasons for hope. It can be argued that excess savings are normal in all mature economies. They need not lead to domestic stagnation if invested abroad in developing countries where investment opportunities are plentiful and returns are high. In the heyday of the old Gold Standard, capital flowed on a substantial scale from Britain and Europe to develop the Americas and foreign empires straddling the globe. For three decades before 1914 Britain ran a current account surplus, which averaged 5% of GDP. Some people now see the prospect of another golden age of international investment. Former communist countries will need foreign funds to help create market economies and to catch up with the West. After a decade in the doldrums, Latin American economies are returning as credit-worthy borrowers to world markets. The old Pacific 'tigers', Hong Kong, Singapore, South Korea and Taiwan, will be joined as rapidly developing economies by new tigers, Thailand, Malaysia, Indonesia and the Philippines. Finally, the sleepy Chinese giant is awakening. In a nutshell, the world faces a shortage of savings, not an excess.

In the 1980s, Japan's excess savings flowed to other OECD countries, such as the US and Britain, which borrowed to consume more than they produced: there is a limit to the amount any country, however rich, can borrow to consume and it has been reached. In the 1990s, Japanese excess savings will be diverted to Eastern Europe, Latin America and the Pacific – to countries which will borrow to produce more tomorrow. A country which uses borrowed money productively can continue, as the US did before 1910, to run payments deficits for decades. So like Britain before 1914, Japan can go on running large current account surpluses and will so do.

While this argument is persuasive, it contains certain flaws. The US current account deficit during the 1980s was an aberration. In every other decade since 1910, when the US reached economic maturity, it ran current account surpluses. Wartime apart, Britain has run surpluses, barring the late 1980s, for over two centuries. Both countries' growth in the past decade derived from falling savings and a build-up of excessive debt. During the present decade these debt levels will be reduced and savings will recover. Both will depend on export-led growth to avoid stagnation, and must move back into current account surplus and start exporting capital again. Despite the prospect of greater capital needs in Eastern Europe and Latin America by the end of the decade, the supply of capital is likely to outpace the demand for it until well into the decade. The US and Europe, like Japan, are now in a deflationary mode. Recovery from the present recession will be painfully slow.

With regional economic rivalry replacing national economic rivalry, the Americas and Europe will form free trade areas, to which Japanese exports will be restricted. US surplus savings will look after the capital needs of Mexico and Latin America; while British and other Western European countries' excess savings will flow to Eastern Europe and the new Commonwealth of Independent States.

Japan faces greater problems in the Pacific. The region is less homogeneous than Europe and America. It is less likely to form a trading block centred on Japan and fed by Japanese capital. Rapidly developing Asian economies tend to generate their own high rates of savings, as Japan did during its miraculous growth years. They are less willing to run persistent trade deficits and politically still reluctant to see the ownership of their assets pass into Japanese hands. The problem of excess Japanese savings will not readily be solved in a world in which the US, Britain and Western Europe are also competing to run payments surpluses.

Even if the problem were solved by continued payments surpluses, the persistence of excess savings would imply uncorrected distortions in the domestic economy. Japanese savings are needed to create a decent social infrastructure and to supply its own citizens with the quality of life they deserve. Politically it will be impossible to deny them this for much longer.

The US, meanwhile, has given notice that its patience with Japan is almost exhausted; President Bush's visit in January 1992 was a warning – Japan must either restrict exports and boost imports or trade sanctions will be imposed. Any move to managed trade between the US and Japan will divert the country's exports to Europe, which in turn will shut them out. Since the bubble economy burst in 1990, the economy has been heading for a recession; how bad it will be and how long it will last remains to be seen – it could be severe and protracted, although the authorities will do everything they can to prevent this. Yet if they succeed, they will merely buy time and the collapse, when it comes, will be worse.

In solving the problem of excess savings, Japan is on the horns of a dilemma: to give its citizens the quality of life they deserve and increasingly demand, resources of land and property must be efficiently used for the benefit of all, and to create a fairer society, wealth must be redistributed from 'haves' to 'have nots' and the rewards from earning raised relative to those from owning. To achieve these ends, land, property and share prices must fall further, endangering the country's financial system, and consensus politics must be abandoned, leading to the demise of the LDP.

Both these processes are under way. Falling asset prices have placed severe strains on the financial system and the economy. Limitless and virtually costless credit encouraged Japanese industry to embark on a massive capital-spending programme during the late 1980s. In 1985, when the financial bubble began to inflate, business investment accounted for 16% of Japan's GNP – a reasonable proportion for an advanced economy. But between 1985 and 1990, investment rose by an average of 11% a year, while real GNP rose by less than 5% a year. Consequently its share of GNP climbed to 22% – a level not seen in Japan since the miraculous growth years and far in excess of that required. Much of the investment was wasteful or non-productive, but nonetheless productive potential was increased so that by 1990 Japanese industry had created new capacity some 10% in excess of current requirements. In the process, capital spending accounted for one third of Japanese GNP growth. This high level of investment could not continue indefinitely; much of the excess capacity will never be needed and in 1991 investment started to fall, checking the growth in the economy.

The slowdown in Japanese growth has already led to a sharp increase in its balance of payments surplus. At the peak of the boom in 1990 Japan's current account surplus shrank to $36 bn or 1% of GNP, down from over 4% in 1986. In 1991 the surplus doubled to around $73 bn and in late 1991 was probably running at a rate of $120 bn a year. The growing surplus led President Bush to turn his January 1992 visit to Japan into a trade mission; while if the Uruguay GATT round fails, demands on Japan to mend its ways, open its markets and compete fairly with other countries, will become intense. Americans have no need to be patient with Japan now that the threat of communism has collapsed. Unscrupulous politicians are already exploiting xenophobic fears of the 'yellow peril' to enhance their own electoral prospects. The American public will be led to demand harsh retaliation against unfair Japanese competition.

Trade sanctions could be the last straw: Japan's battered financial system is in danger of collapse. The bursting financial bubble has left a legacy of debts and losses which will be difficult for banks to absorb. In 1985 the total value of shares and property held by individuals and companies in Japan came to ¥3.2 quadrillion (i.e., ¥3200 trn or $25 trn), ten times national income. Between 1985 and December 1989, national income rose by 24% while the stockmarket climbed by over 200% and property prices rose on average by 70% (land prices in parts of Tokyo and Osaka increased in excess of 100%); total wealth rose to ¥5.8 quadrillion or 14.6 times national income. The paper value of what the Japanese owned increased each year by more than the total of what they earned in those years. When the bubble burst, the Tokyo stockmarket crashed and in early 1992 was trading at around 40% below its peak; property prices declined only some 15% on average, although in parts of Tokyo and Osaka prices have fallen 30% to 40%; private wealth fell by ¥700 trn to around eleven times national income.

It might be supposed that most of the bubble excess has now been eliminated; if property and share prices remain unchanged for the next two years, the ratio of wealth to income will return to its 1985 level. This comforting view assumes that Japanese assets were reasonably priced in 1985. But in that year American and British wealth was only four times national income. Were American and British assets abnormally cheap, or Japanese assets abnormally dear? The value of an asset is inversely related to the yield from it and wealth can only equal ten times national income, if yields are exceptionally low; even a modest 5% yield would reward property owners with half the nation's income and since wealth is inequitably distributed, this would be intolerable. In fact, the rate of return on assets in Japan, whether measured by price-earning ratios, dividend pay-out ratios or rental income, has been miserably low for many years. A Japanese shareholder is lucky to receive dividends of 1–2%. Japanese assets were abnormally expensive in 1985 and remain so today.

The only justification for abnormally low yields is the expectation of much higher returns resulting from capital gains. In the mid-1980s the Japanese believed correctly that absurdly high asset prices would only go absurdly higher (i.e., that low yields would go lower). If asset prices remain unchanged over the next two years, this expectation will be invalidated. The wealth-to-income ratio will then not merely return to its 1985 level, but go much lower. Indeed it must fall to the level at which yields on shares and property become competitive with those obtainable on alternative investments. Unfortunately, rising yields lead to capital losses and once confidence is undermined, people may fear that absurdly low asset prices can only go lower. Japanese asset prices cannot remain at their present level: unless they rise significantly, they will fall substantially.

The bursting bubble has already produced such massive losses that the banking system is in danger of collapse. On the surface, major banks' exposure to property losses is limited. Loans to real estate and construction companies account for only 17% of their assets. This is well below the level of property lending by British and American banks. But most Japanese bank loans to industry or individuals are secured against property. Zaitech operations led industrial companies to speculate with borrowed money on the property and stockmarkets. There are also 35,000 unregulated non-banks, two-thirds of whose funds come from banks, while two-thirds of their lending is property related; total non-bank lending reached ¥90 trn in 1990.

In this environment, the more dubious the loans, the more dubious the lender. While bank lending slowed as the markets approached their peak, non-bank bank lending rose sharply. Loans by the top 200 non-bank banks rose by 47%, over ¥20 trn, in the year to march 1990. Non-bank banks face a crisis on both sides of their balance sheets. Their income is being squeezed by the increase in their non-performing loans, while they are being forced to pay higher rates for their borrowing from banks. As banks curtail their lending, many non-bank banks are being forced to the wall. Unable to raise the money from the banks to carry their loan portfolios, they are obliged to foreclose on troubled borrowers, forcing the sale of the property taken as collateral. This further depresses the price of property, causing more borrowers to default. Bad loans already total 10% on non-banks' lending. This proportion will increase.

The non-bank crisis has turned the Japanese financial system's normal strength into a fatal weakness. Traditionally, no banks and only small companies are allowed to go under. When a medium or large company faces bankruptcy, it is usually rescued by a related company. The keiretsu system looks after its weaker brethren. Where the problem cannot be handled this way, the company's main banker usually comes to its rescue, e.g. Sumitomo has bailed out Itoman. Losses are absorbed within the rescuer's balance sheet, who retain the company's assets rather than unloading them on the market. Debts which cannot be absorbed at lower levels are passed upwards, until eventually they end up on the books of the city banks, long-term credit banks and trust banks. This system has been weakened in recent years; the upward transmission of losses is less automatic and the number of bankruptcies is soaring. In 1991 the total value of debt defaults by failing business rose nearly tenfold. Not all bad debts will translate 100% into loan losses; the sale of bankrupt companies' assets usually repays a part of creditors' loans – but fire sales depress prices causing further losses to others.

Bankruptcies are the tip of the iceberg: most companies are still being rescued. A survey of loan restructuring by thirty-five large companies showed ¥15 trn in non-performing loans, yet so far city banks are reported to have ¥2.8 trn of non-performing loans on their books, trust banks ¥2 trn and long-term credit banks at least ¥2.4 trn. These are already dangerously large amounts: they equal one-third of banks' unrealised portfolio gains, while lost interest, at 5%, equals a fifth of banks' operating profits. The full extent of the problem is being concealed. Easy accounting rules, for instance, allow unpaid interest to be included in profits for six months after the debtor has defaulted, while some bad loans can be parked with related companies. On the worst scenario, non-performing loans could climb to nearly ¥60 trn, enough to wipe out the banking system's hidden reserves.

Big banks are not the only ones in trouble: regional banks, smaller shinkin banks and credit co-operatives have been crippled by interest rate deregulation. They are important: collectively accounting for just under half of the country's ¥390 trn bank deposits. Like the American savings & loans, when forced in the late 1980s to pay higher deregulated interest rates on deposits, they scrambled for higher yielding and hence riskier investments, and were severely hit when the speculative bubble burst. It is reckoned, for instance, that two-thirds of the 445 shinkin banks are insolvent. The proposed solution is mergers and take-overs rather than bankruptcies, but the losses are on such a scale that it is unlikely to work. The 5900 credit co-operatives are better placed, because more of their funds come from small deposits on which they still pay low regulated rates. But they are going to need help when the process of deregulation is completed, and consequently are being consolidated into larger units under their national federations. This shake-up in the banking system could not have come at a worse time. A system where the strong help the weak works only when the strong are many and the weak are few – when all are weak the system collapses.

This tale of woe is not complete: the nominal value of warrant bonds outstanding in March 1991 was ¥18.6 trn. This figure shows how much warrant holders would pay if they exercised their right to buy shares at the warrant price; but it also shows roughly how much the issuers will have to repay if their bonds mature without the warrants being exercised. In November 1991, the market value of the shares on offer to warrant holders was only ¥13.4 trn. Unless the Tokyo stockmarket recovers strongly, most warrants will not be exercised and issuer will have to find funds from elsewhere to repay their bonds. Much of the money borrowed by issuing the bonds was lost in property and stockmarket speculation or wasted installing excess new capacity. The maturing bonds will have to be refinanced at significantly higher interest rates, which will cause serious problems for some issuers.

Bad loans, like scum on water, float to the surface and mostly end up with the big banks, whose ability to support the credit system has been undermined by new Bank for International Settlement capital adequacy requirements. From March 1993 they must hold reserves equal to at least 8% of their risk-adjusted assets. In March 1991 they were comfortably placed: risk assets totalled ¥346 trn and reserves ¥30.4 trn (8.8%). But reserves included nearly ¥10 trn of unrealised stockmarket gains, which have subsequently shrunk and the reserves are perilously close to falling below their BIS limit.

The Japanese credit system has become viciously unstable. In the good old days, when the Tokyo stockmarket was booming, rising share prices boosted bank reserves, allowing them rapidly to expand credit. Zaitech speculation with borrowed money boosted share prices, producing its own rich rewards in higher profits while plentiful credit also helped to stimulate the economy, further increasing company profits. The higher the stockmarket rose, the more it could be fed with further credit: the more the banks lent, the more they were able to lend. It was a fool's paradise. The 1990 stockmarket crash put this process into reverse: the more the market fell, the less the banks could lend. The resulting contraction of credit drove the economy into recession. The credit explosion of the late 1980s has been followed by a credit implosion in the early 1990s.

Confronted with all these problems, it is not difficult to envisage a financial meltdown. But the authorities are not standing idly by: the Bank of Japan has moved aggressively to lower interest rates and while the Ministry of Finance has proposed a cautious general accounts budget for fiscal 1992, public works spending through the off-budget Fiscal Investment & Loan Program is being substantially increased. More vigorous action will be taken if the economy continues to slide; the issue is whether it will work.

The success or failure of aggressive monetary easing depends upon whether the share prices recover. Failure to engineer a sustained recovery in share prices, for whatever reason, will lead directly to a financial collapse which will push the economy into a protracted recession. But even if the stockmarket recovers and the banking system survives its present crisis, the problem will remain. The only way to save the financial system is to reflate the bubble by pushing stockmarket and property prices higher; but the only way to solve Japan's structural problems is to reduce them. Higher land and share prices will work only while they continue to rise, thus a system in which the shareholder and landowner expects to be rewarded by an endless stream of capital gains is fatally flawed. The next bubble, like the last, is bound to burst. The collapse in the Japanese financial system is inevitable, only the timing is uncertain – Japan's economy is doomed.

Political trauma

Against this dismal financial background, how will the political scene evolve? The Taisho generation has regained control over the government in the old way: by deposing Japan's most popular post-war Prime Minister, Toshiki Kaifu, and choosing his successor by means of backroom deals amongst themselves. Reforms aimed at ending corrupt money politics have been postponed and it is back to business as usual. For the sake of appearances, faction leaders are seeking a consensus on electoral reform within the LDP with opposition parties – they will fail. The opposition parties gain from the present system and would obtain fewer seats in first-past-the-post fights, perpetuating the LDP monopoly of power. Within the LDP, weaker factions would lose from any reduction in the number of constituencies; and rural areas would lose much of their political clout. The politicians are unlikely to agree to meaningful reform.

This does not mean that the issue is dead, but that the Japanese will become increasingly paralysed until it is tackled. The creeping paralysis of consensus government has been apparent for some years: it began when the Recruit Cosmos scandal broke and the opposition parties brought normal Diet business to a standstill for almost a year; it eased during Toshiki Kaifu's Premiership; but under Kiichi Miyazawa or any Taisho successor, it can only worsen. Diet proceedings are again being disrupted by old and new scandals; no opposition party will willingly help the LDP to get its legislation through the upper house of the Diet, where it lacks a majority, until after the July 1992 election. The seventy-five LDP Councillors, whose six-year term in the upper house expires, were elected in 1986, at a peak in the LDP's popularity and it is probable that the party will suffer further losses. At present it needs only the support of the twenty Komeito party Councillors for an upper house majority, but some of them will also probably lose; after July it will need help from the small Democratic Socialist party and even the Socialists (renamed Social Democrats). Shin Kanemaru has even hinted at the formation of a grand right-left coalition of all these parties after July; but a merger between the Komeito, Social Democrats and Democratic Socialists is equally likely.

The opposition will continue to exact a high price from the government to allow parliamentary business to proceed; and part of this price will be to hound individual corrupt LDP politicians. The scandals of recent years have produced profound public dissatisfaction with the way the country is governed and deep loathing for those who govern it. As Japan's economic troubles increase, these emotions will be deliberately stirred. As the Kyowa and Sagawa affairs show, the spate of scandals is nowhere near over. Young bureaucrats, tax officials, journalists and the media generally are working to undermine the system from within. Electoral reform will become their rallying cry.

Political paralysis is likely to force the Taisho generation out of office relatively quickly. Kiichi Miyazawa will probably not last a year as Prime Minister; and the knives will be out for his Taisho successor the moment he takes office. Power is likely to be won by the younger generation of Showa politicians before the next lower house election has to be called. They will be forced to yield to public pressure and may even attempt to exploit it. The search for consensus will be abandoned and the battle to force reform through the deadlocked Diet will begin. But with the opposition parties in a majority in the upper house until at least 1995, the new LDP leaders' only hope will be to take the issue to the country at the next lower house election. If the LDP could win a two-thirds majority in the lower house, the upper house stranglehold would be broken.

The reform will replace the present multi-member single-vote system with some form of single-member constituency system, which – like Toshiki Kaifu's proposed reforms – will contain an element of proportional representation. The government will also be forced to re-introduce legislation controlling political donations. The exact details of the reforms do not matter; what does is how they will work.

Cleaner laws make for dirtier politics

Changing the law controlling political contributions will do little to change the behaviour of politicians who believe themselves above the law. Most who have made it to the top of the present corrupt system, including the Showa generation, will never fight clean. The less money they can obtain within the law, the more they will seek outside it. Corruption may become less blatant and more ingenious, gangster connections more carefully disguised; but by far the worst effect of reform will be to increase intimidation in place of bribery – bullies come cheaper than bribes. The cleaner the law says the politicians should be, the dirtier they will fight to retain power. Laws work only when they can be enforced. Under Japan's existing laws, most top politicians should have been locked up long ago. Money politicians must lose power before money politics can be eradicated.

Could electoral reform achieve this? It will not abolish factional politics; it will change its form. At first, the battleground between factions will shift: rival LDP candidates will no longer fight each other to get elected in multi-seat constituencies; they will fight for adoption as the official candidates in the single-member constituencies. The strongest contenders will be those most likely to win locally and the battle for local support will intensify. It would be remarkable if the factions were able to agree the candidates to be included in the LDP's proportional representation list, and their positions on the list.

The powerful Takeshita faction will gain most from electoral reform. By pulling more strings and handing out the largest bribes, it will get its members nominated as candidates in the best constituencies and placed at the top of the party's list. If members of weaker factions cannot win nomination as candidates, they will have little incentive to remain in the LDP. Instead they will break away to form their own parties: there is less advantage in belonging to a large national party in a first-past-the-post fight. Anyone can stand locally for election, fighting on issues, presenting the voter with policy choices and mobilising public opinion to express itself. A new breed of popular demagogues could emerge capable of challenging the grey LDP party hacks. Single-member constituencies mean the end of the LDP.

The death of consensus politics

The LDP split-up will sign the death warrant for consensus politics. In fact it only really operated on economic issues; confrontational politics dominated Constitutional and foreign policy issues. These were the main issues dividing parties before the 1955 set-up and they continued to be contentious. The Prime Minister, Nobusuke Kishi, lost his job in 1960 as a result of riots and demonstrations when he pushed the revised Japan–US Security Treaty through the Diet. The former Prime Minister, Toshiki Kaifu, lost his bid to send Japanese non-combatants to the Gulf because the opposition, supported by public opinion, were strongly against him on this issue. The LDP's recipe for retaining power has been to avoid alienating public opinion on these delicate issues. It has remained middle-of-the-road, forcing the opposition parties to support either extreme. This explains why Japan has remained so puny a force in international affairs. The opposition parties have never been willing to trade ideals for power in the same way.

It was possible for many years to formulate consensus economic policies by dint of barter between rival interest groups. As this process rarely involved the public interest, it was usually a positive-sum game. Each interest group affected by a policy change was consulted. All were expected to give and take in the process of reaching an agreement. All ended up taking more than they gave, partly because of rising economic prosperity and partly at the expense of the consumer. The fudges involved in both the abolition of the Maruyu system and Takeshita's sales tax, explained elsewhere, are good examples of this process. Forming a consensus is time-consuming, but usually there was no need for haste. The result was often government by paralysis. But as long as life was tolerable, the Japanese remained intensely conservative.

This system would not have worked if the opposition parties had come out strongly for the public interest. In the 1960s they did so at local level over pollution, the environment and social welfare. This forced the LDP to address these issues, even at the expense of big business interests. But for the most part, the opposition parties have been more conservative than the LDP. Rather than lead the way forward, they have opposed change of all kinds. They have never come forward with alternative policies. They have waited and rejected those proposed by the LDP. But since the widest possible agreement was sought on policies before the LDP adopted them, there could be little support for opposition to them.

Consensus politics is now doomed. The dangers of a trade war make economic policy changes a matter of urgency. If politicians do not implement radical reforms, foreign retaliation will cause a severe recession and create many losers; if they do implement such reforms, many special interests will get hurt. Nobody will be made absolutely better off by these reforms. Some Japanese will be prevented from becoming worse off. The root of this problem is simple: the only way to eradicate excess savings is to redistribute wealth from the one-third of Japanese who own everything to the two-thirds who own next-to-nothing. This cannot be done without there being winners and losers. There is no way in which a consensus can be achieved to do it. It can be imposed on a powerful minority of Japanese only by the majority of their fellow countrymen. But Japan has no option: if the politicians fail, markets will do the job for them at the expense of impoverishing the nation.

There are several simple rules in politics. The first is that governments always come up with the right solutions, after all other alternatives have been exhausted. This is what is now happening with the problem of excess savings. The second is that, until the pain from doing nothing exceeds the pain from doing something, nothing gets done. Japan's present political and economic system is based on deeply ingrained traditions of history and social behaviour. Changing it is not a matter of passing a few new laws; it involves a revolution in the way people think, act and behave. Social values and morals, relative power, privilege and position, expectations and hopes all have to be altered. Only the greatest of disasters can cause such a change. The struggle will be a long and hard one.

Paralysis and violence

Confrontational politics means that voters must choose between parties offering alternative policies. Parties which democratically secure a majority in the Diet, then have the right to pass laws against the wishes of the opposition, whether or not its members choose to attend Diet sessions. Those who lose because of these laws, still have an obligation to obey them. They can campaign to change the government and thereby rescind the laws they do not like. This is how, in theory, a mature democracy works. They rarely work so well in practice. If a government abuses its power to pass unfair and bad laws – such as the poll tax, introduced by the British government when led by Mrs Margaret Thatcher – it can expect to have difficulty enforcing them. Democratically elected governments know that if they make such mistakes too often they will be thrown out at the next election.

Unfortunately democratic principles are not widely accepted in Japan. Loyalty to whatever group one belongs to requires that anything which threatens its interests must be fought by all means, fair and foul. Consensus politics did not stem from a basic characteristic amongst Japanese to agree, rather than to argue and fight. It is necessary to prevent group violence, lawlessness and intimidation. Confrontational politics will throw Japan into chaos.

It is unlikely that radical break-away groups from the mainstream LDP will achieve any significant victories in the first election under the new system, but they will split the LDP vote, which in marginal seats will let in the opposition parties, denying the mainstream LDP victory. Government will remain paralysed at precisely the moment when resolute action is required to implement radical reform. The Diet will once again be the scene of pitched battles, with the police called in to maintain order. Protesters will take to the streets, demonstrating and rioting. There will be fighting between the supporters of different parties.

It is tempting to compare the 1990s with the late 1920s and early 1930s. There are some similarities. The nation is again economically threatened. There are deep divisions within it that can no longer be papered over. There is a similar concentration of wealth and power in few hands. There are gangs who extort, intimidate and murder. Politicians are corrupt and self-seeking, in league with big business, finance and the criminal yakuza organisations. As political paralysis and social disorder mount, will some group akin to the inter-war militarists be able to take hold of power and form a fascist dictatorship?

Here there is room for hope. In the dark inter-war years, the feeble flickerings of democracy in Japan were extinguished. During the coming crisis, the forces of democracy are likely to prevail. The leaders of industry are no longer the owners of industry. The keiretsu are joint stock companies, whereas the zaibatsu were owned by powerful families. Nobody could touch the pre-war dynasties. Today's giants of industry can be laid low. When Nomura's Setsuya Tabuchi and Nikko's Iwasashi Tabuchi lost their jobs because of the securities scandals, they lost their power. Top managers can be swept aside in a way that the 1930s top owners could not be. The morality of big industry can be changed to meet the standards which the public demands.

There are no generals and admirals, commanding large military organisations, independent of politicians and capable of taking over the country. The Emperor is now a figurehead only. No legitimacy or automatic obedience would follow actions taken in his name. The Japanese are no longer mostly starving peasant or industrial workers under the thumb of landlords and employers. The judiciary is independent and the Public Prosecutor's office has shown itself resolute in pursuing those who break the law regardless of their position and status. Vague laws can be made specific. The system of administrative guidance can be changed. Bureaucrats are on the side of reform.

The political problem for the 1990s will be to suppress extremist minorities of the left and the right, whose weapons are individual intimidation and violence, and to break the organised yakuza. Anarchy, not tryanny, is the danger. These elements in society have neither the public support nor the power which the middle-ranking army and navy officers who belonged to the rival 'Imperial Way' and 'Control' cliques enjoyed. The yakuza gangs have been able to operate because they have been tolerated by politicians, big business and the police. Once these forces are united against them, their power can be broken.

The majority of Japanese know that there are fairer and freer systems of democracy in other countries. The student rebels of the 1960s are today's middle-aged Japanese. The baby-boom generation is leading today's rebellion in favour of democracy and against corruption and exploitation. But it will take some time before strong government can emerge to represent their wishes and impose decency on Japanese society.

In the late 1980s, a great political system collapsed in Central and Eastern Europe. Communism failed to deliver a satisfactory standard of life to its citizens, who would no longer tolerate the lack of political freedom when no economic reward was offered in exchange. Communism's collapse was a consequence and a cause of economic collapse. A period of chaos has ensued during which the old must be pulled down before a new and better system can be built. Everybody recognises the victory which free market democracy has achieved. The same process is at work in Japan. The corrupt old corporatist system was more successful for far longer than communism. Its collapse will not be as catastrophic.

I hope that my gloomiest predictions prove to be false. In setting out what could happen and why, I also hope that in some small measure my analysis of the dangers will contribute to their solution. In the short term, I am a pessimist; I see a sick society, which needs the trauma of an operation to cut out the cancer which has invaded its body politic. But I am also an optimist. I have no doubt that Japan should emerge from this crisis a fairer and freer country, democratically governed, in which the quality of life for the majority of its people will be greatly improved. It should continue to be a good international neighbour, particularly to the Asian countries which surround it. It should be able to play its proper role in the world with confidence. Its GNP growth will be nothing startling and it will never own or dominate the world. It will have balance of payments problems from time to time, like other countries. In fact, a quarter of a century late, Kakuei Tanaka's dream of rebuilding the Japanese archipelago could start to be realised. The coming collapse marks the end of the long cycle in which Japan became economically great; it marks the start of a new long cycle in which it will become socially just.

Index

302

Index

304

Index

Index

Index

Index